ACCOUNTING FOR THE GLOBAL ECONOMY

INTERNATIONAL FINANCE AND DEVELOPMENT SERIES
Published in association with the Institute of Social Studies

General Editor: E. V. K. FitzGerald, Professor of Economics, Institute of Social Studies, The Hague, and Director, Finance and Trade Policy Research Centre, University of Oxford

The *International Finance and Development Series* reflects the research carried out at The Hague and associated centres in Europe, Asia, Africa and Latin America on the relationship between international capital flows and the process of structural adjustment in less-developed economies. The studies in this series share a common analytical approach based on the use of advanced social accounting techniques and the explicit modelling of the economic behaviour of institutional sectors, which in turn permit a new approach to macroeconomic policy design.

Karel Jansen and Rob Vos (*editors*)
EXTERNAL FINANCE AND ADJUSTMENT

Karel Jansen
EXTERNAL FINANCE IN THAILAND'S DEVELOPMENT

Joke Luttik
ACCOUNTING FOR THE GLOBAL ECONOMY

Rob Vos
DEBT AND ADJUSTMENT IN THE WORLD ECONOMY

Rob Vos and Josef T. Yap
THE PHILIPPINE ECONOMY: EAST ASIA'S STRAY CAT?

Howard White (*editor*)
AID AND MACROECONOMIC PERFORMANCE

Accounting for the Global Economy

Measuring World Trade and Investment Linkages

Joke Luttik

in association with
INSTITUTE OF SOCIAL STUDIES

First published in Great Britain 1998 by
MACMILLAN PRESS LTD
Houndmills, Basingstoke, Hampshire RG21 6XS and London
Companies and representatives throughout the world

A catalogue record for this book is available from the British Library.

ISBN 0–333–73099–2

First published in the United States of America 1998 by
ST. MARTIN'S PRESS, INC.,
Scholarly and Reference Division,
175 Fifth Avenue, New York, N.Y. 10010

ISBN 0–312–21330–1

Library of Congress Cataloging-in-Publication Data
Luttik, Joke.
Accounting for the global economy : measuring world trade and investment linkages / Joke Luttik.
p. cm. — (International finance and development series)
Includes bibliographical references and index.
ISBN 0–312–21330–1 (cloth)
1. International trade—Mathematical models. 2. National income–
–Accounting. I. Title. II. Series.
HF1379.L88 1997
382'.01'5118—dc21 97–42694
CIP

This book is printed on paper suitable for recycling and made from fully managed and sustained forest sources.

10 9 8 7 6 5 4 3 2 1
07 06 05 04 03 02 01 00 99 98

Printed and bound in Great Britain by
Antony Rowe Ltd, Chippenham, Wiltshire

Contents

List of Tables

Abbreviations

BOP	IMF, *Balance of Payments Statistics*
CMEA	Council for Mutual Economic Assistance
CMS	Constant market share analysis
DAS	Total net changes in assets
DBs	Diversified borrowers
DFC	FDI income
DLI	Total net changes in liabilities
DRS	Debtor Reporting System (World Bank)
FDI	Foreign direct investment
GDFF	OECD, *Geographical Distribution of Financial Flows to Developing Countries*
GDI	Gross domestic investment
GNS	Gross national saving
MER	Merchandise trade
MOEs	Major oil exporters
MPS	Material product system
MNEs	Multinational enterprises
MOBs	Major offshore banking centres
MULTI	Multilateral development banks
NES	Nonfactor services
OBs	Official borrowers
OCA	Other capital flows
OOECD	'Other' OECD countries
PBs	Private borrowers
PNGLT	Private non-guaranteed debt
PPGLT	Public and publicly guaranteed long-term debt
RES	net charges in reserves
ROW	Rest of the world
RWAMs	Reconciled world accounting matrices
ST	Short-term debt

TRA	Unrequited transfers
(UN)SNA	United Nations System of National Accounts
UNTMS	United Nations Trade Matrices System
WAM	World accounting matrix
WDT	World Bank, *World Debt Tables*
WT	World Bank, *World Tables*

International Finance and Development Series

Series Editor's Introduction

Since the early 1980s, world trade has been growing considerably faster than world output, and international capital flows much faster than trade. Particular historical, institutional and technical factors – such as the end of the Cold War, the completion of the Uruguay Round and satellite telecommunications – have contributed to this acceleration. Although the characterization of this trend as 'globalization' is problematic – in the sense that markets require institutional foundations and global economic institutions are as yet embryonic – it is clear that these factors form part of a profound process of integration within the world economy.

However, the trend is uneven in terms of both the activities and regions involved. One the one hand, while capital and goods seem able to move almost freely throughout the world, services trade is much less developed and labour movements are highly restricted. Goods trade is now almost completely liberalized under WTO arrangements, while the liberalization of domestic financial markets and the diversification of investment portfolios have stimulated cross-border capital flows. Nevertheless, services trade integration is still restricted by the need to harmonize regulatory systems, while the political opposition to unrestricted immigration means that the populations of richer countries can retain their rent on their inherited social capital. On the other hand, while almost all economies have become more open to trade and investment flows, the degree to which they can take advantage of this varies considerably. Middle-income countries with strong skills, institutions and infrastructure enjoy rapid export growth and attract substantial capital inflows, and seem to be converging on (and within) the industrialized countries. Low-income economies, without skills or infrastructure, and industrializing countries with weak institutions, clearly have difficulty in competing internationally and in overcoming endemic poverty; they may be diverging from the global mean.

In the light of these important trends it is perhaps surprising that we know relatively little about the structure of the world economy as a whole. Above all, there does not exist a system of 'world accounts' equivalent to the standard national accounting system. Such a system cannot simply consist of a summation of the national accounts for all the countries in the world for two reasons. First, the transactions between each of the economies must also be identified on both current and capital account of the balance of payments. Second, the inconsistencies between national accounts measured in different ways must be resolved to produce the appropriate balances on a world scale. Work at the Institute of Social Studies on the construction of a 'world accounting matrix' was initiated by Rob Vos and reported in this Series in his volume *Debt and Adjustment in the World Economy*. The present volume by Joke Luttik reflects our progress in the empirical task of constructing such matrices, and her initial analysis of the changing structures in worldwide trade and investment patterns and the relationship between them,

Most of the volumes in this Series are case studies of the effect of international capital flows on individual economies. Logically, these studies consider international capital flows to be largely exogenous to local circumstances, in the sense that the amounts of capital governments and firms in developing countries can borrow from abroad are limited by the demand for these categories of assets. In other words, international capital markets are 'rationed' because there is a systemic shortfall between demand and supply, and thus do not fully clear through interest-rate arbitrage. Modern economic theory recognizes that this shortfall arises from asymmetric information and agency issues between borrowers and lenders; the implication is that the portfolio decisions of international investors as between countries are based on factors such as trade relationships, sovereign risk, and levels of development rather than interest rates. In consequence it is necessary to construct a sound, empirically-based world model of the behaviour of international capital flows in order to understand the position of any one developing country participant. The present volume by Joke Luttik provides a rigorous basis for this task, suggesting that imperfect world capital markets can be seen as involving the 'export of liabilities' where importers' preferences as to asset acquisition reflect not only the type of institution and transaction involved but also the countries involved.

The four 'blocs' of the World Accounting Matrix (WAM) are the current and capital accounts of the balance of payments on the one hand, and gross domestic investment and gross national saving on the other. These blocs also form the backbone of the macroeconomic models used in the country studies reported in this Series. The approach in the present volume also shares with the country studies the analytically powerful assumption that the institutional form taken by capital flows largely determines their behaviour. In the case of the country studies this leads to a disaggregation of the economy between public and private sectors, between large and small firms and households in the private sector on the one hand, and between the various modalities of capital inflow – direct foreign investment, bank loans, portfolio flows and official development assistance – on the other. The WAM contains a parallel institutional disaggregation: between countries or regions of origin and destination derived from the 'Armington assumption' that international transactions can be distinguished not only by kind but by their place of production; and between public capital flows from bilateral and multilateral sources, and direct and financial investment from the private sector. It should be possible in principle, therefore, to link up these country models to the WAM to construct an integrated framework of international trade and investment as part of a future research agenda.

The value of this book goes considerably beyond the patient compilation of data on the origins and destinations of trade and capital flows; it makes significant contributions both to matrix reconciliation methodology and to the analysis of the relationship between trade and investment flows. First, the construction of a single matrix for world trade and investment flows involves the use of many sources of varying degrees of reliability, which are inevitably both mutually inconsistent and fail to sum to the global balances required by social accounting rules, The development of a computerized reconciliation methodology based on the relative reliability of the original sources, derived from an idea originally suggested by Nobel Laureate Richard Stone, represents a key statistical breakthrough. It also suggests that existing unreconciled sources on world trade and payments may contain considerable distortions due to the failure to reallocate large discrepancies in a plausible manner. For instance, there is reason to believe that the US current account deficit may be considerably overestimated due to the underreporting of investment income. Second, the application of 'constant market share' analysis derived from established trade theory to the change in debt stocks and capital flows for a particular region allows us to distinguish clearly for the first time between changes in aggregate demand by investors (in their demand for international assets as a whole), the composition of investors' portfolios between the different instruments available, and the 'competitiveness' of a particular developing country or region in attracting capital flows of a particular type from a particular country or region of origin. For example, this allows us to find out whether US capital inflows into Latin America derive from existing trade links, from changes in the US share of capital export worldwide, from the attractiveness of the bond issues and bank loans involved, or from the risks and returns from investing in that region as opposed to, say, Asia. As this book shows, these two instruments have already led to new insights into the development of the world economy not previously available from official or scholarly sources. In the longer term, I would expect these two contributions to improve the practice of global modelling by international institutions such as the IMF and the OECD.

This book was made possible by the generous support of our research group at The Hague and the Foundation for Research in Economic Sciences (ECOZOEK/NWO), which has made much of our work on the international dimension of capital flows possible. Data was supplied by the World Bank, the United Nations Conference on Trade and Development (UNCTAD) and the United Nations Statistical Office: our only regret is that these institutions have not been able to take on the compilation of WAMs as a regular official publication. This is clearly an appropriate task for an international institution because world accounting is clearly a global public good rather than a proprietary research output. None the less, the necessary methodology is clearly set out in this book and will doubtless be implemented when current concerns about global economic stability are eventually translated into multilateral macroeconomic cooperation.

Valpy FitzGerald
The Hague
March 1997

Author's Preface

This book is based on research conducted within the research project 'Money, Finance and Development' of the Institute of Social Studies (ISS) in The Hague. I am grateful for the institutional and financial support I received from the ISS. I am also grateful for the funding I received from the Foundation for the Promotion of Research in Economic Sciences (ECOZOEK/NWO).

In writing this book, I have received many useful comments from several people. At the ISS, I thank my former colleagues in the Money and Finance group for the opportunity they have offered me to do this research; I am especially grateful to Valpy FitzGerald, Rob Vos and Karel Jansen. When Niek de Jong joined the Money and Finance Group to engage in a similar data exercise we were able to work together, which was not only productive, but also made the data construction work less lonely. I owe special thanks to Henk Jager of the University of Amsterdam for many helpful reviews.

The cooperation between the Money and Finance Group and various other institutions has been very useful. I want to thank Tjeerd Jellema of the Growth Dynamics Institute of Erasmus University for his contribution to the construction methodology. I am also grateful to Mick Riordan and Malvina Pollock of the International Economics Division of the World Bank, for their help in the data collection.

I owe special thanks to the staff of the ISS Computer Department for their valuable support. I am especially grateful to the staff of the ISS Publications Office. My special thanks to Linda McPhee for editing the book; to Joy Misa (without whose help I would still be editing tables) for typesetting and designing the book; and to Teresa Waldin for proof-reading.

Finally, I have been supported and inspired by my friends and family throughout the research period. I thank them all; my particular thanks go to Co, Nel, Herman and Katinka.

Joke Luttik

1 Introduction

1.1 The World Accounting Matrix and Global Policy Analysis

This study undertakes the construction of an accounting framework for the world economy, referred to as the world accounting matrix (WAM), with special emphasis on developing countries. The WAM allows for the consistent presentation of international trade and finance figures, in relation to domestic saving and investment, for groups of countries. A WAM consists of four main submatrices or blocs: (1) current account transactions by origin and destination, (2) capital account transactions by origin and destination, (3) gross domestic investment, and (4) gross national saving.[1] The four main blocs are supplemented with tables for stocks of international assets and liabilities and for GNP.

The WAM is a flexible data framework. It is possible to construct WAMs for many different country groupings, and to focus on different transactions or variables, depending on the purpose of the exercise. It is of course also possible to design a WAM that is more extensive than the WAMs presented in this study. For example, as Leontief (1974) has shown, national accounts can be presented in a global framework that integrates macroeconomic accounts with environmental aspects. Thus a WAM could be designed to study global environmental issues in relation to global macroeconomics. The international flow of labour could also be brought into the WAM framework to study aspects of international migration in a global framework.

All WAMs have in common that they present economic and policy variables in a matrix format. The presentation of policy variables in the form of matrices can be useful because it reveals how a policy move in one country interacts dynamically with other origin and destination accounts. For example, the matrix for foreign aid can be viewed as an instrument of global policy. If Country A makes a policy move and increases its aid to Country B, this has a direct effect on Country B. This effect, in turn, has repercussions not only for Country A, but also for third countries. National policy actions may have significant spillover effects on other countries and to reach a global optimum these spillover effects have to be taken into account in the decision making process. Because the rationale for policy coordination stems from these spillover effects (see e.g. Goldstein 1994) we may condemn the modelling of the impact of foreign aid at the national level as a partial approach as it does not allow for global feedbacks (see e.g. White & Luttik 1994). Similarly, the effect on developing countries of an increase in the demand for world savings is best studied in a global rather than a national context (Allen & Vines 1992: 26).

A first, and inevitable, step in global policy analysis, is the construction of a data framework that explicitly shows the accounting relations between countries. Of course, since identities are not behavioural relationships, a next step is exploratory analysis based on the accounting framework combined with some very simple behavioral assumptions, thus using the WAM as a simple global model. This stage prepares for the final step, analysis with a fully developed global macroeconomic model. A global accounting framework should be an essential ingredient for any global model.

An additional advantage of data presentation in a matrix format based on macroeconomic accounting identities, is the possibility to check for data consistency. The accounting framework reveals instantly where the data do not match and where the gaps in the data are. The accounting constraints themselves provide additional information on the data inconsistencies and the missing data. This is relevant, given the large discrepancies in national and global macroeconomic data. The year-to-year shifts in global discrepancies have become larger than the shifts in aggregated national current account imbalances, which renders the existing statistics highly misleading. If, for example, the global discrepancy in the world current account deficit increases by US$ 20 billion while over the same period the combined deficit increases by the same amount, what has happened? Possibly the increase in the global current account deficit is entirely due to net under-recording in LDCs, but the source of error may also lie in other regions of the world so that there has been a deterioration in the current account positions of LDCs. Due to the poor quality of the statistics, it has become increasingly difficult for policy-makers to base judgement on the macroeconomic statistics published by international organizations like the IMF. A global accounting framework may contribute to a solution for these statistical problems.

This study shows how to build a set of WAMs. In the first place, the study presents a method. To show that the method works and leads to meaningful results, WAMs are constructed for 1970, 1975, 1980 and 1985. These four WAMs were built to illustrate and test the method. For WAMs for more recent years, I refer to de Jong, Vos et al. (1993a & b) who constructed WAMs for 1985–90 following the same method.

Section 1.2 of this introductory chapter sketches developments in international trade and finance and the concomitant problems in the recording of international transactions that have created a need for a WAM. Section 1.3 describes the efforts of others to solve these problems. Section 1.4 indicates the contribution of the WAM to the statistical problems described in section 1.2. Section 1.5 deals with the contribution of the WAM towards the solution of analytical problems. Section 1.6 clarifies some elements of the approach adopted in this study that have not been dealt with in earlier sections.

1.2 The Problem Setting

Patterns of trade and finance have changed dramatically since the early 1970s. Firstly, with the quadrupling of the price of oil in 1973 a series of unprecedented and growing current account imbalances, i.e. large surpluses in some countries and large deficits in others, began to emerge. Secondly, since the beginning of the 1970s, and progressively in the 1980s and 1990s, there has been a strong growth in the volume and complexity of international financial transactions. This growth has exceeded the financing requirements of the large current account imbalances. Thus, while international linkages through trade and finance have increased, trade and finance have, at least to some extent, become de-linked. These changes have been accompanied by a significant deterioration in the coverage and quality of the data on international transactions. At the global level, this can easily be seen by comparing the aggregated reported trade and financial flows for all countries in the world. The sum of world exports should equal the sum of world imports of trade and capital, but in practice this is not the case. Both the global current account and capital account have shown large discrepancies. Moreover, balance of payments statements of many individual countries show large discrepancies between current and capital account positions. Trends in trade and finance and statistical problems challenge both theories of international trade and finance, and statistical systems.

The purpose of this section is to identify the major developments in international trade and finance and the major problems in international macroeconomic statistics that have created a need for the WAM. It will be shown that the growing statistical problems are closely linked to rapid changes in the patterns of international trade and finance.

Rapid changes in international trade and finance

World trade in goods and services is larger than ever and imbalances on current account have increased significantly in the last 25 years. By definition, a current account surplus must equal the combined deficit on capital and reserve accounts. In other words, a surplus on current account does not cause an export of capital, but *is* an export of capital, either an increase in claims against foreigners or a decrease in liabilities to foreigners.[2] If there is neither a surplus nor a deficit on the current account, there is no (net) capital flow according to balance of payments definitions. In the 1980s shifts in savings and investment patterns resulted in large shifts in capital flows in the industrialized countries: the sum of the current account deficits of the industrial countries increased from an average of US$ 60 billion[3] in 1982–83 to more than US$ 200 billion by the end of the 1980s (IMF 1992). Alternatively, when we look at the size of capital flows in the reconciled WAMs as represented by the ratio capital flows to merchandise trade, both according to balance of payments definitions, there is an increase from 15 per cent in 1970 and 1975 to 24 per cent in 1980 and 1985 and 31 per cent in 1990.[4]

In a balance of payments context, we look at *net* capital flows, i.e. net changes in assets and net changes in liabilities. When we look at *gross* flows, it becomes clear that the increase in international financial movements has greatly exceeded the increase in trade finance. For example, cross border bank lending, measured by the total of outstanding international bank credit (net of interbank claims) rose from US$ 175 billion at the end of 1975 to 3,430 billion at the end of 1990.

This increase is the equivalent of a jump from 5 per cent (1975) to 20 per cent (1990) of industrialized countries' annual GDP (IMF 1992). The Eurodollar market is estimated to have had a turnover of US$ 300 billion per working day, which implies a yearly turnover of 25 times world trade in 1986 (Drucker 1986). An estimate for 1989 for foreign exchange transactions in London, New York and Tokyo alone places the daily turnover at US$ 431 billion (see Walter 1991) which amounts to a yearly turnover of 32 times world trade transactions. Thus, there are large capital movements unconnected to trade and largely independent of it.

One of the most dramatic changes in the world economy that have occurred over the last two decades is the increase in the mobility of capital. This increase is related to the abandoning of capital controls and the development of telecommunications and computer technology; new financial instruments have appeared, information now spreads instantaneously throughout the world and transactions can be carried out without delay (Solomon 1991: 73). This allowed the large US current account deficits in the 1980s to be financed easily by liquid funds coming from all over the world. The trading world is now strongly linked through financial movements, including direct and portfolio investments. At the same time, trade and finance have not become quite uncoupled, but the link has become loose and unpredictable. Financial movements were previously regarded as following the trade imbalances. Now financial movements are themselves generating these imbalances through shifts in demand and prices. Thus, financial movements are becoming more active than passive in the balance of payments and some argue (for example, Behrman 1989) that capital movements rather than trade have become the driving force of the world economy.

Another major tendency in international economics is the increasing impact of the world economy on national economies. It has become increasingly difficult to distinguish country-specific transactions. While most economic theory still focuses on national economies, and international macroeconomic statistics are still based on national economies as reporting units, multinational enterprises (MNEs) and international organizations are increasingly important transnational actors. This tendency for internationalization requires a (partial) shift in focus in economic theory and statistics from a country-specific level to a firm-specific level. In other words, although national economies, or groups of national economies like the EU will remain important economic units for the formulation of national, or coordinated, economic policies, as observed by Kindleberger almost three decades ago: 'the nation-state is about through as an economic unit' (Kindleberger 1969: 207). Root (1990) stresses the need for a synthesis of trade and investment theories which centres on the firm operating in the world economy. The WAM could contribute by providing an appropriate statistical data base, should the required data be made available, which is not now the case. Thus, while WAMs presented in this study are constructed for groups of countries, if the required statistics become available, they can be extended quite easily with a separate category for multinational firms.

LDCs and international trade and finance

This section examines how the problems sketched above relate to LDCs, and how LDCs give rise to specific statistical and analytical requirements for the WAM. Most countries of the world are LDCs and most people of the world live in LDCs. Yet LDCs are relatively small transactors in the world economy, which is dominated by industrialized countries. The recent rapid changes in international trade and finance, though originating in industrialized countries, have affected LDCs. Similarly, the effects of these changes in LDCs have had repercussions in the industrialized countries. For example, the increase in international financial flows to LDCs in the 1970s was related to the rapid internationalization and liberalization of international financial markets (see for example Das 1986). Also, the debt-servicing problems of LDCs in the 1980s were considered a considerable risk to the security of the international financial system (Cline 1983: 31).

Although LDCs receive a small share of global capital flows, and are small as exporters of capital, they are no longer only a passive receiving party. For example, as we shall see in the reconciled WAM for 1985, the country group labelled 'private borrowers' – a group of mainly middle-income LDCs which had access to foreign finance in the 1970s and 1980s – financed a substantial share of the US current account deficit.

The working hypothesis for this study is that capital flows to LDCs are largely exogenous: LDCs are constrained in their foreign exchange levels by credit rationing in international capital markets and by donor stringency in the supply of official development assistance (see Fitz-

Gerald & Vos 1989). The increase in foreign private flows to LDCs in the 1970s was directed at a relatively small group of LDCs; most LDCs remained dependent on official flows. It is argued that different types of foreign finance have a different impact on the recipient economies. Therefore, LDCs are classified according to the major source of foreign lending: official or private, and LDCs' foreign debt and interest payments, as well as capital flows to LDCs, are disaggregated into official and private components. Thus, the focus on LDCs demands specific classifications of countries and transactions for the WAMs constructed in this study.

The increase in private capital flows to LDCs has been accompanied by an outflow of private assets from LDCs often referred to as capital flight from LDCs. This capital flight may be considered by the national authorities as a capital outflow that is disadvantageous to the national economy (Lessard & Williamson 1987a: 2). However, it is not within the scope of an accounting framework to make a distinction between desirable and undesirable transactions. Therefore, capital flows from LDCs in the WAM are treated as foreign asset accumulation, just like capital outflows from other regions in the world.

Discrepancies in statistics for international trade and finance

In the last two decades, macroeconomic statistics have shown rapidly growing discrepancies. There are different types of statistical discrepancies that occur at both the national and the global level, and both between and within data sources. At the national level, the difference between savings and investment should by definition be equal to the current account position. In a national balance of payments, a surplus (or deficit) on the current account is by definition equal to the combined deficit (or surplus) on the capital and reserve accounts. At the global level, the sum of the current account incomings of all countries should by definition be equal to the sum of all current account outgoings of all countries. There are similar definitions of relationships for capital account transactions, as well as for each category of international transactions.

Despite these above definitions, in practice, there are large and growing statistical discrepancies which are closely connected to the changes in patterns of international trade and finance described above. A clear example of this is found in the link between the liberalization or abolition of exchange controls and the recording of international financial transactions. When exchange controls are abolished, new systems of data collecting have to be developed and implemented but this takes time and may well lead to a (temporary) deterioration in the quality and coverage of statistics (IMF 1992). Thus against the background of liberalization, many new financial instruments were developed and many new transactors entered the markets; these changes have made it increasingly difficult for statisticians to trace the flows, and statistical systems have not kept pace.

The increasing importance of the role for MNEs in the world economy has also posed problems for international and national macroeconomic statistics. Conventional statistics aim to measure balance of payments transactions between the reporting countries and the rest of the world. In national income statistics, foreign-owned production is not distinguished from locally-owned production. In trade statistics, transactions between parent companies and their foreign affiliates, or between affiliates with a foreign parent in a third country, are not distinguished from transactions between independent exporters and importers. On the capital account of balance of payments statistics, the transactions of MNEs are distinguished from other financial transactions, but there are significant statistical problems in the recording of financial transactions of MNEs. In essence it has become increasingly difficult, not to say impossible, for national compilers of statistics to cover all the worldwide activities of MNEs.

International organizations account for substantial and growing international capital flows. Until recently, these flows were not recorded at all in a balance of payments context (IMF 1987). Since 1987 a start has been made in the recording of these transactions, but it is still very incomplete (IMF 1992). Given this incompleteness, the increasing share for international organizations in international capital flows has also contributed to the increasing gaps in global statistics.

1.3 What Have Others Done to Solve These Problems?

The international organizations that collect and publish macroeconomic statistics have expressed their growing concern in various publications. Some of the most important examples are noted below. The IMF has regularly published discussions of the causes of discrepancies in balance of payments statistics, both in its regular publications (see for example IMF 1983, 1990) and in special reports (IMF 1987, 1992). Some forms of cooperation have been established, for example between the Bank for International Settlements (BIS) and the OECD that jointly publish debt stock figures on export credits and figures on bank claims adjusted to eliminate double counting.[5] To promote convergence of debt recording practices, an International Working Group on External Debt Statistics was set up by the international organizations that collect and publish data on LDC debt. These organizations jointly published a report that discussed the recording of stocks of external debt (World Bank, IMF, BIS and OECD 1988), which was followed by another report published in 1994 which extends this discussion focusing on measurement and reconciliation of stock and flow data. The IMF has actively participated in the ongoing revision of the United Nations' *A System of National Accounts* to achieve a greater degree of coordination in the statistical field with other international agencies (see Galbis 1991). The Transnational Corporations and Management Division of the UN – formerly known as the United Nations Centre on Transnational Corporations – has recently started to publish stock and flow data for foreign direct investment, including a classification by origin and destination (UNCTC 1992).

All these efforts promote quality, consistency and a greater coverage of the data systems. However, they remain fragmentary and directed only at certain aspects of trade, finance and debt statistics. These partial efforts to improve the existing data systems are insufficient to deal with the increasingly complex patterns of trade and finance, and the concomitant, increasingly serious data problems. A helpful method to solve the data problems would be to integrate the statistics of trade, finance and domestic accumulation in a global data framework based on solid accounting concepts. In a global accounting framework, various data sources can be combined, and discrepancies may be systematically traced and solved. A global accounting framework may also provide a statistical basis for the analysis of the increasingly complex patterns of trade and finance.

The idea of developing a global accounting framework is not new. Meade examined the problem of simultaneously restoring equilibrium to balances of payments in a many-country world (Meade 1951). To analyse how the authorities of each country should behave to attain a final state of world equilibrium, he used matrices that show the relationships between each country's imports, exports, national income and domestic expenditure. Leontief formulated an input-output framework for the world economy (Leontief 1974), in which the world consists of a developed and a less developed region, and production is divided into an extraction industry, all other production, and a pollution abatement industry. Another example is the accounting matrix for the world economy constructed by Weale as a basis for the analysis of world trade (Weale 1984). In this accounting matrix the national accounts for ten regions are combined and the regions are linked through a trade matrix. Another attempt is the Global Accounting Framework (GAF) which is currently being developed (McCarthy et al. 1989). This system integrates balance of payments data with national account data and debt statistics for individual countries, but aims at reconciling the data at the national level, while the remaining discrepancies at the global level are recorded on separate discrepancy lines. Other examples of 'accounting for the world economy' are found in world models that model economic linkages among countries, like the pioneering Project LINK. One of the basic principles of Project LINK is that world accounting identities should be preserved: world exports = world imports (Klein 1984). In the model, and in most of the global models that were to follow Project LINK, a world trade matrix ties together the regions of the world, while there is an indirect financial linkage through the interest rate and the exchange rate.

1.4 The Contribution of the WAM: The WAM as a Statistical Tool

In the WAM, countries and regions are linked through both trade and financial matrices. Contrary to the approaches discussed in the previous section, the WAM explicitly describes the structure of financial flows between countries and regions. The WAM presents flows of goods and services and financial flows and stocks in matrix format, thus integrating various data sources and economic aspects in one accounting framework. It can therefore be placed in the tradition of existing integrated statistical systems for national economies like the United Nations System of National Accounts and social accounting matrices.

In the construction of a WAM, the statistical discrepancies between and within the data sources become immediately clear. In an accounting framework, a statistical discrepancy cannot be swept under the carpet because it will always show up elsewhere in the system. Obviously, a WAM does not solve discrepancies; its purpose is to provide a framework for the identification and analysis of inconsistencies, and the systematic treatment of discrepancies. The reconciliation methods developed for national accounting systems can be adapted to fit a global accounting system, taking advantage of the work of Stone and many others on national accounting systems. These methods consist of a combination of data collection, data confrontation, data judgement and mathematics, so that the result is a set of complete and consistent tables. Of course, consistency must not be confused with accuracy: it is not true that the reconciled estimates are accurate because they are consistent. But 'if our judgements are at all correct, such estimates will be an improvement on the inconsistent set of data with which we started and provide a firmer basis for analysis than the initial estimates could provide' (Stone 1977: xxi).

1.5 The WAM as an Analytical Tool

Market shares and economic analysis

The origin and destination matrices that describe international trade and financial flows are important features of the WAM. These matrices not only show current and capital account positions of a country group *vis-à-vis* the rest of the world, but also *vis-à-vis* each country group. The latter is referred to as the 'pairwise' current and capital account balances between groups of countries.

The importance of origin/destination matrices and 'pairwise' balances for analysis depends on imperfect competition in the geographic distribution of flows. If a product is traded in a perfectly competitive world market, its origin and destination are not important and market shares have no explanatory power. A central assumption in this study is that the 'Armington assumption' (Armington 1969) holds, not only for merchandise trade, but also for services and capital flows. Armington argues that products can be distinguished not only by their kind, but also by their place of production. Buyers differentiate each good according to the supplier's area of residence. In other words: a Japanese car is not a perfect substitute for a European car. A similar point can be made for nonfactor services, a balance of payments category that largely consists of transport and travel. At least to some extent, the geographic distribution of transport will be related to trade and, assuming imperfect competition in merchandise trade, a portion of transport will also be subject to imperfect competition. For travel we may well assume that a journey to Japan is no perfect substitute for a journey to Europe.

Perfect competition in international capital markets implies perfect capital mobility. Under this assumption capital moves freely following rates-of-return differentials between countries. Empirical studies on foreign direct investment (FDI), have shed doubt on the validity of the perfect competition assumption for FDI. These studies have suggested that much direct investment takes place through large multinational firms operating in oligopolistic markets and that the capital flow appears dependent on strategic firm decisions rather than on immediate cross-country yield differentials at the margin.

In a truly competitive international market for bank and portfolio lending, borrowers have ready access to loans at a given interest rate. A central assumption in this study is that LDCs do not have free access at all times to international capital markets. Access to international capital markets differs for countries according to their degree of creditworthiness. The supply of finance to LDCs, or their capacity to sell international liabilities, is sensitive to credit rationing rules by international banks and donor agencies (see FitzGerald & Vos 1989). Obviously, official flows to LDCs are no reflection of rate-of-return differentials, they rather reflect geopolitical or humanitarian interests.

In spite of the enormous upswing in bank and portfolio lending between developed countries, capital markets have not yet become fully integrated. The question of whether there is a single global market for capital is still controversial. The concepts are not easily defined. How should international capital flows be measured and how should integration be defined? Empirical studies have tried to solve the issue by looking at the different definitions of integration, and the tests associated with it, but no clear picture has emerged. Therefore we assume that there is imperfect competition in international capital markets, not only for FDI and for capital flows from the developed countries to developing countries, but also for capital flows between developed countries. Consequently, there is imperfect competition for interest payments.

Since there is imperfect competition in the geographical distribution of merchandise trade, services and capital flows, it is useful for economic analysis to construct an accounting framework with origin and destination matrices.

The WAM as a simple world model

To see which insights origin and destination matrices, and the 'pairwise' balances that follow from these matrices, may give for global policy analysis, I will now give an example using the reconciled WAM ('RWAM') for 1985 developed later on in the study. The example shows how a policy move in one country or country group will work its way through the system and will influence other economies through directional patterns of trade and finance, and 'pairwise' balances.

In the WAM for 1985, Japan has a surplus on the current account of the balance of payments of US$ 59 billion. Let us assume that Japan increases its imports of merchandise trade so that the gap on the current account is equal to zero, with these additional imports distributed in proportion to the markets shares for Japanese imports in 1985. Because a current account deficit is a capital account surplus, and the Japanese current account is set at zero, Japan has to decrease its capital outflows. Japan's deficit on the capital account amounts to US$ 58.8 billion – the difference with the current account is of course matched by a change in reserves. Again, we assume that the decrease is distributed among the country groups according to their shares for 1985. There is no reason for the preferences on the current account to be equal to those on the capital account, and in the 1985 RWAM they are in fact clearly different. The difference between the market shares for Japanese exports of merchandise and those for capital exports from Japan leads to massive imbalances on the balances of payments of some country groups. For example, the EU needs to fill a gap on its balance of payments of US$ 15.9 billion and the US would need US$ 6.1 billion in additional finance. The global sum of this additional required finance would add up to zero so that other country groups would 'benefit' from capital inflows in this hypothetical scenario. A large share of the gain would go to the LDCs and major oil exporters (MOEs).[6] Together they would receive US$ 22.1 billion in additional foreign finance. These country groups account for a relatively large share of world exports to Japan, but receive a small share of Japan's capital exports and therefore lose only a small share of their capital imports.

To keep things simple it is assumed that the difference between the increase in export earnings and the decrease in capital inflows is absorbed by a change in foreign reserves holdings of the country groups. For example, the US increased its reserves in the 1985 WAM with US$ 1.8 billion, but due to its additional required foreign exchange of US$ 6.1 billion the US reduces its reserves with US$ 4.3 billion in the above example. In a next 'round of effects', the US will regain some of its loss because of a reduction in interest payments, which will amount to approximately US$ 1.4 billion per year due to the decrease in capital inflows from Japan.

According to national accounting rules, the increase in imports to Japan must be matched by an increase in domestic investment or a decrease in savings, or a mix of the two. For the other country (groups) the increase in exports means a decrease in domestic investment, an increase in saving or a mix of the two. No matter how the new equilibrium is reached, there will always be implications for the national economies, which in turn are likely to have repercussions for other country (groups). For example, if domestic investment decreases, this may involve a decrease in imports of capital goods, and so on.

The above is example is a hypothetical event based on 1985 data. The event did not happen, nor is the example intended as a forecast of what will happen. It only illustrates the type of relations a WAM may reveal and what we may learn from the matrices. It also shows that the scale of the adjustments that may result from differences in adjustment patterns between current and capital account transactions is enormous. This conclusion is of interest for the discussion of today's international monetary system (or non-system as is it referred to by some; see Kenen et al. 1994).

The WAM, developing countries and global modelling

The WAM only has accounting relations. Accounting frameworks come to life as economic models when some entries become variables to be explained by behavioral relations. The above example of what may happen to the world if Japan closes its current account deficit is a tentative step into this direction. What is really needed to study these interactions is a fully developed global model, which could be used to indicate how country X's efforts to reach its policy targets will be affected by what countries Y and Z are doing with their policies as well as to simulate the aggregate effects of varying degrees of policy synchronization (Goldstein 1994: 313).

Global macroeconomic modelling is a relatively new field – the pioneering Project LINK was launched in 1968. In global models, developing countries are generally represented by a finance constraint current account equation. A common assumption is that an inflow of external finance increases import capacity, and, assuming that additional imports are capital goods, that the inflow increases investment by the same amount. Hence, aid – or any other inflow of foreign finance – contributes to growth.

Many models do not distinguish between private flows and official flows. In other models the supply of official finance to developing countries – usually a fixed proportion of GDP in industrial countries – is different from the supply of private external flows, but the mechanisms through which official and private flows affect the economy are the same. In some models, for example the FUGI model, official flows are assumed to go to the public sector of the receiving economy, which behaves differently from the private sector, receiving only private flows (Kaya et al. 1983). Where most models link financial flows to developing countries to GDP in industrialized countries, the MSG2 model, developed by McKibbin and Sachs (1991), sets the scale of borrowing for LDCs exogenously under the assumption that the amount of loans available to LDCs is rationed by considerations of country risk. Also in MULTIMOD II finance from industrialized countries to developing countries is assumed to depend on the ability of developing countries to service debt (Masson et al. 1988). The 'measure for solvency' in this model is the ratio of interest payments on debt, corrected for inflation, to exports. This approach to the modelling of financial flows comes close to the approach advocated in this study where international capital markets are considered as imperfect, and 'sales of liabilities' are considered to reflect preferences not only by type of transaction but also by place of transaction. Thus we suggest a portfolio approach including a variety of assets, domestic and foreign. Portfolio preferences may differ according to the country where the liability is issued. There is no reason that financial preferences should mirror trade preferences. This notion should be an essential feature of the model.

A trade matrix is a common ingredient for global models. For example, the LINK model ties together the national macroeconomic models of the major countries and regions of the world through a world trade matrix. Financial variables however, are linked through interest rates and exchange rates, but never through matrices for financial transactions.

As a first step in a more elaborate modelling of financial interactions in Project Link, a series of balanced WAMs has been constructed for 1985–90, based on the methodology also used in this study (de Jong, Vos et al. 1993a & b). Now that these matrices are available, it will also be possible to link countries through financial matrices. However, this is not a simple task, given the complexity of the financial links between countries, and between trade and finance. Perhaps the WAM-based analysis in this study may be of some use in specifying the relationships for a global WAM-based model.

WAM-based analysis in this study

The WAM can be used as a database for a world model, but this study will also show that a WAM alone can be used as an analytical tool for the descriptive analysis of patterns of trade and finance. Due to its specific aggregation the WAM can reveal patterns that are not easily discovered elsewhere. Depending on the purpose of the exercise, it is possible to construct WAMs for different country aggregations and to focus on other policy-relevant details.

Firstly, simple coefficients are calculated that measure the shares of a particular transaction or country group in the total. This type of analysis takes advantage of the WAM as a 'one-page-summary' of the world economy and the availability of information on the origin and destination of all international transactions. Secondly, the directional patterns of trade and finance are examined and the two are linked by establishing directional 'biases' in trade and finance, and by assessing the link between pairwise current and capital account balances. As an exploratory step in the analysis of global patterns, the directional biases and links in international trade and finance are quantified, examined and interpreted.

Finally, patterns of trade and finance are examined in more detail by constant market share analysis, whereby growth in exports, capital inflows and debt stocks for a particular group of LDCs is decomposed into four components: (1) the world effect, (2) the composition effects, (3) the market effect, and (4) the competitiveness term, which for capital flows and stocks is interpreted as a creditworthiness effect. Constant market share analysis is a popular technique for the analysis of export growth (see for example Leamer & Stern 1970), but now that we have the origin and destination matrices it can also be applied to financial flows and stocks. For example, when growth in capital inflows for a country group is slow, the constant market share analysis shows whether this can be ascribed to slow growth in global capital markets, concentration on slowly growing financial instruments or markets, or a decrease in perceived creditworthiness.

1.6 Some General Observations

First of all, it *is* possible to construct consistent and reasonable WAMs, despite the existing enormous data deficiencies; the WAM is a helpful tool in global policy analysis and finance and in the solution of the rapidly growing statistical problems. The complexity of international trade and finance and the related statistical problems have increased since 1985, and the desirability of constructing WAMs is thus even greater now than it was a decade ago. This is underlined by an IMF report which observes that 'the world capital account statistics are in a state of crisis' (IMF 1992: 2).

The data for the WAMs constructed in this study are drawn from existing data systems, mainly from those published by international organizations (IMF, World Bank, OECD, and the UN). Without the Debtor Reporting System (DRS) of the World Bank, the actual construction of WAMs focusing on LDCs would not have been possible. The DRS is the only systematic data source for the origin and destination matrices for capital flows. Unfortunately, the DRS is limited to flows *into* LDCs. A global extension of the DRS would greatly improve the data availability and hence the quality of WAMs. Since matrices for financial transactions by origin and destination are an essential feature of the WAM, a large part of the construction work consisted of tracing bits and pieces of information in this field, while the remaining 'missing entries' have been estimated using a mathematical reconciliation procedure.

The WAM does not present gross capital flows, but does present new loans minus repayments, or net capital inflows (net changes in liabilities) and net capital outflows (net changes in assets); this way of presenting capital transactions is common to flow-of-funds frameworks and balance of payments statistics. Moreover, the availability of estimates for gross flows is rather limited. The use of this particular definition of capital flows implies that the dramatic increases in international financial flows are not captured in the WAM as far as they are netted out. It also implies that the matrices for trade and other current account transactions are conceptually different from the matrices for capital flows since current account transactions are always presented on a gross basis. This has posed problems in both in the mathematical reconciliation procedure and in the analytical applications of the WAMs, because net changes in assets or liabilities may be negative, and consequently, it is not possible to calculate meaningful shares in the total. To solve this problem, the availability of matrices for stocks of assets and liabilities has been very helpful.

In the construction of the WAMs, the approach has been to include all countries of the world, including those for which statistical recording is sparse. Missing entries have been estimated, either from additional data sources, or from group or world ratios. Also, matrix presentation is helpful in tracing missing information because one cell in a matrix by origin and destination shows two sides of a transaction at once. If the US has reported an import from Taiwan, one does not necessarily need a report by Taiwan to fill the cell in the matrix, although the report from Taiwan would be helpful in checking the data for consistency. The data have been reconciled for groups of countries but – with the exception of the US and Japan – not at the individual country level. This implies that in the aggregation stage discrepancies may be netted out. For example, summing the errors and omissions in the balances of payments for the EU members may result in small errors and omissions for the EU, which may conceal large errors and omissions for individual countries.

2 Concepts, Definitions and Classifications for the World Accounting Matrix

2.1 Introduction

The World Accounting Matrix (WAM) is based on the concept that related variables – international trade, financial flows and stocks, and domestic savings and investment – should be presented in one framework that explicitly takes the relationships between the variables into account. The WAM has its conceptual roots in the various accounting systems that have been developed for national economies. Each of these systems describe specific aspects of national economies. When combined in one system, they are referred to as integrated data frameworks. The most widely-used example of an integrated data framework is the United Nations System of National Accounts (SNA) which is designed for application at the country level. In the WAM, the principles of integrated data frameworks for national economies are applied at the level of the world economy, for country groups.

The WAM describes specific aspects of the world economy by aggregating macroeconomic variables in a way that fits the proposed analysis. The WAM can be considered as a specific aggregation of the SNA, based on SNA-concepts. The definitions of the variables that are included in the WAM are operational, in other words the defined variables are measurable and can be found in the statistical sources that will be used to construct the WAM. Similarly, the level and type of disaggregation for the WAM is constrained by data availability. This chapter explains the main concepts, definitions and classifications for the WAM.

2.2 From National Accounting to World Economic Accounting

National accounting systems are based on the national income identity which states that, in a closed economy, the value of output produced must equal the disposition of output in terms of consumption and investment.[1] It is an identity because it includes the actual, rather than the planned values for consumption and investment: if there were an excess ex ante supply (demand), it is ex post interpreted as forced inventory accumulation (forced savings or inflation tax).[2]

In an open economy, demand for goods and services includes demand for both domestically produced and imported goods. The demand for imported goods leads to demand for the productive resources of other countries, thereby generating income in these countries. Similarly, demand from foreigners for home-produced goods generates demand for domestic output. Therefore, to derive income in an open economy, exports have to be added to and imports have to be subtracted from consumption and investment in the national income identity for a closed economy:

$$GDP \equiv C + I + X - M \tag{2.1}$$

where:

C = total consumption
I = total gross domestic investment
X = total exports of goods and non-factor services
M = total imports of goods and non-factor services
GDP = gross domestic product

To derive total national disposable income, net foreign factor payments from abroad and unrequited foreign transfers have to be included in the definition. Here, analogous to the treatment of imports, net factor payments to abroad and net factor transfers to abroad are deducted from the GDP. Identity (2.2) shows this:

$$GNP \equiv GDP - R - Tr \equiv C + S \tag{2.2}$$

where:

GNP = gross national product
R = net factor payments to abroad

Tr = net transfers to abroad
S = total gross national savings

Deducting identity (2.2) from identity (2.1) gives:

$$S - I \equiv X - M - R - Tr \qquad (2.3)$$

Identity (2.3) is the balance between domestic savings and investment on the one hand and the balance on the current account of the balance of payments on the other hand. An external surplus, i.e. a surplus on the current account of the balance of payments, implies that savings exceed investment. A deficit on the current account of the balance of payments implies insufficient savings relative to investment. By definition, an external surplus (deficit) equals the net capital outflow:[3]

$$F \equiv S - I \equiv X - M - R - Tr \qquad (2.4)$$

where F = net capital outflow.

Identity (2.4) is the key identity to the study of finance, trade and accumulation. It integrates the balances for the principal transactions that take place within an economy: commodity transactions (production and acquisition of goods and services) and financial transactions (the acquisition of financial assets and the use of sources of investment finance).

The national income identities for a single economy are also true at a more aggregated level: for any group of national economies or for the world as a whole. Identity (2.4) shows that, by definition, at every such level the goods surplus $(S - I)$, the balance of payments on current accounts $(X - M - R - Tr)$ and net foreign savings (F) are identical.

World exports of goods, services and transfers should equal world imports of goods, services and transfers. Therefore, the world current account, the sum of the current accounts of all individual national economies, should add up to zero. The current balances of individual countries are either in surplus or in deficit. Consequently, each year countries will be net borrowers or net savers, but the sum of the world foreign savings equals zero by definition. Similarly, global savings must equal global domestic investments. Some countries may have excess domestic savings, while others receive foreign savings. The world total of savings, however, must equal the world total of investments. Summed over all countries j, these relations can be summarized as follows (Vos 1986, 1989):

$$\Sigma F_j \equiv \Sigma (X_j - M_j - R_j - Tr_j) \equiv \Sigma (S_j - I_j) = 0 \tag{2.5}$$

Just as national income identities form the basis for national accounting, the relation summarized in identity (2.5) may serve as a basis for world economic accounting. In the WAM, countries and regions are linked through the matrices F, X $(=M)$, R and Tr. These matrices are linked with the matrices for S and I so that the WAMs present the world totals for saving and investment.

2.3 General Features of the World Accounting Matrix

In this section, a step-by-step method is used to show how a WAM is constructed for four hypothetical countries, under the assumption that the world consists of these four countries only. Table 2.1 gives the income and expenditure accounts for four countries W, X, Y and Z. These accounts are arranged along the lines Meade and Stone set out for income and expenditure accounts for a single country in their 1941 article, and can be found in the SNA as the four 'standard accounts' which relate to production, consumption, accumulation and 'rest of the world' (or external) transactions. The accounts are balancing statements with outgoings on one side and incomings on the other side of each account. The table shows how the accounts are interrelated; every transaction is recorded twice: once as an outgoing on one account and once as an incoming on another account. For example, outgoings on the production account consist of gross income payments (or value added) on line 1 and purchases of imports on line 2. The contra-entry to line 1 is found on line 8, gross income receipts from domestic production on the consumption account. The contra-entry to line 2 is found on line 15, sales of imports, under incomings on the rest of the world account. The basic accounting relations of trade, finance and accumulation on a world scale can be found on the accumulation account and on the rest of the world account: global exports (line 13) equal global imports (line 15), global investments (line 10) equal global savings (line 12) and the sum of foreign finance (line 11 or 16) equals zero.

In a matrix format, where incomings are shown in the rows and outgoings are shown in the columns, the number of entries can be reduced from 16 to 8 per country. Furthermore, in a matrix, the interrelations between the different accounts stand out very clearly. This can be seen from Table 2.2, which gives the 'four accounts of the nation' for each of the countries W, X, Y and Z in matrix form. This table demonstrates two advantages of presenting data systems in matrix format. Firstly, the number of entries can be reduced by half. Secondly, the nature of the transaction can easily be seen from its position in the matrix.

The focus of the WAM is not on domestic interrelations but on international interrelations. Therefore, the four matrices are rearranged and combined in order to show the interrelations between the four countries. The interrelations are found in the 'rest of the world' columns and rows. In Table 2.2 only totals or net positions are given. In the WAM, more detail is required, in order to show the origin and destination of the international transactions. Each entry in Table 2.2 can be interpreted as a matrix, or submatrix (of the main matrix). By subdividing the accounts into four categories, i.e. one category for each of the four countries, one matrix is obtained that represents all transactions for W, X, Y and Z. The submatrices that result from this extension take two forms: (1) matrices that record national transactions only, with all cells empty apart from the cells on the diagonals and (2) matrices with only empty cells on the diagonals, while the other cells record bilateral transactions. Entries in the latter category record an incoming transaction from one country that is an outgoing transaction for another country. In the example, there are three forms of international transactions: (1) transactions with a contra-entry on the production account: imports and exports, (2) transactions with a contra-entry on the consumption account: foreign factor income and payments, and (3) transactions with a contra-entry on the accumulation account: foreign lending and borrowing. Table 2.3 gives the three matrices that show the international transactions between W, X, Y and Z.

Table 2.3a presents transactions in goods and services. The column totals are the incomings from trade (exports); the row totals are the outgoings (imports). The net position for each country can be derived by subtracting the row total from the column total. Table 2.3b presents the factor income payments between the four countries while Table 2.3c shows foreign borrowing and lending among the four countries. The purpose of the WAM is to show international interrelations and interactions between domestic accumulation balances and balances of foreign

Table 2.1 The national accounts for countries W, X, Y and Z

PRODUCTION

outgoings							incomings					
line		W	X	Y	Z	total	line		W	X	Y	Z	total
1	(8)	120	205	215	305	845	3	(6)	100	150	200	250	700
2	(15)	40	50	60	60	210	4	(10)	30	45	5	65	145
							5	(13)	30	60	70	50	210
total		160	255	275	365	1055	total		160	255	275	365	1055

CONSUMPTION

outgoings							incomings						
line		W	X	Y	Z	total	line		W	X	Y	Z	total
6	(3)	100	150	200	250	700	8	(1)	120	205	215	305	845
7	(12)	25	30	40	50	145	9	(14)	5	-25	25	-5	0
total		125	180	240	300	845	total		125	180	240	300	845

(Continued)

Table 2.1 (Continued)

ACCUMULATION

outgoings							
line		W	X	Y	Z	total
10	(4)	30	45	5	65	145
11	(16)	-5	-15	35	-15	0
total		25	30	40	50	145

incomings						
line		W	X	Y	Z	total
12	(7)	25	30	40	50	145
total		25	30	40	50	145

REST OF THE WORLD

outgoings						
line		W	X	Y	Z	total
13	(5)	30	60	70	50	210
14	(9)	5	-25	25	-5	0
total		35	35	95	45	210

incomings						
line		W	X	Y	Z	total
15	(2)	40	50	60	60	210
16	(11)	-5	-15	35	-15	0
total		35	35	95	45	210

1 Gross income payments	=	8 Gross income receipts from domestic production
2 Purchases of imports	=	15 Sales of imports
3 Sales of consumption goods	=	6 Purchases of consumption goods
4 Sales of capital goods	=	10 Purchases of capital goods
5 Sales of exports	=	13 Purchases of exports
7 Saving	=	12 Saving
9 Net factor incomes from abroad	=	14 Net factor income payments
11 Net lending to abroad	=	16 Net borrowing from abroad

Table 2.2 National accounts in matrix format for countries W, X, Y and Z

Country W

in \ out	P	C	A	R	total
P		100	30	30	160
C	120			5	125
A		25			25
R	40		-5		35
total	160	125	25	35	

Country X

in \ out	P	C	A	R	total
P		150	45	60	255
C	205			-25	180
A		30			30
R	50		-15		35
total	255	180	30	35	

Country Y

in \ out	P	C	A	R	total
P		200	5	70	275
C	215			25	240
A		40			40
R	60		35		95
total	275	240	40	95	

Country Z

in \ out	P	C	A	R	total
P		250	65	50	365
C	305			-5	300
A		50			50
R	60		-15		45
total	365	300	50	45	

Table 2.3 International transactions between countries W, X, Y and Z

(a) Trade

	W	X	Y	Z	total
W		5	10	15	30
X	5		30	25	60
Y	25	25		20	70
Z	10	20	20		50
total	40	50	60	60	210

(b) Factor income from/to abroad

	W	X	Y	Z	total
W		10	0	0	10
X	0		0	5	5
Y	5	15		10	30
Z	0	5	5		10
total	5	30	5	15	55

(c) Foreign lending

	W	X	Y	Z	total
W		5	10	0	15
X	5		10	5	20
Y	0	0		5	5
Z	5	0	20		25
total	10	5	40	10	65

transactions. Therefore, a WAM in its simplest form has to include foreign balances and national accumulation balances. Table 2.4 gives a world accounting matrix in a simple form for countries W, X, Y and Z. For the sake of simplicity, transactions on current account have been aggregated by adding up matrices (a) and (b) of Table 2.3. The world accounting matrix consists of four submatrices (or quadrants):

- North-West quadrant: all transactions on the current account
- North-East quadrant: domestic investment
- South-West quadrant: domestic savings
- South-East quadrant: records foreign lending and borrowing

From Table 2.4 it is easy to see that global exports equal global imports: for the North-West quadrant the sum of the subtotal of ingoings equals the sum of the subtotal of outgoings. Similarly, global investment equals global savings: the sum of the subtotals of the North-East quadrant equals the sum of the subtotals of the South-West quadrant. The South-East quadrant shows that the sum of foreign finance equals zero: the sum of the subtotals of the ingoings equals the sum of the subtotals of the outgoings. Furthermore, the table shows that the national accounting identity that states that for each country the balance of payments on current account must equal the financial surplus (equation (2.3) in section 2.2) holds: the row total of ingoings (exports and factor income plus investment) equals for each country the column total of outgoings (imports and factor payments plus savings). Similarly, for each country, the total of outgoings in the North-East quadrant and the South-East quadrant (investment plus foreign lending) represents total financial and fixed investment. For each country, total investment equals total available investment finance, as represented by the total of ingoings in the South-West quadrant and the South-East quadrant (domestic savings plus foreign borrowing). Thus, sources and uses of world payments are identified simultaneously. Table 2.5 is a generalization of Table 2.4; it gives a world accounting matrix for m countries (or country groups). Matrix CT presents the aggregated current account transactions, matrix S presents domestic savings, matrix I presents domestic investment and matrix F presents the aggregated capital account.

Ideally, any WAM should provide a direct link between stocks, flows and investment income. This link is not only useful for statistical checks but also for analysis. Table 2.6 shows how this can be done.

Table 2.4 A world accounting matrix for countries W, X, Y and Z

		Current Account					Capital Account					
		W	X	Y	Z	subtotal	W	X	Y	Z	subtotal	total
Current Account	W		15	10	15	40	30				30	70
	X	5		30	30	65		45			45	110
	Y	30	40		30	100			5		5	105
	Z	10	25	25		60				65	65	125
	subtotal	45	80	65	75	265	30	45	5	65	145	
Capital Account	W	25				25		5	10	0	15	40
	X		30			30	5		10	5	20	50
	Y			40		40	0	0		5	5	45
	Z				50	50	5	0	20		25	75
	subtotal	25	30	40	50	145	10	5	40	10	65	
	total	70	110	105	125		40	50	45	75		

Table 2.5 *A world accounting matrix for m countries*

matrix CT

countries	1	2	3	.	.	m	
1	A_{11}	A_{12}	A_{13}	.	.	A_{1m}	X_1
2	A_{21}	A_{22}	.	.			
3	A_{31}	.					
.	.	.					
.	.						
m	A_{m1}					A_{mm}	X_m
	M_1					M_m	CT

matrix I

	1	2	3	.	.	m	
	I_1						I_1
		I_2					.
			I_3				.
				.			
					.		
						I_m	I_m
	I_1	.	.			I_m	I

matrix S

countries	1	2	3	.	.	m	
1	S_1						S_1
2		S_2					.
3			S_3				.
.				.			
.					.		
m						S_m	S_m
	S_1	.	.			S_m	S

matrix F

	1	2	3	.	.	m	
	B_{11}	B_{12}	B_{13}	.	.	B_{1m}	C_1
	B_{21}	B_{22}	.				.
	B_{31}	.					
	.						
	B_{m1}					B_{mm}	C_m
	D_1	.	.			D_m	F

This table has stocks of assets and liabilities and the corresponding revaluations. Stocks of assets and liabilities are incorporated in the system by opening and closing balance sheets. A balance sheet shows (1) the recorded value of tangible assets held plus the excess of financial claims held as assets over financial claims issued as liabilities and (2) the net worth of the national economy. These two amounts are always equal. Net assets at the end of a period are equal to net assets at the beginning plus net investment at home and abroad in the period plus revaluations needed to adjust assets previously acquired, or liabilities previously issued, to prices relevant at the closing date. Unfortunately, the construction of balance sheets at the global level is not a workable option given the enormous data problems, especially with regard to revaluations. Therefore the stock tables for the WAMs in this study are 'simple' satellite tables that are not directly linked to the core table. However, in the construction process where possible the link between the variables has been made to make the best possible use of the available statistical information.

Table 2.6 also shows how a consumption account can be introduced to record demand and supply for consumption. Thus GNP, a variable indispensable for economic analysis, can be derived as the sum of consumption and saving. As a result, in the construction of the WAMs, the GNPs derived from Table 2.6 may differ considerably from the GNPs in primary statistical databases. A large share of the statistical discrepancy is absorbed by saving, because saving is a residual in national accounting and is therefore considered as a relatively unreliable variable.

2.4 Units of Analysis

Obviously, for a world accounting system, transactors, transactions and stocks have to be aggregated, and the particular aggregation chosen should be in accordance with the purpose of the study. Transactors, transactions and stocks are closely related and their aggregation has to be consistent. If, for example, official lenders engage in a long-term loan, the immediate result is an official, long-term flow and an increase in long-term, official assets/liabilities. There are statistical and analytical reasons for disaggregations of transactions and stocks. To disentangle discrepancies some variables have been disaggregated during the construction process, but they are no longer differentiated in the final

Table 2.6 An extended world accounting matrix

	1	2	3	4	5	6
1				A_0		
2			C			
3		C	CT	I		
4	A_0		S	F	R	A_1
5				R		
6				A_1		

A_0 : opening assets
A_1 : closing assets
C : domestic consumption
CT : transactions on the current acct. of the balance of payments
I : domestic investment
S : domestic saving
R : revaluations
F : transactions on the capital acct. of the balance of payments

presentation of the WAMs because they have no analytical relevance. Table 2.7 presents the categories of transactors, transactions and stocks in the final presentation of the WAMs.

Categories of transactors

In this study, countries are classified to facilitate an analysis of patterns of trade and finance of LDCs in a global context. As Table A2.1 shows, all countries of the world are included, but the emphasis in the country classification for the WAM is on LDCs. The classification of developing countries is based on the hypothesis that there is a difference in debt characteristics, economic structure and capacity to absorb shocks between countries that borrowed primarily from official sources and those that borrowed primarily from private sources. An important difference between official flows and private flows is found in the lending conditions. Official loans are usually more stable in terms of interest rates and availability than private loans, but, unlike private loans, official loans are usually subject to conditionality. Because of these differences in lending conditions, official and private flows are likely to have a different impact on the receiving economies. Finally, there are likely

Table 2.7 Disaggregation of transactors, transactions and stocks

Regional breakdown	Institutional breakdown
US	Multilateral development banks
Japan	
EU	
Other OECD countries	Official creditors
CMEA	Private creditors
Major oil exporters	
Official Borrowers	
Diversified Borrowers	
Private Borrowers	
Rest of the world	

International transactions	Domestic transactions
Trade	Consumption
• food and beverages (SITC 0–1)*	Gross domestic investment
• raw materials (SITC 2+4)	Gross national saving
• fuels (SITC 3)	
• manufactures (SITC 5–9)	
Non-factor services	
Unrequited transfers	
• from official sources	
• from private sources	
Investment income, capital flows and stocks	
• foreign direct investment	
• other capital	
– from official sources	
– from private sources	
Changes in reserves	

* Defined according to Revision 2 of the Standard International Trade Classification (SITC).

to be differences in the sectoral allocation of different types of flows; it is hypothesized that official flows and private flows tend to finance different types of investments in the receiving economies. Different types of international capital flows are thus likely to lead to different patterns of investment and growth.

Most capital flows to LDCs consisted of official flows until the 1970s, when there was a considerable increase in private lending. Official lending in the 1970s remained significant, but its share in the total declined until private lending began to shrink in 1982. Even when private lending boomed in the 1970s, access to private lending was restricted to a small group of LDCs while most LDCs remained dependent on official lending as the main source of foreign capital.[4]

The classification used here is primarily based on long-term data from the *World Debt Tables* of the World Bank.[5] This is the only data source that classifies long-term LDC debt according to the source of foreign lending: the creditors are subdivided into official and private creditors. Short-term external debt data are used as an additional source of information, but the World Bank does not distinguish between public and private short-term debt due to inadequacy of the available data. Here it is assumed that short-term debt mainly stems from private sources.

Three country groups are distinguished. In principle, countries are classified as 'Official Borrowers' if the ratio of official long-term debt to total long-term debt is greater than 67 per cent. Countries are classified as 'Private Borrowers' if the ratio is less than 33 per cent and the countries that fall in between these categories are regarded as 'Diversified Borrowers'. The classification is based on World Bank data for stock values of long-term external official and private debt in the period 1970–87. The classification is quite stable: about two thirds of all countries remained in one class throughout the period 1970–87. For countries with a more volatile record, or with values close to either 33 or 67, the ratios for the 1980s were taken to be decisive. In a few cases, countries were categorized as Private Borrowers because of their large short-term debt from private sources. Table A2.2 summarizes the values for the ratio of official debt to total debt in four period averages for each country. The first three columns of the table show period averages that only include long-term debt, while the last column also includes short-term debt, a debt category that is reported by the World Bank from 1980 onwards.

An important aspect of the analysis involves the geographical distribution by origin and destination of LDC trade and finance in the world economy. The study analyses both intra-LDC flows and flows between LDCs and the 'rest of the world'. To analyse patterns in trade and capital flows between LDCs and the 'rest of the world' it is useful to subdivide the world into blocs that represent the origin and the destination of trade and capital flows of LDCs. Three major blocs are distinguished: the Western industrialized countries (OECD), the Eastern European and some other countries that used to comprise the Council of Mutual Economic Assistance (CMEA) and the major oil exporters (MOEs), a group of countries mainly situated in the Middle East. The OECD, by far the largest group in terms of international trade and finance, is further subdivided into the US, Japan, the EU and 'Other OECD countries' (OOECD). Finally, there is a residual category, the rest of the world (ROW).

In addition to the regional breakdown there is also an institutional breakdown relating to the source of foreign lending of LDCs which corresponds to the country classification of LDCs. Foreign loans are subdivided into loans from international organizations (multilateral loans), loans from governments (bilateral loans) and loans from private creditors. For multilateral loans an institutional category is added to the regional groups; for bilateral and private loans the institutional breakdown is incorporated by a subdivision into a private and an official sector within the country groups that are the major creditors for LDCs.

Categories of transactions and stocks

The current account consists of three major types of transactions: trade, services and unrequited transfers.[6] Given the differences in market structure for different categories of trade some further disaggregation is desirable. For the analysis of debt problems of developing countries it is useful to incorporate information on the import and export structure of various regions. This further classification is based on the assumption that there is a relationship between the type of trade dependency and debt problems through the level of diversification of exports and the terms of trade. Countries with a more diversified export structure are less vulnerable to price changes in commodity markets. In the

WAM, separate matrices are constructed for food and beverages (SITC 0 – 1), raw materials (SITC 2 + 4), fuels (SITC 3) and manufactures (SITC 5 – 9).

There are analytical and statistical reasons for a disaggregation of services on the current account. Firstly, for analytical reasons services are disaggregated into factor services and non-factor services. From an economic perspective, non-factor services are similar to goods, i.e. they are outputs whose demand is subject to influences such as income and prices. Factor services are a reflection of stocks of assets and liabilities. The discrepancies on the service balances are large for both factor and non-factor services. To trace the discrepancies in non-factor services they have been disaggregated into relevant categories in the construction stage, but in the final presentation they appear as one category. For factor services there are both statistical and analytical reasons for further disaggregation. Investment income is related to capital flows and stocks. To disentangle the discrepancies in investment income, different categories are distinguished in the construction stage. A strategy during construction is to compare reported income flows with estimated income flows from stock data. Disaggregation is needed to estimate income flows from stock data as a different rate of return is applied to different types of stocks. In the final presentation, disaggregation of investment income remains limited to two major categories: foreign direct investment and other capital. For LDCs interest payments related to other capital are disaggregated into payments to official creditors and private creditors.

The same disaggregation is made in capital flows. The basic distinction between foreign direct investment and other investment is that a direct investor has an ownership claim that involves control of the asset. The distinction between capital flows from official and private sources follows from a central hypothesis in this study: different types of foreign finance have a different impact on receiving economies. Further disaggregation of capital flows would be interesting from an analytical perspective, but it would not be feasible given the lack of data that describe the origin and destination of these transactions.

There are two major types of capital stocks: physical capital and financial assets or liabilities. Physical capital can be domestically or foreign owned. A stock of foreign investment consists of the accumulated value of flows of foreign investment over the years. For receiving countries, accumulated foreign investments are a liability, for investing countries they are an asset.[7] Financial assets or liabilities may take various forms, but what they have in common is that the outstanding amounts result from capital outflows (assets) or capital inflows (liabilities). The types of financial assets and liabilities distinguished in the WAM correspond to the distinctions made in investment income and capital flows.

Unrequited transfers on the current account refer to transactions whereby one party provides goods, services or cash to a non-resident, without the recipient assuming any obligation for payment. Unrequited transfers may stem from official or from private sources. Most official transfers refer to transfers to LDCs, such as development assistance, debt cancellation and contributions to international organizations. Private transfers include migrants' transfers, a category that has played an important part in the earning of foreign exchange for some LDCs.

Exchange rates

The WAM includes information from different data systems for all countries in the world. In international data sources, national accounting data are usually presented in units of domestic currencies, while international transactions and stocks of foreign assets and liabilities are usually presented in US dollars or Special Drawing Rights (SDRs). The WAM presents data expressed in US dollars, converting where necessary using official exchange rates. This has a number of implications. Exchange rate conversions of domestic transactions to US dollars implicitly assume that price levels are the same in all countries, while in fact there are wide and systematic differences across countries (see for example Kravis et al. 1981). Also, price structures differ across countries. Consequently, exchange rate conversions of expenditures often give a distorted impression of the real quantity composition of the GDP in one country compared with another (Kravis et al. 1981: 339). This type of problem is particularly relevant for comparisons between LDCs, and between LDCs and industrialized countries, because of the large differences in economic structures. Another consequence of presenting the WAMs in US dollars is that shifts in the patterns of trade and finance partly reflect changes in exchange rates. No attempt is made in this study to solve the conceptual problem of exchange rate conversion. The purpose of this section is only to indicate that comparison of shifts in the shares of country groups in total trade, finance and domestic accumulation is influenced by the method used for exchange rate conversion. Therefore, the shifts should be interpreted with some caution.

2.5 Concluding Remarks

The Statistical Office of the United Nations has developed a coherent framework for recording and presenting the main flows relating to production, consumption, accumulation and external trade known as the 'System of National Accounts' (SNA). The WAM is a specific aggregation of the SNA, so the basic concepts of the SNA variables – saving, investment, consumption and international trade and finance – constitute the foundation of the WAM.

The SNA provides only a conceptual framework and is not a data source for the WAM. As no single data source covers all the required information for the WAM, data for the WAM are collected from many different sources. Obviously, data availability constrains the disaggregation of WAM variables. For example, a more detailed disaggregation of capital flows would have strengthened the usefulness of the WAM as an analytical tool, but the limited availability of financial data by origin and destination does not allow for more detail in the classification of financial variables than proposed in this chapter. The definitions of the variables of the WAM rely on the definitions of the various statistical sources. The various data sources are not integrated; they are set up to serve different objectives, and consequently, use different definitions. This gives rise to practical problems when combining different data sources in one framework.

3 Data Sources and Data Problems

3.1 Introduction

For some WAM variables, several possible data sources are available, while for others, there is no systematic source. The macroeconomic statistics published by international institutions (IMF, World Bank, UN, BIS) serve as the major source for data on international and domestic transactions, while for some data only national sources are available. This chapter explains the selection of data sources and identifies the major data problems in the construction of the WAM. When more than one data source is available, the basic criteria for the selection of data sources are: (1) completeness, (2) level and type of disaggregation, and (3) reliability. For the completeness of a data source, the most important criteria are the country and time coverage. The level and type of disaggregation in a data source should be as close as possible to the level and type of disaggregation that is desired for the WAM, which means that the availability of a distribution by origin and destination is important. Reliability is more difficult to assess.

These three criteria correspond to three major data problems. Firstly, there is the problem of missing data: some of the entries of the WAM cannot be filled with information supplied by the international institutions. Usually, the databases of the international organizations do not provide data for non-member countries. For example, for the period under consideration the USSR and most other former CMEA countries are largely excluded from IMF and World Bank statistics. For some countries data coverage is poor. This applies to a large number of small LDCs (for example Cape Verde, Bhutan, Nepal, Equatorial Guinea and Burundi), as well as countries involved in armed conflicts, like Angola,

Mozambique, Afghanistan, Iran and Iraq. For some variables, for example short-term debt, the time coverage is limited. In many instances, a disaggregation by origin and destination is either not available at all or available only to a limited extent. This problem applies mainly to data on financial variables. The publications of the international institutions do not provide a geographical classification by origin and destination of financial variables. They report time series, for example for foreign direct investment by the US, but they do not give the geographical destination of foreign direct investment by the US. For some countries, a geographical breakdown for financial variables can be found in national publications, mainly in reports from the central banks.

The second major data problem emerges when combining data from different sources in one framework. While the estimates in publications of international organizations have been harmonized, data from individual country sources differ strongly in their coverage, definitions and level and type of disaggregation. Statistics are always collected with a particular purpose in mind. Depending on the purpose, the statistics are organized according to the most appropriate definitions and disaggregations and collected from the most appropriate source. Also, statistics are constantly subject to revision, and there may be differences in timing (of the revisions) or valuation of transactions. This makes it difficult to compare and combine similar variables from different sources; it also explains discrepancies between the data sources.

A third major problem is the existance of discrepancies within a single data source. These may be caused by misspecification and omission of data. The international organizations provide guidelines and recommendations for their member countries for the compilation of statistics. Misspecification of a transaction occurs when a country reports a transaction under a heading that differs from the recommendations of the international institution that publishes the statistics. When for a particular transaction the misspecified amounts of debtor countries are not equal to the misspecified amounts of creditor countries, this results in a discrepancy at the international level. Misspecification affects the balances of disaggregated transactions, but it has no effect on the overall balance of a category of transactions. However, omission of data may lead to discrepancies in overall balances. If, for example, a direct investment transaction is reported as a portfolio transaction, this will lead to discrepancies on both global accounts, but it does not affect the global balance of capital account transactions. If a direct investment transaction is omitted, there will be a discrepancy on the global capital account.

3.2 Merchandise Trade

For the matrices for merchandise trade the United Nations Trade Matrices System (UNTMS)[1] has been selected for the WAM because of the extensive country coverage, the availability of the series in constant prices and the type and level of disaggregation. There are four commodity groups in the system: SITC 0 – 1 (food, beverages and tobacco), SITC 2 + 4 (crude materials, animal and vegetable oils etc.), SITC 3 (mineral fuels, lubricants and related materials), and SITC 5 – 9 (manufactures). According to the UN definition, merchandise trade (valued f.o.b.) includes:

> All goods which add to or subtract from the material resources of a country as a result of their movements into or out of the country. It includes the market value of related distributive services up to the customs frontier of the exporting economy.

Compared with the other data sources for merchandise trade, the UNTMS is a fairly complete data base; all major countries are covered. The matrices are built on the basis of reported exports (valued f.o.b.) by origin and destination. Thus, country X's imports in the matrices are represented by all exports to country X as reported by trading partners, and not on imports reported by country X itself.

The UNTMS only covers merchandise exports. In the WAM, the trade matrices are combined with estimates for other balance of payments transactions from other data sources that differ in their definitions and country coverage. The major data source for balance of payments transactions is the IMF, *Balance of Payments Statistics* (BOP). The BOP includes time series for merchandise exports f.o.b., and imports f.o.b.. World flows reported in the UNTMS are generally larger than those reported in the BOP. This can largely be explained by a difference in country coverage.[2] The trade matrices of the WAM are based on reported exports. In the BOP, global reported exports exceeded reported imports in 1970, 1975 and 1980, while in 1985 reported imports were larger than reported exports. Other trade reporting systems are likely to have a similar bias. Consequently, the use of an export-based reporting system will render larger world trade values in 1970, 1975 and 1980 than will an import-based reporting system, and vice versa in 1985.

The world trade imbalances in the BOP follow from a discrepancy between global recorded exports and imports.[3] Table 3.1 gives the global balance of payments discrepancies in the BOP. It follows from the table that the surplus on the global trade balance in 1970, 1975 and 1980 has 'helped' to balance entries on the global current account, while the shift towards a deficit on the global trade balance at the beginning of the 1980s has been an important factor behind the sharp increase in the world current account discrepancy. Thus, a consequence of the use of the UNTMS matrices in combination with BOP data is that the deficit on the world current account in the WAM will tend to be higher in 1970, 1975 and 1980, and lower in 1985.

3.3 Transport and Other Nonfactor Services

The main component of nonfactor services is international transport. The global deficit on the account for international transport greatly contributes to the world current account discrepancy (see Table 3.1). In order to analyse the discrepancy on this account, and if possible make adjustments for it, it is necessary to calculate the different transport items separately, using the BOP that provides sufficient detail on transactions in nonfactor services. In the BOP, the definitions are (IMF 1977):

> *Shipment* covers freight, insurance and other distributive services. *Other transportation* includes international passenger fares, expenditures by international carriers in other countries than that of the operator of the carrier, charter fees and other transportation services. *Travel* includes goods and services acquired in a foreign country by travellers during their stay in that country.

There are several data problems related to international transport and travel. There is a large difference between world income and payments. There is a problem of country coverage, mainly for CMEA countries (which are non-members), but also for a few major oil exporters. There is no systematic information on the origin and destination of international transport and travel. Discrepancy on the shipment account is large but stable (see Table 3.1). Discrepancies within data sources may either: (1) affect the balance on the current account, usually reflecting

Table 3.1 Global balance of payments discrepancies (in US$ billions)

	1970	1975	1980	1985
Current Account	-3.6	-0.3	-55.0	-83.4
Merchandise trade	8.1	20.6	4.6	-12.6
Nonfactor services:				
– Shipment	-3.0	-14.2	-28.3	-24.5
– Other transportation	-2.4	-1.9	-3.0	-1.7
– Travel	0.4	-0.4	-2.7	6.5
Investment income FDI:				
– Reinvested earnings	2.5	7.6	9.4	19.7
– Other	-1.1	-3.0	-5.1	-8.8
Other investment income	-3.4	-5.1	-18.7	-54.1
Unrequited transfers:				
– Official	-3.0	-8.7	-17.4	-15.6
– Private	-0.6	1.4	10.7	13.0
Other current account	-1.1	3.4	-4.5	-5.3
Capital Account	1.3	-5.9	27.8	64.8
Foreign direct investment	-1.9	-5.6	-7.5	-14.9
Other capital flows:				
– Long-term	2.8	14.1	34.2	32.4
– Short-term	8.9	-8.7	20.8	15.8
– Portfolio	2.2	1.9	8.1	40.6
Net changes in reserves	-10.7	-7.7	-27.7	-9.1
Errors and Omissions	2.3	6.2	27.2	18.6

Note: Columns may not tally due to rounding.

omission of data or (2) affect the balance of two accounts, reflecting misspecification of data. According to an analysis by the IMF: ‘it is virtually certain that the large discrepancy on the shipment account reflects mainly the omission, on the credit side, of the revenues of a large portion of the world shipping fleet – principally the earnings of fleets operated by Hong Kong, Eastern European and Greek enterprises – from recorded balance of payments data' (IMF 1987: 90).

A smaller part of the discrepancy may be explained by misspecification between merchandise trade and 'freight and insurance'. Imports are usually recorded c.i.f. and are converted to f.o.b. for the BOP. The difference between imports c.i.f. and f.o.b reflecting 'freight and insurance' is shifted from reported imports to the shipment account of the BOP. The IMF (1983 & 1987) suggests that overestimation of 'freight and insurance' may explain a part of the deficit on the global accounts for transport and a part of the global surplus (in 1970, 1975 & 1980) for merchandise trade.

The main component for 'other transportation' is the expenditure of foreign carriers in domestic ports, such as fuel costs and port charges. The expenditure of 'missing fleets' in ports in countries other than their own should be recorded as debits on the account for 'other transportation'. The lack of reported debits on this account may explain some of the negative discrepancy (IMF 1987). The relatively small but volatile discrepancy on the world account for travel has never been analysed.

In the construction of the WAM, the category 'other goods, services and income' has been added to nonfactor services purely for practical reasons. The 'rest' category refers to all transactions that could not be classified under merchandise, shipment, other transportation, travel, unrequited transfers or investment income. The transactions refer, for example, to payments made by embassies, military units, seasonal workers or advertising abroad by exporters.[4]

3.4 Investment Income, Capital Flows and Stocks

Since the financial variables investment income, capital flows and stocks of assets and liabilities are closely related it is obviously preferable to use for the WAM one data source for the three variables and where possible, this has been done. In Chapter 2 the conceptual relations between investment income, capital flows and stocks were defined: a net capital outflow (inflow) is equal to net changes in the stock for foreign assets (liabilities) adjusted for revaluations. Year-to-year changes in stocks of foreign assets or liabilities reflect the yearly capital flows, although changes in the external stocks are also influenced by revaluations of the existing stock. Investment income is a reflection of stocks built up in the past. Some statistical systems use these conceptual relations in the compilation of debt statistics. Investment income is sometimes estimated by applying a relevant interest rate to investment positions; sometimes stocks are compiled by cumulating the flow figures over a relevant time period (Ulan & Dewald 1989, Williamson & Milner 1991). There are large statistical problems in this type of data compilation and hence also in the construction of the WAMs. The major problem is that revaluations (reflecting price changes, exchange rate changes or debt reorganizations) are rarely estimated systematically. Revaluations may be large and may therefore have a significant impact on the difference between capital flows and year-to-year changes in stocks, and on the link between investment positions and investment income.

Foreign direct investment

The BOP is the most comprehensive data source for direct investment, providing estimates for a large sample of countries. The BOP reports direct investment income and payments on the current account of the balance of payments and direct investment flows of the capital account. The stock tables of the BOP record net direct investment abroad and net direct investment in the home country, but the stock tables are only available for 34 – mainly industrialized – countries.[5] In the BOP, *direct investment* is defined as:

> Investment that is made to acquire a lasting interest in an enterprise operating in an economy other than that of the investor, the investor's purpose being to have an effective voice in the management of the enterprise. (IMF 1977)

The first data problem for direct investment stems from the interpretation of this definition; some countries, for example the US, use as a threshold an ownership as low as 10 per cent of the shares of an enterprise, while other countries use much higher thresholds.[6] This problem may lead to misspecification and asymmetry in reporting if one country classifies a transaction as direct investment, while another country classifies the same transaction under the heading of other investment. In the BOP *direct investment income* comprises:

> The parent company share in (1) the earnings of foreign subsidiaries and other unincorporated foreign affiliates, (2) the earnings of unincorporated

branches in foreign countries, and (3) interest received from (or paid to) foreign-incorporated affiliates and branches. (IMF 1977)

In the BOP direct investment income is split into two parts: (1) reinvested earnings and (2) other direct investment income. This distinction gives rise to further statistical problems. In most countries, reinvested earnings are unrecorded, and even where they are recorded, statistical reporting systems in a number of countries may not fully capture the activities of their multinationals abroad or of foreign companies within their jurisdiction (Turner 1991). In many cases, multinational enterprises minimize tax payments by manipulating the earnings of their various subsidiaries, and this may well diminish the meaningfulness of statistical reports.

The US, the UK, Germany and the Netherlands report non-repatriated profits as foreign direct investment flows, and income on non-repatriated profits as direct investment income, while most other countries do not. In the period 1970–85, these countries were large net creditors[7] and, consequently, there has been an excess of income credits over debits, while net changes in direct investment assets have exceeded net changes in direct investment liabilities. Another factor explaining global discrepancies in direct investment, is the treatment of direct investment inflows in offshore centres. Statistics of major creditor countries suggest that a significant portion of direct investment flows is directed towards offshore centres, whereas reported inflows are negligible (Turner 1991). This is because some offshore centres (Bermuda, the Cayman Islands and Hong Kong) are not included in the BOP, while others (the Netherlands Antilles, Panama, Switzerland) may not consider the transactors (local branches and subsidiaries of foreign enterprises which engage only in international transactions) as residents for balance of payments purposes (IMF 1987).

The IMF (1987) analysed the global discrepancy on the account for direct investment income for 1983. It found that the relatively small discrepancy (minus US$ 1.6 billion) concealed widespread under-reporting and significant asymmetries in reporting. Bilateral comparison on the basis of reports by four major creditor countries (US, UK, Germany and the Netherlands) traced large amounts of 'credits not matched by debits', indicating that a large portion of debits is entirely omitted from global balance of payments statistics.[8] Other bilateral comparisons with the major creditor countries showed that in 1983, misspecification between direct investment income and other investment income was widespread.[9]

There is no data source that provides 'harmonized' information on the geographical origin and destination of direct investment though many countries publish a geographical distribution for their direct investment flows and stocks, and in a few cases also for investment income. In a number of projects,[10] data from national sources, private enquiries and international institutions (OECD and UNCTC) has been collected and published. Although this is helpful in the search for information, the data are not harmonized, and the concepts and definitions may differ considerably with those in the BOP.

Other foreign capital

For the category 'other foreign capital' two major data sources have been selected: (1) the World Bank *Debtor Reporting System* (DRS), as a primary source for LDCs and (2) the BOP, as a primary source for other countries. An additional data source is the IMF *International Banking Statistics* (IBS included in the IMF, *International Financial Statistics*), for stock data that are not covered by the DRS and the BOP. To a limited extent, the OECD data system on third world debt has been used. The BOP gives information on investment income and capital flows for a large group of countries. The DRS only covers LDC debt and related flows and payments, but the classification of the data is more suitable for the WAM, and the World Bank has provided a geographical distribution by origin and destination of LDC debt and related payments.[11] The BIS gives data on international assets and liabilities of banks in the BIS area,[12] while the OECD data give some insight in the make-up of LDC short-term debt.

There are differences in the definitions for external debt as used by the World Bank, the IMF, the BIS and the OECD. A helpful contribution to the comparison of definitions of external debt is made in a joint publication of these four organizations (World Bank, IMF, BIS, OECD 1988). The report provides, a 'core' definition of external debt as follows:

> Gross external debt is the amount of disbursed and outstanding contractual liabilities of residents of a country to non-residents to repay principal, with or without interest, or to pay interest, with or without principal. (World Bank et al. 1988: 12)

The report also indicates where definitions used by each of the participating institutions differ from the core definition. The concept of financial liabilities used in the BOP is wider than that embodied in the core definition, mainly because the BOP includes equity-type liabilities.[13] The coverage of types of loans in the DRS is smaller than in the core definition, primarily because: (1) loans to non-residents in the borrower's own currency have not to date been included in the data on external debt; (2) information on arrears of capital and interest has only partially and indirectly been reflected in the statistics. The stock of debt is only reduced by a principal payment actually made, not by one due; arrears of amortization are indistinguishably included in the total. Interest arrears are not included and not shown, unless and until they are capitalized under a debt organization agreement; and (3) notes and coins held by non-residents are not reported in the DRS. An additional difference between the BOP and the DRS is the classification of external long-term lending to overseas subsidiaries that in the DRS is included as part of the host country's foreign debt, while in the BOP long-term intra-company financing is treated as part of foreign direct investment. The definition of total external debt in OECD debt statistics is similar to the core definition. The BIS data system does not attempt to measure total external debt; the BIS banking statistics record external positions – amounts of assets and liabilities – of all reporting banks *vis-à-vis* individual countries.

Differences in the definitions of external debt of the DRS and the BOP are reflected in the definitions for long-term and short-term debt given by the World Bank and the IMF. The DRS defines long-term external debt as a:

> debt that has an original or an extended maturity of over one year and that is owed to non-residents and repayable in foreign currency, goods or services.

The BOP definition for long-term external debt (cf. IMF 1977) is:

> capital with an original contractual maturity of more than one year, or with no stated maturity (for example, corporate equities);

and, finally the BOP definition of short-term debt is:

> debt that has an original maturity of one year or less, including currency.

The difference in definitions for long-term and short-term debt between the DRS and the BOP on the one hand, and the BIS on the other, are more fundamental: in the BIS statistics, all debt that is due in one year, regardless of the original maturity, is classified as short-term debt. The OECD definitions are similar to those of the BOP, excluding the equity component.

The sectorization of external debt is different in the BOP and in the DRS. In the DRS, the three main categories of long-term external debt are:

public debt, which is an external obligation of a public debtor;
publicly guaranteed debt, which is an external obligation of a private debtor that is guaranteed for repayment by a public entity; and
private non-guaranteed debt, which is an external obligation of a private debtor that is not guaranteed by a public entity.

The two main categories of creditors are:

official creditors, disaggregated into multilateral and bilateral; and
private creditors, disaggregated into suppliers, financial markets, foreign parent company, and other private sources.

A breakdown by creditor is given for interest payments, disbursements, principal repayments and outstanding amounts of external debt, for public and publicly guaranteed debt, and, where available, for private non-guaranteed debt, but not for short-term debt.

The BOP classification differs for investment income on the one hand, and stocks and capital account transactions on the other hand. For investment income, two sectors are identified: the resident official sector (including inter-official) and the foreign official sector. For stocks and capital account transactions, the BOP makes a distinction between 'portfolio' and 'other capital'. Portfolio transactions are split into transactions concerning bonds and those concerning equities. In the category 'other capital' of the BOP, domestic creditors for assets and domestic debtors for liabilities are identified. Transactions are split into long-term and short-term. Further, the domestic sector is split into three parts: the resident official sector, deposit money banks and other sectors. Thus, the classification of LDCs based on the source of foreign capital, can only be derived on the basis of the DRS; this is another reason for choosing it and not the BOP as the primary source for LDCs. A further important reason is of course the availability of a distribution by origin and destination. There is no sectoral disaggregation in the BIS banking statistics whereas the sectoral classification in OECD debt statistics is similar to that in the DRS; in addition to the DRS, total external outstanding amounts of short-term debt are split into a bank and an export credit component.

Differences in definitions and in coverage between the various reporting systems for external debt inevitably lead to discrepancies between the data sources, but even when there are no (or very small) differences in definitions and coverage, there may be sizeable discrepancies. An example of discrepancies between data sources is found in reporting of external debt of LDCs in the DRS and the BOP. This is disturbing because the DRS has been selected as the major data source for LDC debt but the DRS series have been supplemented with BOP series for short-term debt because the time coverage for short-term debt is limited in the DRS.

For private non-guaranteed debt, country coverage in the DRS is incomplete, but the list of countries covered grew rapidly in the 1980s. When private non-guaranteed debt is not included in the DRS, it may be derived as the residual between reported long-term amounts in the DRS and the BOP.[14] When it is included, total long-term debt reported in the DRS and the BOP should by definition be equal. In practice, however, the difference is large in some cases. The time series for short-term debt in the DRS start in 1978 for interest payments and outstanding amounts and in the 1980s for disbursements and principal repayments. Where DRS data on short-term debt are available, the differences with the BOP are sometimes large, in particular for Private Borrowers. Another problem is the combination of stock data from the BOP and the DRS with banking data, which provide estimates for countries not covered in the BOP or the DRS, but are based on a less extensive definition of external debt.

While the DRS only shows 'one side of the coin', i.e. liabilities and related flows and interest payments, the BIS data on stocks, and the BOP data on capital flows and investment income can be checked for internal consistency at the global level. There was a spectacular increase in global discrepancy in investment income and capital flows between 1970 and 1985 as recorded in the BOP. The discrepancy on the account for other investment income rose from circa US$ 5 billion in the 1970s to US$ 18.7 billion in 1980 and US$ 54.1 billion in 1985 (see Table 3.1); since 1982 it has been the largest factor explaining discrepancy on the world current account. The rising excess of debits over credits corresponds to the bias in the reporting of other capital flows: the net inflow of capital indicates that countries receiving capital were more capable of measuring the flows than the creditor countries, and were thus better able to record related investment income flows (IMF 1987: 46; see also Table 3.1). Although the increase in the discrepancy in capital flows exceeds the rise in discrepancy in investment income, the latter has received more attention from the IMF. The IMF Working Group that published the *Report on the World Current Account Discrepancy* (1987) focused on the accounts for investment income and the role of offshore financial centres.

The report claims to have reduced the discrepancy on the investment income account in the period 1979–83 to a minor amount. This was achieved by (1) revisions for country-specific problems, (2) reclassification between direct investment and other income (see the discussion earlier in this chapter), and (3) a check of reported income with income calculated from investment positions, applying estimated appropriate interest rates. This last approach gave rise to the largest adjustments. It was found that interest payments related to interbank positions were fairly correct. Interest income from bank deposits received by non-banks was found to be severely underestimated. This category explained the largest portion of discrepancy in other investment income. Under-recording of investment income of non-banks was found to be widespread, and not limited to certain areas or countries.

A similar check was performed on income related to securities. For bonds, reporting of debits seemed to be relatively good, but it was found that interest receipts are recorded, at most, to the extent that bond holdings are known to the statistical authorities. It was estimated that 40 per cent of holdings is unknown, and probably 45 per cent of receipts unreported. Also, for the much smaller category of equities some missing credits were identified. There is no apparent bias in the geographical allocation of the discrepancies, which means that, because of their large share in world transactions, the largest share of the discrepancies has been located in industrialized countries.

Dooley (1988) defines capital flight as the stock of claims on non-residents that do not generate investment income receipts in the creditor's BOP data: since residents have chosen to acquire financial assets that are outside the control of domestic authorities, it is reasonable to assume that the residents involved do not report the associated investment. Following this line of argument,[15] a considerable share of the adjustment in investment income is probably neither reported nor repatriated. However, this makes no difference for recording in the BOP because, according to BOP recording conventions, these unrepatriated receipts should still be reported as investment income credits, just as reinvested earnings are in the case of foreign direct investment (FDI).

Existing problems for BOP compilers have been emphasized by the rise of 'major offshore banking centres' (MOBs). One major statistical problem, mentioned in the discussion of international transport, but an even greater problem where international banking is concerned is that some MOBs do not include in their balance of payments statistics the transactions of certain intermediaries that they regard as essentially non-resident. Another problem is that the classification of transactions may be transformed when offshore banking is involved in the transaction. If, for example, country X pays an insurance premium to an insurance company in country Y, this is reported as a current account transaction in nonfactor services for both countries. If country X pays an insurance premium to an MOB which is then placed in a bank account in country Y by the insurance company, it will appear as a short-term capital account transaction in country Y, while it remains unrecorded by BOP compilers in the MOB who consider these transactions non-resident. Consequently, the link between the current account transaction and the capital account transaction remains unregistered and this will generate discrepancies in both the global current and the capital account. Thus, the involvement of MOBs in international transactions tends to obscure geographical patterns, and makes bilateral comparisons less meaningful.

Financial innovations create statistical problems because of the increase in speed of the transactions and the number of stages that may be involved in what is essentially a single operation. The substitution of marketable, highly liquid financial instruments for direct bank lending ('securitization') makes it more difficult to identify cross-border assets or liabilities; sometimes the borrowers or lenders do not even know that the counter-party is a non-resident.

Differences in recording practices for debt reorganization may also lead to asymmetry in debtor and creditor reporting. Most forms of debt reorganization affect the sectoring of debt; for example a refinancing loan from an official agency may replace loans from the private sector. There will also often be resectoring on the debtor side, especially where the central bank or the government has taken over debt previously owned by the private sector. In most cases, the maturity breakdown is clearly affected (World Bank, IMF, BIS, OECD 1988: 29). These forms of debt reorganization should only affect the categorization of debt totals: a debt previously recorded as a debt of the private sector will be changed into a debt held by the official sector, or a short-term debt has been changed into a long-term debt in the process of debt reorganization. Apart from these agreed forms of debt reorganization, there are unilateral actions which may affect the reported totals of debtors or creditors; there may be asymmetrical reporting in the case of write-offs or provisioning, if the creditor reports only the residual value of the asset, while the debtor continues to report the whole liability. Similarly, repudiation on the debtor side will lead to asymmetry if the debtor no longer reports the liability, while the creditor continues to report the asset.

There are many gaps in information on the distribution by origin and destination for investment income, capital flows and external assets and liabilities. The major source of information for the WAM is the DRS for matrices for LDC interest payments, principal repayments, disbursements and external debt. These matrices refer to public and publicly guaranteed, long-term debt, disaggregated into debt from official and from private creditors. There is no information available on the origin and destination for the components 'private non-guaranteed debt' and 'short-term debt'. For countries other than LDCs there are no systematic international data sources. Some information can be found in national sources. This information, however, is usually restricted to a distribution by origin and destination for flows of bonds or total portfolio transactions and investment positions, either for banks only or for banks and non-banks, while for investment income very little information is available.

In the US *Federal Reserve Bulletin* tables are shown for a geographical distribution of US portfolio transactions (flows) and investment positions of banks and non-banks; these tables have been published regularly since the 1960s. The Bank of Japan collects and publishes information on the geographical distribution of Japanese capital account transactions that corresponds closely to the BOP. These data have been traced for 1980 and 1985. For a number of other industrialized countries (see Table A.3.1 for a list of data sources), data on the geographical distribution of investment positions and portfolio transactions have been collected for 1985.[16]

3.5 Unrequited Transfers

The major data source for unrequited transfers is the BOP because it gives detailed information for a large sample of countries; the major distinction is between private and official transfers. A supplementary data source is the annual OECD publication *Geographical Distribution of Financial Flows to Developing Countries* (GDFF) that gives the origin and destination of grants from the US, Japan, the EU, the Other OECD Countries and Major Oil Exporters to LDCs, based on reports from the donor countries. The BOP and the GDFF are partially overlapping data sources, the BOP covering total unrequited transfers, and the GDFF covering the distribution by origin and destination for that portion of unrequited transfers that is received as a grant in LDCs. In the BOP, the definition for an *unrequited transfer* is:[17]

> the provision of a good, a service or cash, without the recipient assuming any obligation for payment. (IMF 1977)

According to the GDFF, an *official grant* comprises:[18]

> gifts, in money or in kind, for which no repayment is required.

Although the definitions are similar, there are differences in the sectorization and in the inclusion of specific items in official transfers in the BOP and official grants in the GDFF. In the BOP, official transfers refer to transfers where one or both parties belong to the official sector, while official grants in GDFF refer to grants from a foreign official sector. The main items in both systems are development assistance, such as subsidies to current budgets, grants of technical assistance and contributions to international organizations. Unlike transfers in the BOP, grants in the GDFF include loans extended in currencies of the donor countries, repayable in currencies of recipient countries. Also, the BOP includes indemnities imposed under peace treaties (reparations) to private individuals but the GDFF does not. Another difference is that the

OECD system is a creditor-reporting system, while the BOP is a debtor-reporting system for official grants to LDCs.

On the global account for transactions in official unrequited transfers there has been a persistent excess of debits over credits (see also Table 3.1). According to an analysis for 1983 (IMF 1987), and a similar analysis for the 1970s (Tims & Waelbroeck 1982), the most important factors causing the discrepancy are that: (1) international institutions receive larger amounts from their member countries than they pay out to them in the form of transfers. The imbalance partly reflects the financing of overhead costs; (2) coverage of development assistance by recipient countries is less complete than by donor countries; recipient countries might have difficulty in identifying and valuing non-cash development assistance, particularly technical co-operation; and (3) on the account for pension payments, coverage of recipient countries is incomplete, reflecting the difficulties of receiving countries in measuring and identifying the flows.

In the BOP, private unrequited transfers include migrants' transfers, workers' remittances and others. With migration, i.e. change of residence for at least one year, the personal belongings of migrants are actually transferred to the new economy, and claims issued in the country from which the migrants have migrated become foreign claims. These transactions are to be reported under the appropriate categories of the current and the capital account, and migrants' transfers are contra-entries to the flows of goods and the changes in financial items that arise from migration of individuals from one economy to another. Workers' remittances are unrequited transfers by those migrants employed by their new country, of which they are considered to be residents. Other private transfers refer to other unrequited transfers between individuals, between non-official organizations and between an individual and a non-official organization.

Except for a small deficit in 1970, the global account for private unrequited transfers has been in surplus. The discrepancy on the account for private transfers partly offsets the discrepancy on the account for official transfers. This suggests classification problems that may emerge when a private recipient has difficulty in allocating a transaction to a foreign official sector, leading to a registration of a private transfer, but the sources of discrepancy are largely independent, except for minor classification problems (IMF 1987). The data problems related to workers' remittances are large. To some extent these problems may be definitional and related to residence, leading to misspecification, but the largest factor explaining the discrepancy is omission of credits (IMF 1987).

For some 'labour-exporting' LDCs like Egypt, Jordan, Pakistan, Turkey and the Yemens, remittances were more than 50 per cent of exports in 1978 (Russell 1986). Omissions of credits in 'labour-exporting' countries may be due to the fact that workers' remittances are not recorded at all; or they may be only partially recorded, because in certain countries (such as India) transactions below a certain amount do not have to be reported, or because in-kind transactions (i.e. in goods or natural produce, not in money) are not recorded. The greatest source of problems, however, is that only a portion of workers' remittances moves through formal channels. The rest goes either through informal channels that may well, but not necessarily, use the official banking system, or is personally transported. To give an example of the possible scale of the problem, Brown (1992) estimated that recorded workers' remittances for the Sudan in 1983–84 were about one quarter of actual workers' remittances. The counterpart of the under-recording of remittance credits is the under-recording of remittance debits in the major oil-exporting countries.

3.6 Net Changes in Reserves and Errors and Omissions

The BOP is the obvious data source for *net changes in reserves*. Reserves in the BOP are defined as those assets (monetary gold, SDRs in the Fund, reserve position in the Fund, use of Fund credit, and existing claims on non-residents) that are conceived of as available for use by an economy's central authorities in meeting balance of payments needs (cf. IMF 1977).

Reserves may take the form of various assets that may be held abroad. If a part of the reserves is held abroad, this will involve capital account transactions that for the partner countries may fall under different categories of the capital account. Therefore, summed over all countries, the sum of the capital transactions, including reserves, should equal zero. As is shown in Table 3.1, although the discrepancy on the world capital account is smaller than on the world current account, it is still sizeable.

Table 3.2 *The geographical distribution of errors and omissions (in US$ billions)*

	1970	1975	1980	1985	1975-85*
US	-0.2	5.8	25.0	18.5	189.6
Japan	0.2	-0.6	-3.1	4.5	15.0
EU	1.3	0.3	0.3	2.6	4.8
OOECD	0.5	6.2	13.0	-2.2	48.8
CMEA	0.0	-0.3	-0.2	0.9	0.5
MOE	-0.4	-1.4	-2.6	-2.4	-25.6
OB	-0.0	-0.9	-1.0	0.2	-4.7
DB	-0.2	-0.4	-0.5	0.2	-5.9
PB	0.7	-2.0	-1.5	-2.7	-39.3
ROW	0.3	-0.6	-2.1	-1.2	-9.0
Total**	2.3	6.2	27.2	18.6	174.2

Notes:
* Cumulative.
** Columns may not tally due to rounding.

Source: IMF, *Balance of Payments Statistics.*

Conceptually, the difference between 'net changes in liabilities' and 'net changes in assets', plus 'net changes in reserves' should equal the balance on the current account of the balance of payments. In practice, the balance will always show a net residual, which is the result of errors and inconsistency in recording. In the BOP, the residual is shown under the heading 'net errors and omissions'. Since some of the errors and omissions will offset each other, the size of the item does not necessarily indicate how accurate reporting has been. Table 3.2 gives the errors and omissions for the country groups of the WAM in the years 1970, 1975, 1980 and 1985. The table shows that net errors and omissions in the BOP have been largely positive in the industrialized countries, and largely negative in other countries. Of course, for country groups, positive and negative net errors and omissions are likely to be netted out. This is clearly the case for the EU, where the low positive

Table 3.3 *Positive errors and omissions in a BOP statement for country X*

	recorded	A	B	C	D
Current Account	-30	-25	-25	-30	-30
incomings	80	85	80	80	80
outgoings	110	110	105	110	110
Capital Account	25	25	25	30	30
net changes in liabilities	35	35	35	40	35
net changes in assets	10	10	10	10	5
net changes in reserves	0	0	0	0	0
Errors and Omissions	5	0	0	0	0

figure hides the large positive net cumulative errors and omissions of the UK – amounting to US$ 28 billion in the period 1975-85 – and also for the Other OECD Countries, where the large net figure for Switzerland – US$ 75 billion in the period 1975-85 – is compensated by negative amounts for other countries.

A simple example (Table 3.3) will clarify the possible explanations for positive errors and omissions. Country X has recorded current incomings ('exports') of 80 and outgoings ('imports') of 110; consequently, the recorded current account deficit is 30. On the capital account, country X has a surplus of 25, made up from recorded net changes in liabilities ('inflows') of 35, and net changes in assets ('outflows') of 10. Because the sum of the capital account and the current account is -5, positive errors and omissions of +5 would be required for the balance of payments statement to be equal to zero, assuming zero reserve changes. If the capital account is taken to be correct, it follows from the example that positive net errors and omissions represent (1) under-recorded current account credits; or (2) overstated current account debits. If the current account is correct, positive net errors and omissions represent (1) under-recorded capital inflows; or (2) overstated outflows. Obviously, the errors and omissions may simultaneously reflect a combination of underrecording and overrecording on both current and capital accounts.

The fact that positive errors and omissions arise in the major financial centres suggests that the main explanation may lie in the existence of unrecorded capital inflows taking the form of acquisitions of financial assets (Turner 1991). Global net positive errors and omissions have increased and this increase has coincided with a growing world current account deficit which originates, to a large extent, from underrecording of investment income credits in industrialized countries. There is hence reason to assume that underrecording of investment income may also be an explanatory factor.

For developing countries, the net negative errors and omissions are often associated with capital flight. In studies that measure capital flight from BOP (flow) accounts, errors and omissions are assumed to stem mainly from errors in the measurement of private short-term capital flows, and are therefore added to the short-term capital flows as recorded in the BOP.[19] The data problems discussed in the previous sections suggest, however, that there is also reason to assume that current account transactions of developing countries may contribute to the net negative errors and omissions.

The interpretation of the net errors and omissions item is important for the construction of the WAMs, because, as will be shown in the next chapter, during the construction process adjustments are made that affect both the current and the capital account balances of the country groups. This will result in a residual different from the reported item net errors and omissions in the BOP.

3.7 Domestic Transactions

For the domestic transactions of the WAM, the World Bank publication *World Tables* (WT) is used as the major data source because it provides deflators for various components of GNP, and it covers a large sample of countries. The WT provide country estimates used by the World Bank in its dialogue about economic and social trends in developing countries, with the emphasis on countries that have borrowed from the World Bank; for the 'origin and use of resources', national sources, as collected by World Bank regional country economists, are the main source of information. Other economies are covered in the WT, based on data from the OECD, the IMF and national publications, but these data are not subject to scrutiny by World Bank staff.[20]

The basic concepts and definitions for the time series of national estimates in the WT are those of the United Nations System of National Accounts (UNSNA).[21] Gross domestic investment and gross national savings are central variables in the WAM, which uses the following definitions from the *World Tables*:

- *gross domestic investment* (GDI) is defined as:[22] the sum of gross domestic fixed investment and the change in stocks;
- *gross national savings* (GNS) is estimated as a residual derived from gross domestic product, consumption, net factor income and net current transfers from abroad;
- *gross domestic product* (GDP) is defined as: the sum of the value added in the agriculture, industry, and services sectors;
- *consumption* consists of the sum of private consumption and government consumption;
- *private consumption* is defined as: the market value of all goods and services purchased or received as income in kind by individuals and non-profit institutions. The category is called 'private consumption, etc.' because it includes any statistical discrepancy in the use of resources;
- *government consumption* is defined as: the sum of (1) purchases, less sales, of consumer goods and services, reduced by the value of the own-account production of fixed assets, (2) compensation of employees, (3) consumption of fixed assets, and (4) any payments of indirect taxes;
- *net factor income from abroad* includes the net compensation of employees (with less than one year of residence in the host country) and the net property and entrepreneurial income components of the UNSNA;
- *net current transfers* comprises net transfer payments – between residents and the rest of the world – that carry no provisions for repayments; and
- *gross national saving* equals GDP minus total consumption, etc. plus net factor income and net current transfers from abroad.

In the *World Tables* the data are expressed in national currency units, in current and in 1980 constant prices. For the WAM, the data have been converted into US dollars, using line *rf* in the *International Financial Statistics* of the IMF. The *rf* series refers to period averages of market exchange rates.

The problem of missing data in the WT is mainly a problem of country coverage. Industrial countries are completely covered and the coverage for LDCs is extensive.[23] Brunei, Iran, Iraq and Syria are missing from the major oil exporters. The CMEA is not covered, with the exception of Hungary and Poland. None of the other former CMEA countries belonged to the member countries of the World Bank in the period under consideration. To fill the gaps for missing countries some additional data sources are used: (1) the DEC Analytical Database of the World Bank (Riordan 1991) for the CMEA, (2) the UN *National Accounts Statistics* (various years) for some of the major oil exporters and a few LDCs and (3) the World Bank *World Development Report* (various years) for some other LDCs.

As discussed in the previous chapter, CMEA countries have used the Material Product System for the recording of national macroeconomic aggregates instead of the UNSNA. Because of the conceptual differences between the UNSNA and the Material Product System, it is difficult to make estimates from CMEA countries comparable to the World Bank UNSNA-type estimates. Another problem is the selection of the most appropriate exchange rate for the conversion of CMEA estimates from domestic currency to US dollars.

In addition two types of statistical discrepancies concerning GDI and GNS are likely to occur. Firstly, in the WAM, data on GDI and GNS are linked to balance of payments data from other data sources. By definition, according to the world accounting identities (see Chapter 2), the difference between GDI and GNS should equal the balance on the current account of the balance of payments for each country (group). In the WAM, the estimates for GDI and GNS from the WT are combined with current account data from other sources, mainly from the IMF *Balance of Payments Statistics* (BOP). In principle, the BOP is included within the UNSNA (IMF 1977) and the term 'net foreign investment' (GNS minus GDI in national accounting) is conceptually equivalent to the current account surplus. However, the differences between BOP and national income accounting practices inevitably lead to differ-

Table 3.4 *Discrepancies between national accounts and balance of payments statistics (in US$ billions)*

	1970		1975		1980		1985	
	S – I	CA	S – I	CA	S – I	CA	S – I	CA
US	7.3	2.3	30.1	18.1	30.9	1.9	-79.6	-114.9
Japan	2.2	2.0	-0.5	-0.6	-10.0	-10.7	49.8	48.7
EU	4.4	2.5	2.0	-0.1	-36.3	-39.5	25.9	18.6
OOECD	-0.2	-0.7	-8.1	-9.8	-10.9	-14.2	-5.7	-5.2
CMEA	-1.9	0.0	-0.9	-0.8	-4.2	-6.4	-0.8	0.2
MOE	1.2	0.2	30.6	28.1	73.4	65.2	7.3	-6.8
OB	-3.3	-1.9	-10.2	-6.9	-19.6	-11.2	-24.2	-12.2
DB	-1.1	-1.2	-6.2	-6.9	-4.0	-8.0	-19.3	-20.3
PB	-5.6	-4.4	-18.3	-16.7	-30.7	-32.6	-0.5	3.8
ROW	-2.5	-2.4	-6.7	-4.7	2.2	0.5	4.9	4.6
Total	0.5	-3.6	11.8	-0.3	-9.2	-55.0	-42.2	-83.5

Source: 'S – I' is the difference between GNS and GDI calculated from the World Bank, *World Tables*; 'CA' is the balance on the current account of the balance of payments, calculated from the IMF, *Balance of Payments Statistics.*

ences between the actual values in system. Table 3.4 gives the actual values for the current account balances calculated from BOP statistics and the goods surplus from the WT for the WAM country groups in 1970, 1975, 1980 and 1985. The table shows that the discrepancy may be considerable. At first sight, the discrepancies are particularly large for the US, Major Oil Exporters and Official Borrowers. In Japan, the two data systems seem to be consistent, while in the other country groups the differences are not particularly large for the group totals, but they may of course be netted out. There is also the problem of internal consistency: it follows from the world accounting identities presented in Chapter 2 that, summed over all countries, GDI should equal GNS. The total of the columns 'S – I' in Table 3.4 shows that the difference between world GNS and world GDI ranged from US$ 0.5 billion in 1970 to US$ 42.2 billion in 1985. With the exception of 1975, the difference is large but considerably smaller than the discrepancy on the world current account discrepancy, the total of column 'CA'.

3.8 Concluding Remarks

This chapter explains the selection of data sources. (See Appendix A3 for a complete list of the selected data sources.) The most important sources are: (1) World Bank, *World Tables* (WT), (2) UNDIESA, *United Nations Trade Matrices System* (UNTMS); (3) IMF, *Balance of Payments Statistics* (BOP); World Bank, *Debtor Reporting System* (DRS); and OECD, *Geographical Distribution of Financial Flows to Developing Countries* (GDFF). The major supplementary data sources are the international banking statistics of the BIS and the IMF, the OECD debt statistics and various national sources. The major 'gaps' in the data are in the distribution by origin and destination of foreign 'other' investment, nonfactor services and unrequited transfers.

For the geographical distribution of LDC debt there is more information than for foreign investment among industrialized countries or for LDC assets. The major weakness in LDC foreign debt data is the limited availability of time series on short-term debt, and the lack of information on the distribution by origin and destination of short-term debt and non-guaranteed debt from private sources.

The BOP is the 'central' data source for the WAM. It covers all international transactions and is fairly complete in terms of coverage and the level of disaggregation. However, while it has been used for most international transactions, a number of other data sources were used where necessary either as a substitute or supplement. The other major data sources for international transactions are (1) data on merchandise trade from the UNTMS, (2) data on LDC debt from the DRS, and (3) data on grants to LDCs from the GDFF. This combination affects the values for the world accounting identities. For example, as shown in section 3.2, the substitution of trade data from the BOP by the UNTMS not only affects the current account positions of individual countries and country groups, but also the world current account discrepancy.

Discrepancies within data sources mainly relate to the BOP and the WT. In the BOP, the major examples on the global level are the world current and capital account discrepancies. At the national level, the net errors and omissions indicate the size of the discrepancies between current and capital account transactions. Because Gross National Saving (GNS) is a residual in national accounting, a solution to the discrepancy between world Gross Domestic Investment (GDI) and world GNS is to assume that reported GDI is more reliable than reported GNS. It has often been emphasized (cf. World Bank *World Tables* 1989) that statistical systems in many developing countries are weak and that this affects the availability and the reliability of data. The data analysis in this chapter has shown that inconsistencies in data of industrialized countries probably account for a large share of the discrepancies in the world current account and in the world capital account. As will be shown in the next chapter, there are no ready solutions for the many data problems. The problems can only be solved by making certain assumptions based on a careful analysis of the data.

4 The Construction of World Accounting Matrices for 1970, 1975, 1980 and 1985

4.1 Introduction

This chapter describes how the data sources discussed in the previous chapter have been used in the construction of the WAMs, and how the data problems have been solved. WAMs have been constructed for the years 1970, 1975, 1980 and 1985, for ten country groups and one institutional sector, the multilateral development banks (multi). The construction process consists of several stages of data processing.

In *stage 1*, the 'raw aggregates' are calculated from the international data sources. If they are expressed in SDRs or units of local currency they have been converted to US dollars, using period average exchange rates. This results in a set of submatrices and row and column totals, from (partially) overlapping sources, each describing a particular variable such as the 'trade in fuels in 1975', or 'direct investment income in 1985'. These tables show many inconsistencies and gaps.

In *stage 2*, adjustments are made for gaps and inconsistencies in the row and column totals. For example, adjustments are made for 'missing countries', either by taking data from additional data sources or by making an estimate based on country group or world ratios. The adjustments in stage 2 are made on the basis of the analysis of the causes of the discrepancies outlined in the previous chapter, but only if there is sufficient ground for doing so.

In *stage 3*, 'second estimates' are calculated from related variables for variables that show large global inconsistencies. For example, estimates for interest income are derived from stock tables. The data processing in stages 2 and 3 lead to a set of row and column totals that is more consistent than the raw aggregates in stage 1, but large gaps and inconsistencies remain.

In *stage 4*, the row and column totals are made entirely consistent using a Stone/Byron type of mathematical reconciliation procedure.[1] This procedure, which was originally developed for input-output tables and social accounting matrices, has been adapted to fit the constraints of the WAM as derived from the accounting identities formulated in Chapter 2. As explained in Chapter 3, the data is not equally reliable. In the reconciliation procedure different degrees of reliability of the data can be taken into account; it is also possible to include more than one estimate for the same entry.

In *stage 5*, adjustments are made to fill a number of the gaps in the interiors of the matrices. This is done by relating missing variables to related aggregates. For example, the (unknown) interiors of the matrices for nonfactor services are related to the matrices for merchandise trade, or the (unknown) geographical distribution of US interest payments is related to the tables that describe the geographical distribution of US international liabilities. The interiors are estimated on the basis of the reconciled row and column totals produced in stage 4.

Finally, in *stage 6*, the complete WAMs are reconciled. This stage serves to reconcile the interiors with the row and column totals that were reconciled in stage 4, and to fill in the remaining empty spaces. One of the characteristics of the procedure is that it allows for the simultaneous reconciliation of the complete WAMs. Because the interiors are in general much weaker than the row and column totals, in stage 6 the degree of reliability assigned to the row and column totals is much higher than that assigned to the different degrees of reliability for the interiors. Thus, the spillover from the relatively weak interiors to the row and column totals is largely prevented.

Section 4.2 briefly clarifies the mathematical reconciliation procedure which plays a crucial role in the construction of the reconciled WAMs. Sections 4.3 to 4.8 describe the construction of the matrices for merchandise trade, nonfactor services, foreign direct investment income, flows and stocks, investment income related to other capital, and flows and stocks of other capital, unrequited transfers and domestic transactions. The degree of reliability assigned to each category of transaction is noted; reliability ranges from 'degree 1' for the most reliable data (which remain unchanged in the reconciliation procedure), to 'degree 5' for the least reliable data, where the largest adjustments were allowed. Appendix A4 gives a formal presentation of the reconciliation procedure as far as it is based on the work of Stone.

4.2 The Mathematical Reconciliation Procedure

In general, statistical accounting systems impose a set of constraints on the data that they contain. For example, the savings investment balance and the external balance represent accounting constraints in a national accounting system. The statistical problems described in Chapter 3 are thus not unusual. In any statistical system there are endless problems which stem from the incompleteness and inconsistency of the data, differences in classifications and definitions used by different collecting agencies. Most statistical agencies employ methods for reconciliation, and these can range from very crude to very sophisticated. Any method for reconciliation consists of a systematic strategy to extract the best possible description of the economy from the available data. Stone et al. (1942) first suggested the use of a formal, mathematical treatment of the problem of how to meet the accounting constraints by adjusting the estimates contained in what are considered to be the less reliable sources. The point of the method is to adjust what are believed to be the weaker estimates, and to preserve as far as possible those believed to be the stronger estimates.

To reconcile the WAM, the balancing method originally proposed by Stone et al. (1942), which was further developed by Stone (1977), and extended by Byron (1978) has been adapted to fit the constraints of the WAM. This method allows us to assign a degree of reliability to the data input, so that the greatest adjustment takes place in the data that are believed to be the least reliable. It is possible to use multiple estimates for one cell, but it also allows the option of 'non-availables', i.e. no estimate for a cell. Although it has been developed to balance large accounting systems like national accounts or social accounting matrices, the method is generally applicable to the solution of any reconciliation problem with linear accounting constraints. To date, the literature on this method has been mainly concerned with application of the method to national accounts and Social Accounting Matrices (SAMs), which have a relatively simple set of accounting constraints. However, the method can be applied to the complex and large accounting structure of the WAM.

Byron (1978) has formalized and extended the method proposed by Stone for adjusting initial unbalanced estimates of the components of a matrix so that they optimally satisfy the accounting requirements. Stone's proposal is based on linear combinations of initial unbiased estimates where the procedure represents the first order conditions resulting from a minimization of a quadratic loss function. Byron developed an alternative procedure for minimizing the constrained loss function, based on the conjugate gradient algorithm. Because Byron's contribution is more efficient in terms of time and storage requirements, it is particularly useful for the balancing of large data systems like the WAM.

Regarding the balancing method, the crucial difference between the WAM and the data systems for which the Stone/Byron balancing method was developed is found in the accounting constraints. In order to adapt the method to fit the WAM, the independent accounting constraints specific for the WAM were identified (Jellema 1992) from the accounting identity that forms the basis for the WAM. Then a computer program was developed, based on the 'Stone/Byron' method and the WAM constraints. The purpose was to design a program in which the number of countries and the number of disaggregations can vary, so that WAMs at different levels of aggregation can be constructed. So far this program has been used to construct the WAMs described in this study and to construct a series of WAMs for 1985–90 for a larger number of country groups (see de Jong et al. 1993 a & b).

4.3 The Construction of the Matrices for Merchandise Trade

The matrices for merchandise trade are built with data drawn from the United National Trade Matrices System (UNTMS) and based on reported exports, presented in US dollars. The matrices describe transactions by origin and destination, disaggregated into four trade categories. The system of the UNTMS allows for the aggregation of the 79 country/region series into the 10 countries/country groups of the WAM. The system includes data for 71 individual countries, while the data for all other countries in the world for which trade data are available have been aggregated into eight regional groups. It was not in all cases self-evident where to fit these regions into the classification, but the deviations are assumed to be small, particularly because the regional groups consist of small countries.

The matrices for merchandise trade, which are considered as relatively reliable and complete, are based on reported exports and recorded by origin and destination: the imports of country X are represented by the exports to country X of all other countries. Thus the matrices are internally consistent. Given the consistency and the completeness in terms of coverage, in stage 2 of the construction procedure no adjustments have been made for the matrices for merchandise trade. Given the relative reliability of the data, in the mathematical reconciliation procedure, the highest category ('degree 1') has been assigned to the data for merchandise trade which are consequently not altered in the construction process.

4.4 The Construction of the Matrices for Nonfactor Services

The BOP is the data source for nonfactor services which consist of three major categories: shipment, other transportation and travel. The world shipment account has shown sizeable deficits that have contributed considerably to the world current account discrepancy. The global discrepancy on the shipment account has been relatively stable, with the ratio between the discrepancy on shipment and total shipment debits around 40 per cent. Given the size and the stability of the discrepancy, it can be argued that it is both worthwhile and feasible to make adjustments for it. In a report on the world current account discrepancy, the IMF (1987) made adjustments for the discrepancy on the world shipment account that reduced it to a negligible amount in 1983. The procedure followed in the IMF report has been used to estimate adjustments for the WAM.

In the IMF report, the first step was of a close examination of the reported data and additional information from a questionnaire[2] in order to correct for inaccuracy and inappropriate classification. The adjustments that follow from this examination involve a decrease of both earnings and payments resulting in a small increase in the discrepancy, from US$ 31.8 billion to US$ 32.5 billion. This excess of payments over earnings is assumed to represent revenues earned by fleets not covered by IMF data. The adjustments for the 'missing fleet' data have been allocated by country according to the UNCTAD data that attribute the tonnage of five open registry economies (Liberia, Panama, Cyprus, Bermuda and the Bahamas) to the country of 'true management' which is defined as 'the person, company or organization responsible for day-to-day management of the ship concerned' (IMF 1987: 93).

For the WAM, it is simply assumed that in 1970, 1975, 1980 and 1985 the discrepancy on the shipment account represents revenues of the 'missing fleet'. In addition, it is assumed that the geographical distribution of the missing earnings related to the 'missing fleet' in 1983 is similar to the geographical distribution in 1970, 1975, 1980 and 1985.[3] The justification for this assumption is the stability that the discrepancy on the shipment account showed in the period 1970–85; the share of the discrepancy in total shipment payments (outgoings) was 30 per cent. The IMF report also analysed the discrepancy in the account for other transportation, but because the adjustments derived for the discrepancy in this account involved large changes in both payments and earnings without affecting the level of the discrepancy, this information has not been used to adjust the WAM. For the other nonfactor services no information about the causes of the discrepancies has been found.

The elimination of the discrepancy on the shipment accounts reduces the discrepancy on the accounts for nonfactor services to US$ -3.1 billion (in 1970), 1.1 billion (in 1975), -10.2 billion (in 1980) and -0.5 billion (in 1985). A second adjustment is required for CMEA data for nonfactor services because most CMEA countries are not covered in the BOP. CMEA total nonfactor services have been estimated assuming that, as a percentage of merchandise trade, they equal the global average percentage.[4] This results in a set of adjusted row and column totals for nonfactor services.

There is no systematic data source for the origin and destination of nonfactor services flows. To estimate the matrix for nonfactor services it has been assumed that the ratio of nonfactor service earnings to merchandise trade earnings is equal for each of the trading partners of a country group.[5] For example, if 20 per cent of the exports of Official Borrowers goes to the US, it is assumed that 20 per cent of the exports of nonfactor services of Official Borrowers also goes to the US.

The results of this data processing are firstly a set of adjusted row and column totals that are still inconsistent, but with discrepancies smaller than those reported in the BOP, and secondly, a set of interiors that are consistent with the row totals (nonfactor services earnings were set proportionally to merchandise trade earnings) but not with the column totals. The row and column totals and the interiors were balanced in the mathematical reconciliation procedure. A fairly high degree of reliability ('degree 2') has been assigned to the matrices for nonfactor services as they are allowed to vary in order to achieve consistency, but the degree of variation is limited because they are considered as more reliable than the matrices for financial variables.

4.5 The Construction of the Matrices for Foreign Direct Investment: Income, Flows and Stocks

The BOP is the data source for the row and column totals of the matrices for foreign direct investment (FDI) income and flows. As noted in the previous chapter, there is a global discrepancy in FDI. There is (1) widespread omission of reinvested earnings by a large number of countries, (2) omission of certain activities of international companies, in particular in offshore financial centres, and (3) omission of countries. Concentration in FDI is large: a small number of creditors account for a large share in the world total. In the previous chapter, creditor reporting was found to be more complete, and therefore more reliable, than debtor reporting.

In stage 2 of the construction procedure, no adjustments have been made for the row and column totals for FDI. There are no entries for FDI for CMEA countries in the BOP, and it has been assumed that there is no FDI in or from the CMEA.[6] In the reconciliation procedure, as creditor information is more reliable than debtor information, 'degree 3' has been assigned to FDI income and net changes in assets, and 'degree 4' to FDI income payments and net changes in liabilities. FDI is considered as less reliable than trade and nonfactor services, and more reliable than other capital flows (OCA), in particular where net changes in assets and income are concerned. The difference in degree of reliability between FDI assets and liabilities and the type of discrepancies in the BOP mean that the outcome of the reconciliation procedure will tend to lead to higher FDI income payments than those reported in the BOP and higher net changes in liabilities than those reported in the BOP.

A second data problem is the lack of information on the origin and destination of investment income. For the geographical distribution by origin and destination, much more information is available for *stocks* of FDI than for FDI flows and income. The stock matrices constructed for 1975 and 1982 are based on the tables that show the distribution by origin and destination of inward and outward investment positions in Dunning and Cantwell (1987).[7] Because of the bias in reporting, creditor information is preferred to debtor information; information on inward positions has only been used when data on outward positions were not available.

To estimate the interiors of the matrices for FDI flows and income, the interiors of the stock matrices for 1975 and 1982 have been used as a starting point.[8] The geographical distribution of FDI income is assumed to be equal to the geographical distribution of assets. If, for example, 20 per cent of the assets of the US are in Japan, then 20 per cent of US income is earned in Japan. This assumption thus implies an equal rate of return on FDI. The geographical distribution of net changes in assets (outflows) is assumed to be equal to the geographical distribution of stocks of assets. The impact of this assumption is significant because it implies a stable pattern in the direction of FDI. In the final reconciliation stage, the interiors of the matrices have been made consistent with the row and column totals. The estimated matrices for flows have been checked with data from individual sources, for 1970 and 1975 (US data only), for 1980 (data for US and Japan), and for 1985 (data for US, Japan, UK, Germany, the Netherlands, Canada, France, Italy, Belgium/Luxembourg, Spain and Australia). For FDI income, this is not possible due to a lack of data.

Of course, the lack of a matrix for stocks of FDI for 1970 makes the matrix for 1970 FDI income – and the FDI flow matrix – very weak. There are virtually no data for stocks of FDI for 1970 and it was not possible to estimate a matrix for 1970. Fortunately, for 1975 it has been possible to estimate a stock matrix making the ground for the construction method for income and flow matrices more solid. For 1980 and 1985, matrices for FDI have been estimated taking the stock matrix for 1982 as a point of reference. Row and column totals are drawn from the BOP stock tables. However, these tables are only available for 34, mainly industrialized, countries. For other countries, row and column totals have been estimated from the values for 1982, adjusted with growth rates derived from the estimates for the 34 countries included in the BOP. Subsequently, the interiors of the stock matrices for 1980 and 1985 have been estimated with the reconciliation programme for individual matrices. It is obvious that the interiors of the matrices for FDI in 1980 and 1985 are very rough estimates that should be interpreted with great caution.

4.6 The Construction of Matrices for Other Capital: Income, Flows and Stocks

This section describes the construction of the matrices for all capital other than foreign direct investment referred to as 'other capital' (OCA).

LDC debt

For other capital (OCA) the DRS and the BOP have been used, with the DRS covering LDC debt (stocks, flows and interest payments). The main categories of LDC Debt in the DRS are: (1) public and publicly guaranteed long-term debt (PPGLT), which is split into debt from official and debt from private sources, (2) private non-guaranteed debt (PNGLT), and (3) short-term debt (ST). In the WAM, the DRS data on LDC debt and related payments are integrated with data from the BOP for OCA of other countries, and for LDC assets and related payments. As shown in Chapter 3, the major difference in definition and coverage between the BOP and the DRS is the coverage of short-term debt, but the different figures reported in the two sources cannot be reconciled. Short-term debt is relatively important for Private Borrowers, and not so important for Official Borrowers and Diversified Borrowers. A comparison of the actual values in the BOP and in the DRS shows that the estimates for Official Borrowers and Diversified Borrowers are quite close, while for Private Borrowers the differences are too large to be neglected. Therefore, in the reconciliation procedure for row and column totals, the BOP estimates for Private Borrowers have been taken into account as a second estimate for total interest payments and net capital inflows. No other adjustments have been made for the row and column totals.

The geographical distribution by origin and destination for LDC debt and related flows (i.e. outstanding amounts of foreign debt, new disbursements, principal repayments and interest payments) is from the DRS. The matrices refer to the PPGLT category and describe the distribution by origin and destination of LDC debt and related flows between Official, Diversified and Private Borrowers on the one hand, and the US, Japan, EU, Other OECD Countries, CMEA and Major Oil Exporters on the other hand. The matrices are disaggregated into two categories: official and private (referring to the source of capital). The allocation is not complete, i.e. there is a (small) 'unallocated' category. The 'unallocated' total of this debt category has been allocated according to the structure of the matrix for official PPGLT for 'unallocated official' and private PPGLT for 'unallocated private', assuming that the distribution by origin and destination of unallocated PPGLT is similar to the allocated PPGLT. If, for example, 20 per cent of allocated interest payments on official PPGLT by Official Borrowers goes to the US, it has been assumed that 20 per cent of Official Borrowers' unallocated interest payments on official PPGLT goes to the US as well.

The PNGLT category is also disaggregated into a private and an official component. The private component is further disaggregated into 'foreign parents', 'financial markets' and 'suppliers'. For this category no distribution by origin and destination exists. From the nature of the four components of PNGLT four assumptions can be derived for estimating the distribution by origin and destination of PNGLT:

1. The geographical structure of the official component resembles the structure of the matrix for the official part of PPGLT. This is based on the assumption that the donor preference for certain regions is equal for guaranteed and non-guaranteed loans.
2. The geographical structure of the financial markets component resembles the structure of the matrix for the private part of PPGLT. This is based on the assumption that a guarantee for repayment by a public entity does not affect the geographical direction of lending.
3. The geographical structure of the foreign parent component resembles the structure of the matrix for foreign direct investment flows or stocks. This is based on the assumption that borrowing from the foreign parent by the host country is proportionally distributed over all direct foreign investors.

Table 4.1 Private, non-guaranteed debt by type of creditor

	PPGLT options			
	Private	Official	Merchandise trade	Total
Undistributed public & publicly guaranteed debt				
Official		100		100
Private	100			100
Private, non-guaranteed debt				
OBs & DBs	50		50	100
PBs	100			100
Short-term debt				
OBs & DBs	81		19	100
PBs	91		9	100

4. The geographical structure of the suppliers component resembles the structure of the matrices for merchandise trade. Suppliers' credits are defined as export credits extended by the exporter.[9] If an export from country X is financed by a suppliers' credit, the credit comes from country X as well. An additional assumption for outstanding amounts of suppliers' credits is that the geographical structure of merchandise trade does not change over the period for which the loans have been extended.

The distribution of PNGLT by type of creditor is only available for a small number of countries. The available information has been summarized in Table 4.1 which gives the shares as a percentage of total PNGLT. 'Suppliers' and 'Financial Institutions' are the major categories for the countries in the table. It is therefore assumed that PNGLT is linked to these two categories. For Official Borrowers and Diversified Borrowers both categories seem to be equally important; the assumption is therefore that 50 per cent of Official Borrowers' and Diversified Borrowers' PNGLT consists of 'suppliers' and another 50 per cent of 'financial institutions'. For Private Borrowers, 'financial institutions' is the major category and Private Borrowers' PNGLT is therefore assumed to consist of this category only.

Table 4.2 Implicit interest rates in the DRS

	US	Japan	EU	OOECD	CMEA	MOE	Multi	Creditor countries
1970: official interest rates								
OB	1.2	5.1	3.0	2.2	2.0	1.1	2.8	2.2
DB	1.7	2.6	3.0	1.8	0.1	1.8	4.5	2.4
PB	2.8	3.3	3.7	3.8	0.2	2.0	5.4	3.7
1970: private interest rates								
OB	5.8	5.8	5.1	5.3	4.2	3.2	..	5.1
DB	5.2	6.0	4.7	5.0	5.6	5.7	..	5.1
PB	7.2	6.5	5.4	7.0	3.5	7.5	..	6.3
1975: official interest rates								
OB	1.5	3.9	2.4	1.4	1.8	1.7	2.3	2.0
DB	2.0	2.5	2.8	2.7	0.7	2.3	5.0	2.9
PB	3.3	3.6	3.4	5.5	1.6	3.7	6.4	4.5
1975: private interest rates								
OB	7.1	5.8	5.0	6.4	3.2	5.9	..	5.5
DB	4.5	2.9	4.3	4.3	3.1	3.4	..	4.0
PB	10.5	10.6	10.4	10.3	8.2	6.6	..	10.4

(Continued)

The WDT does not disaggregate ST into sub-categories. The OECD publication *Financing and External Debt of Developing Countries* disaggregates ST into 'banks' and 'export credits'. According to the OECD, 81 per cent of Official Borrowers' and Diversified Borrowers' ST and 91 per cent of Private Borrowers' ST consists of 'banks'. On this basis it has been assumed that 19 per cent of Official Borrowers' and Diversified Borrowers' ST, and 9 per cent of Private Borrowers' ST is linked to trade payments and can therefore be allocated according to the structure of the matrices for merchandise trade while 81 per cent of Official Borrowers' and Diversified Borrowers' ST and 91 per cent of Private Borrowers' ST can be allocated according to the structure of the matrices for private PPGLT. This can be summarized as in Table 4.1.

Table 4.2 (continued)

	US	Japan	EU	OOECD	CMEA	MOE	Multi	Creditor countries
1980: official interest rates								
OB	2.4	2.5	2.2	1.4	1.3	2.0	2.4	2.2
DB	3.0	2.6	2.2	3.7	1.4	3.3	5.9	3.6
PB	4.9	3.8	5.1	6.7	3.9	2.8	7.7	6.1
1980: private interest rates								
OB	10.1	15.5	5.6	7.2	7.7	6.4	..	7.5
DB	13.3	14.1	8.6	9.1	8.3	10.7	..	10.0
PB	12.1	11.9	9.2	10.5	8.9	8.5	..	10.4
1985: official interest rates								
OB	4.5	2.9	3.1	2.9	2.1	1.7	2.3	2.9
DB	4.3	3.3	3.8	5.6	6.0	1.6	5.7	4.5
PB	6.2	3.5	3.3	7.6	5.1	20.7	6.9	5.9
1985: private interest rates								
OB	11.9	5.6	6.4	8.6	5.9	6.4	..	7.1
DB	14.1	8.6	7.8	9.7	7.7	11.6	..	9.3
PB	8.6	7.7	11.0	7.4	4.1	11.2	..	9.4

Source: Calculated from the World Bank, *World Debt Tables* (various years).

Table 4.2 explores the internal consistency of the DRS. The DRS includes stocks of foreign debt and interest payments. The ratio between the two represents the interest rate that has on average actually been paid on outstanding loans. Since this rate is implicit in the reported stocks and interest payments, it is referred to as the implicit interest rate. As is to be expected, overall implicit interest rates for Private Borrowers tend to be higher than for Diversified Borrowers, and for Diversified Borrowers higher than for Official Borrowers while private rates are higher than official rates. The rates vary quite significantly among creditor countries, but in general the implicit rates seem to be quite plausible. In the mathematical reconciliation procedure, the highest degree of reliability ('degree 1') has been assigned to the data from the DRS because they are reliable and complete compared with other financial data. Thus, spillover from the large inconsistencies in investment income and capital flows elsewhere in the system (see Chapter 3 and the next section) is prevented.

Global discrepancy in other capital

Where the DRS has been selected as the major source for LDC debt (stocks, net changes in liabilities and interest payments), the BOP is the major data source for other capital (OCA) flows and interest income and payments for countries other than LDCs, and for net changes in assets and interest income for LDCs. As indicated in the previous chapter, the BOP publishes data on OCA income, OCA flows and OCA stocks. These have been used to calculate the row and column totals for the OCA matrices. The calculated totals show large global discrepancies. For OCA income, an IMF report (IMF 1987, see Chapter 3) has assessed the credibility of OCA income in the BOP for 1983. It was found that the payment side of the account was reasonably reliable. The 'missing earnings' were subsequently assigned to particular countries using information on stocks and flows from other data sources: IMF and BIS data on bank positions and OECD and World Bank data on bonds and equities. As the WAM is a data framework that includes investment income, capital flows and international investment positions, it is a suitable tool for a similar consistency check between investment income and investment positions. This check on consistency should also indicate how to make adjustments for the global discrepancies. However, as will be shown below, both the data requirements and the data problems are large.

A first step is to explore the statistical relation between reported stocks, flows and payments in the major data sources for other capital. The BOP reports stocks of assets and liabilities which by definition cover all loan types reported in BOP tables for investment income and capital flows. However, BOP data are only available for 34, mainly industrialized, countries. Table 4.3 gives stocks of assets and liabilities in OCA, total investment income related to OCA from the BOP and the corresponding calculated implicit interest rates for 1975, 1980 and 1985 for the largest industrialized countries (the G-7 countries). It is not possible to do this at a more disaggregated level, because the classification of investment income differs from the classification for stocks (and flows) in the BOP.

Table 4.3 *Investment positions, investment income and implicit interest rates for G-7 countries (in US$ billions)*

	Total assets			Total investment income receipts			Implicit interest rates		
	1974/75	1979/80	1984/85	1975	1980	1985	1975	1980	1985
US	145.7	335.2	648.9	8.8	35.4	55.7	6.0	1.6	8.6
Japan	0.0	106.5	312.2	3.1	9.8	19.5	—	9.2	6.3
France	38.8	135.8	162.3	4.5	19.3	20.0	11.6	14.2	12.4
Germany	43.6	174.8	205.4	4.4	12.3	13.2	10.0	7.0	6.4
Italy	2.3	69.3	75.1	1.6	5.3	5.1	69.4	7.7	6.8
UK	141.6	394.5	662.4	10.2	43.4	57.3	7.2	11.0	8.7
Canada	0.0	30.0	52.5	1.2	2.2	3.7	—	7.4	7.0
G-7	372.0	1246.1	2118.8	33.8	127.7	174.5	9.1	10.2	8.2
	Total liabilities			Total investment income payments			Implicit interest rates		
	1974/75	1979/80	1984/85	1975	1980	1985	1975	1980	1985
US	185.2	391.9	782.1	10.3	33.5	56.8	5.6	8.6	7.3
Japan	0.0	124.0	275.1	3.6	9.7	14.4	—	7.8	5.3
France	40.2	122.0	183.8	4.0	16.0	21.5	10.1	13.1	11.7
Germany	33.7	184.6	195.7	3.0	8.7	9.8	8.8	4.7	5.0
Italy	3.7	83.8	118.3	2.8	6.0	9.1	75.0	7.1	7.7
UK	153.3	407.5	620.4	11.2	44.5	54.1	7.3	10.9	8.7
Canada	20.6	84.8	133.5	2.7	7.5	13.0	13.0	8.8	9.7
G-7	436.7	1398.6	2308.9	37.6	125.9	178.7	8.6	9.0	7.7

Source: Calculated from the IMF, Balance of Payments Statistics (various years).

Table 4.3 shows that implicit interest rates vary significantly between the G-7 countries. The stocks probably vary in terms of types of lending and time structure, and therefore some variation is to be expected. Shifts in exchange rates and inflation rates are therefore likely to be largely incorporated in the implicit interest rates. Also, real interest rates may vary between countries, but this difference is marginal compared with the differences in Table 4.3.[10] The large differences in implicit interest rates indicate that reported stocks and investment income in the BOP are, to some extent, inconsistent. This may of course be due to the underestimation of stocks – as is clearly the case for Italy in 1975 – or to overestimation of stocks, or to errors in the reporting of investment income.

The statistical relationship between reported flows of OCA and year-to-year changes in reported assets and liabilities is more difficult to assess. In the BOP, the differences between the two are generally very large. This may of course partly be due to errors in reporting, but as set out in Chapter 2, it is largely due to valuation adjustments caused by exchange rate movements and other asset revaluations (like debt conversion or cancellation). To estimate the revaluations, detailed information on the currency composition of investment positions is required, and this information is unavailable.

One strategy to reduce the discrepancy in investment income related to OCA is to trace unreported investment income by comparing reported income with reported stocks of foreign assets. In order to do this, BOP stock data have to be supplemented with data from other sources, because of the limited country coverage in the stock tables. One additional source of information is the statistics of the BIS, which give the external positions of banks in the BIS reporting area. Country coverage in the BIS is large, but the coverage of types of foreign investment is limited compared with the BOP. Where available, the BOP tables are used, because the tables correspond conceptually to the investment income flows that have been used for the construction of the row and column totals. BOP tables are available for the US, Japan, most EU countries and most other OECD countries. For assets of other countries, BIS banking statistics have been used. Using BIS data to derive an estimate for investment income implies a *minimum* estimate, as the data base only covers bank loans.

In addition to the problem of country coverage, there is a problem of time coverage. Generally, the availability of statistics on other foreign investment positions has greatly increased; with the exception of the DRS, stock data for 1970 are virtually non-existent and the lack of data makes the exercise impossible for 1970. The series are available from 1975 onwards. The level of disaggregation, and also the country coverage in the BOP, is better in 1985 than in 1975.

To assess the accuracy of reported stock data, the income check is based on the assumption that asset reporting is better than income credits reporting. In the case of capital flight, this is doubtful because both assets and income credits are likely to be equally ill-recorded. It would be better to perform the investment income check for different categories of capital, but this is not possible because of a lack of disaggregation in investment income reported in the BOP; income is calculated from different categories of foreign assets, and then the sum of the calculated income has been compared with total investment income reported in the BOP.

Another problem is the structure and the composition of stocks of foreign assets and liabilities. There are numerous instruments of foreign lending, terms of lending vary not only for different types of loans but also for different borrowers, and loans are denominated in different currencies. To assign the appropriate interest rate to each type of stock requires more detail in the database than is currently available. It is therefore necessary to make some simplifying assumptions:

1. There are four types of foreign assets for OECD countries (bank lending, straight bonds, flexible rate bonds and equities); there is one type of foreign assets for all other countries: bank loans.
2. Interest rates on US dollar-denominated assets are a suitable proxy for all interest rates. This can partly be justified because most foreign lending is denominated in US dollars,[11] and partly by assuming that interest rates tend to equalize across countries.
3. Rates of return on equities (dividends) are equal to 50 per cent of the rate of return on all other assets.[12]
4. The maturity structure of straight bonds can be reduced to two types: short-term (less than one year) and long-term (seven years on average). To simplify the calculations, it is further assumed that maturity (n) for long-term loans is seven years; all long-term loans are

being repaid within seven years, each repayment amounting to one seventh of the original loan. It is also assumed that the rate of growth in the period 1975–85 (g) of the world stocks (S) and the new loans (L) is the same in each year (t) of the period:

$$S_t = (1 + g)^n S_{t-n} \qquad (4.1)$$

5. Interest is paid over the average of the value of the stock of straight bonds at the beginning and at the end of year t. The average stock AS_t consists of loans (minus repayments) that were contracted in the previous years:

$$AS_t = S_{t-1} + \frac{S_t - S_{t-1}}{2} = \frac{L_t}{2} + \sum_{i=1}^{n} \frac{2(n-i)+1}{2n} \cdot L_{t-i} \qquad (4.2)$$

6. The rate of interest (r) prevailing in the year the bond was extended can be assigned to that portion of the bond that is still outstanding in year t.

Using equations (4.1) and (4.2), loans minus repayments in previous years can be expressed as a percentage of AS_t, and a weighted interest rate can be applied to AS_t to calculate interest payments in year t.[13] Table 4.4 presents the results of the calculations. The interest rates for long-term and short-term assets is LIBOR (from the IFS); the interest rate for bonds is the Eurodollar bond rate.

According to OECD estimates,[14] the proportion of straight bonds in total bonds has declined from approximately 100 per cent in the 1970s, to 80 per cent at the beginning of the 1980s and 50 per cent in 1985. For rates of return on variable rate bonds in year t, the Eurodollar bond rate prevailing in year t has been used,

The generated estimates presented in Table 4.4 are generally higher than the estimates from BOP statistics. Substitution of the generated estimates would considerably reduce discrepancy on the account for investment income in 1985, but this would increase it in 1975 and 1980.[15] Given the large number of assumptions, the degree of credibility is not likely to be higher than that of the BOP estimates. The generated estimates have therefore been used as a 'second estimate' in the reconciliation procedure, with both estimates assigned a similar level of reliability. OCA is the least reliable category in the WAM, while liabilities and income payments are considered as more reliable than assets and interest

Table 4.4 *Reported investment income and generated investment income (in US$ billions)*

	Interest payments			Interest receipts			Generated interest receipts		
	1975	1980	1985	1975	1980	1985	1975	1980	1985
US	10.3	33.5	56.8	8.8	35.4	55.7	12.0	52.1	53.7
Japan	3.6	9.7	14.4	3.1	9.8	19.5	3.1	16.2	31.5
EU	28.4	106.7	132.9	28.1	108.5	127.2	20.7	138.6	110.8
OOECD	5.9	19.3	34.6	5.3	12.7	23.1	1.4	14.2	11.1
CMEA	0.4	4.2	4.5	0.1	0.7	0.5	2.0	8.6	6.4
MOEs	0.6	1.1	1.1	4.3	14.7	18.9	0.5	3.5	5.9
OBs	1.1	4.8	6.9	0.6	2.6	1.7	0.9	3.1	4.3
DBs	1.3	9.3	10.7	0.5	1.4	3.2	0.9	4.1	6.4
PBs	5.0	38.6	42.3	3.2	14.5	12.9	6.9	38.2	51.4
ROW	1.8	5.1	6.8	0.5	1.7	1.8	2.8	13.5	22.0
Total	58.4	232.3	311.0	54.5	202.0	264.5	51.2	292.1	303.5
Discrepancy				-3.9	-30.3	-46.5	-7.2	59.8	-7.5

Sources: Calculated from IMF, *Balance of Payments Statistics* (various years), and own calculations.

income. In the mathematical reconciliation procedure 'degree 4' has been assigned to liabilities and income payments and 'degree 5' has been assigned to assets and interest income.

A geographical network for other capital?

There is no systematic information on the geographical distribution by origin and destination (geographical network) of capital flows of industrialized countries in international data sources. Some national sources, mainly reports by Central Banks, do provide a geographical breakdown of their international capital flows, or stocks of foreign assets or liabilities. For the US, the geographical distribution of other capital transactions, and a geographical distribution of investment positions for banks and non-banks has been used to estimate the geographical distribution of US capital flows in 1970, 1975, 1980 and 1985. For Japanese capital flows, a geographical network is available for 1980 and 1985. Based on data for other capital transactions and investment positions of banks and non-banks for a number of other industrialized countries the interiors of the matrices for capital flows for the EU and 'Other OECD' have been estimated. However, with the exception of Japanese data, which correspond closely to the BOP estimates for Japan, the differences between flows as reported in the BOP and other capital flows reported in national sources are generally large. As was shown in the previous section, year-to-year changes in stocks and flows are not easily comparable, due to exchange rate fluctuations, valuation adjustments and debt restructuring. However, since there is no other source of information, the geographical distribution of capital flows of industrialized countries has been derived from the available stock data. The estimates should be interpreted very cautiously.

The strategy for the construction of the interiors of matrices for OCA is as follows:

1. For the US, there are data on the geographical distribution of portfolio transactions for 1970, 1975, 1980 and 1985.
2. The geographical distribution of other US capital flows has been estimated from the tables for assets and liabilities of banks and non-banks, using the year-to-year changes as a proxy for capital flows; the tables are available from 1969 onwards.

3. Japan reports a geographical distribution of capital flows for 1980 and 1985. This information corresponds closely to the BOP data for Japan.
4. For other industrialized countries, some information has been found for 1985 on portfolio transactions and assets and liabilities of banks, and in a few cases also for non-banks. As with the US, estimates for the geographical distribution of flows have been derived from the stock data.
5. In some cases two estimates are available for the same cell, for example when Japan reports an outflow to the US and the US reports an inflow from Japan. If both inward and outward estimates are available, the inward estimates are assumed to be more reliable, because of the general tendency for undervaluation of (changes in) assets.

Finally, in estimating stock matrices for other capital, the best data source for LDC debt is the DRS. The BOP has been used as the data source for row and column totals for countries covered in the BOP, and the BIS statistics have been used for countries not covered in the BOP. BOP and BIS tables are unavailable for 1970. For 1975, 1985 and 1985, some of the entries in the interior have been estimated with information from national sources (US, UK, Germany, the Netherlands, France and Switzerland). The matrices have been reconciled using the program for individual matrices. The estimates are considered weak because of the huge gaps in the available data.

4.7 The Construction of Matrices for Unrequited Transfers

The row and column totals for these matrices have been calculated with BOP data. The only systematic data system that gives information on the origin and destination of unrequited transfers is the OECD's *Geographical Distribution of Financial Flows to Developing Countries* (GDFF). This publication covers net grants to LDCs from governments or official agencies in the donor countries and has hence been used to compile the matrices for development grants and technical assistance. Based on the analysis of the data problems in the previous chapter, in the reconciliation procedure 'degree 3' has been assigned to the data on unrequited transfers. The data are less reliable than the data for merchandise trade and nonfactor services, but more reliable than most other financial variables in the WAM.

A problem in combining the OECD data with BOP data is a difference in definitions: the BOP definition of an unrequited official transfer is much wider than the definition of a (net) grant of the OECD. Furthermore, the OECD data base is a *creditor* reporting system, with the disadvantage that creditor estimates of development grants tend to be considerably larger than the amounts reported by receiving countries, especially where technical assistance is concerned. In an attempt to bring the BOP and the GDFF estimates closer together, technical assistance has been deducted from total official grants as reported in the GDFF.[17] Since this did not seem to be very helpful, the OECD interiors of the matrices for total official grants have been used in combination with the row and column totals for unrequited transfers from the BOP, assuming that every transaction in the GDFF is included in the BOP. Since the coverage of transactions in the BOP is much larger than in the GDFF, this means that the distribution by origin and destination was available for only a small share of total transfers while the remainder has been allocated through the mathematical reconciliation procedure. This was necessary because there is no information on the geographical network for official and private transfers not covered in the GDFF. As suggested by Russell (1986), and in line with the WAM approach, in order to construct a better database for private unrequited transfers, it would be necessary to collect numbers, wage rates and occupational distribution of workers, and to attempt to construct matrices that describe the distribution of flows between labour-sending and labour-receiving economies. This requires further research.

4.8 The Construction of the Matrices for Domestic Transactions

Two domestic transactions are included in the four main blocs of the WAM: gross national savings (GNS) and gross domestic investment (GDI). Consumption (C) and gross domestic product (GDP) are presented in supplementary tables. The domestic tables use the *World Tables* (WT) of the World Bank as the major data source. Because the WT lack data for CMEA countries other than Hungary, Poland and Rumania, and because estimates for domestic aggregates derived from the Material Product System used in the CMEA countries are not comparable to the WT estimates based on UNSNA definitions, the GDI estimates for CMEA countries of the *DEC Analytical Database* of the World Bank (Riordan 1991) are used to complete this part of the WAM. These estimates are weak, but better estimates are not available. To prevent spillover from the weak CMEA estimates to other country groups and the current account balances, GNS has been derived as the residual from the CMEA's GDI and current account balances, assuming that the goods surpluses of the CMEA are equal to the current account balances of the CMEA. Thus, there is no statistical discrepancy in the CMEA accounts on this level, which 'neutralizes' the CMEA accounts.

Another problem of country coverage exists for a few Major Oil Exporters and Official Borrowers. For most of these countries, estimates for GDI, GNS, C and GDP can be found in other data sources. The *United Nations National Account Statistics* provide data for the missing Major Oil Exporters, while World Bank publications other than the WT (*World Development Report*, *World Debt Tables*) present data for most of the missing Official Borrowers. In the few instances where only a GDP estimate was available, the country group ratios for GDI, GNS and C on the one hand and GDP on the other, have been used to estimate GNS. Thus, the data for Major Oil Exporters and Official Borrowers have been supplemented for countries missing in the WT with (1) estimates from the *United Nations National Accounts Statistics* where available; and (2) estimates derived from group ratios for GDI, GNS and C. The adjustments based on additional data published by the UN for missing Major Oil Exporters, including Iran and Iraq are large: they add 70 per cent to the GDP for Major Oil Exporters from the WT in 1980. For Official Borrowers, the adjustments for missing countries is much smaller (5 per cent of GDP in 1980), because the missing countries are small. Apparently, the compilers of the WT consider the data reported in the UN statistics for the 'missing countries' unreliable. Obviously, the adjustments that are derived from the country group ratios are even less reliable. The global discrepancy in GDI and GNS tends to be smaller than the global discrepancy in balance of payments statistics (see the previous chapter). This may be justified, since the national income statistics are more reliable than balance of payments statistics, but some doubt remains because the difference in global discrepancy could not be explained, and it is possible that the statistical discrepancies are netted out on the global level. Generally, estimates for GNS are considered weaker than estimates for GDI, because GNS is usually derived as a residual in national income statistics. 'Degree 2' has been assigned to GDI in the mathematical reconciliation procedure, while 'degree 4' has been assigned to GNS.

4.9 Concluding Remarks

The first step in the construction process was to calculate aggregates for the country groups from the data sources selected in the previous chapter. These aggregates show many gaps and inconsistencies. In the subsequent stages of the construction process the gaps were filled and the inconsistencies were eliminated. Where possible, this has been done using estimates from comparable data sources or from related variables as well as the results of the data analysis in the previous chapter. Finally, a mathematical reconciliation procedure was applied to achieve completeness and consistency.

For merchandise trade, a set of matrices was calculated from a consistent and relatively reliable data system and required no adjustments. For nonfactor services a number of adjustments were made to eliminate the large global discrepancy in recorded shipment transactions and compensate for unrecorded CMEA data. The remaining discrepancy on this account has been eliminated in the mathematical reconciliation procedure. The interior of the matrix for nonfactor services has been estimated using the mathematical adjustment procedure, and assuming that the geographical network of nonfactor services closely resembles that of merchandise trade. For foreign direct investment no adjustments were made in stage 2. Consistency has been achieved using the mathematical reconciliation procedure. A central assumption in the construction of the matrices was that creditor reporting is more reliable than debtor reporting. Matrices for stocks of foreign investment were used as a basis for estimating the interiors of the matrices for foreign direct investment income and flows.

For other capital flows and investment income and payments, there is more information available for LDCs than for other countries; as the LDC debt crisis has greatly enhanced the availability and quality of data on LDC debt and related flows. For interest payments by LDCs, capital inflows and foreign debt of LDCs matrices that are relatively consistent and reliable were constructed and these were not altered in the reconciliation procedure. Data problems for other entries in the matrices for other capital are significant. There are large inconsistencies at the global level and large parts of the interiors are empty. For investment income 'second estimates' have been calculated from stock data. These data are compared with 'first estimates' from reported data, and jointly used in the mathematical reconciliation procedure. Ideally, a similar procedure should be followed for capital flows, comparing net changes in assets and liabilities with stocks of assets and liabilities, but the data requirements have proved to be too large. Instead, capital flows have been made consistent in the mathematical reconciliation procedure. For the geographical distribution of capital flows and stocks, some information was found in national sources; stock data were used to estimate the geographical network for investment income and also for capital flows, where only stock data were available. Using this information as a basis and combining it with the data on foreign debt of LDCs, the matrices were estimated in the mathematical reconciliation procedure.

For unrequited transfers no manual adjustments were needed in stage two; the mathematical reconciliation procedure solved the discrepancies on this account. To fill in parts of the matrices, LDC debt statistics that give the geographical distribution of official grants to LDCs were used. The complete interiors of the matrices were estimated in the mathematical reconciliation procedure. For domestic transactions, some adjustments were made for missing countries. Subsequently, the estimates were made consistent in the mathematical reconciliation procedure.

Clearly, the data requirements for the WAM are large. A major problem is the lack of a geographical network for international financial transactions. The WAM is based on the concept that related variables – international trade, international financial flows and stocks, and domestic savings and investment – should be integrated in one framework that explicitly takes the relationships into account. One advantage of the approach is that it allows for the estimation of entries that are not directly available in existing statistics; the conceptual link between stocks, flows and interest payments has been used to estimate missing entries in the interiors of the matrices.

Major inconsistencies within and between reported macroeconomic data mean that published data sources are sometimes highly misleading.

In the construction of a WAM, these inconsistencies are analysed and eliminated, taking advantage of the world accounting identities that form the basis for the WAM. In the mathematical reconciliation procedure any remaining discrepancies among variables are eliminated simultaneously.

The construction process produced a set of consistent WAMs which, on the basis of certain assumptions, make the best possible use of existing statistics; however, the quality of the results is of course dependent on the quality of the initial data input. It is clear that large parts of the WAMs should be interpreted very cautiously. The WAMs presented in this study should be seen as a set of provisional matrices that have been constructed with limited resources.

5 A Presentation and Interpretation of the Reconciled WAMs

5.1 Introduction

The previous chapters described the construction of a set of reconciled WAMs (RWAMs). Before interpreting these matrices, it would be useful to clarify their interpretive potential and limitations. This chapter presents both the 'raw' and reconciled WAMs, but rather than describing the processing of each WAM cell, it provides representative illustrations of the adjustment method. The first details the construction of two financial variables: because (FDI income in 1970 and EU (other) investment income from the US) the statistical problems for financial variables are much larger than for other variables. The second uses the WAM to identify global discrepancies, assess their size, delineate the necessary adjustments and evaluate the sensitivity of the reconciliation method for different degrees of reliability.

This allows the patterns of flows and global balances as described in the RWAMs, to be compared with those in unintegrated, unreconciled data sources, like the *Balance of Payments Statistics* (BOP) of the IMF, and reveals differences that are sufficiently large to affect policy analyses; the world economy is not as it is usually perceived. The balance of payments positions of the country groups in RWAM, and the large US current account deficit in 1985, are presented as cases in point.

The first four tables in Appendix A5 (Tables A5.1–A5.4) give the balance of payments transactions by origin and destination and the marginal totals computed on the basis of statistics published by international organizations. These tables were constructed in 'stage 1' of the reconciliation procedure, i.e. no adjustments are made, a large share of the transactions has not been allocated by origin and destination, and there are considerable discrepancies between the row and the column totals. Tables A5.5 to A5.8 present the four main blocs of the RWAMs. In these tables there are no discrepancies and all transactions are allocated by origin and destination.

5.2 Two Examples of the Construction of Financial Matrices

The construction of the matrix for FDI income in 1970

The construction of financial matrices involves much 'educated' guesswork. In stage 1 of the construction of the matrix for FDI income in 1970 the 'raw marginals' are calculated from the BOP. There are no adjustments in stage 2, because although there are numerous gaps in the data on account of 'missing countries', possibilities for gap-filling are too limited. Nor can adjustments be made in stage 3, since there are no second estimates available. In stage 4 the marginal totals of the complete WAM in 1970 are made consistent through the mathematical reconciliation procedure; the result for FDI income is shown under the heading 'adjusted marginals' in Table 5.1. Both the sum of the column totals and the sum of the row totals increase when adjusted. It is also clear that the adjustments are not spread evenly over the countries: a large part of the adjustment is attributed to Major Oil Exporters and Private Borrowers column totals (indicating a change in Major Oil Exporters' and Private Borrowers' FDI income from FDI assets) and US row totals (indicating a change in US FDI payments).

In stage 5 the interior of the matrix (the 'raw matrix' in Table 5.1) is estimated, relating the matrix for FDI stocks in 1975 to the row totals derived in stage 4 (the adjusted marginals). The income matrix has *income receipts* on the rows, and the stock matrix has *inward investment*, or liabilities, on the rows. Therefore, to relate the two variables one matrix has to be transposed. For example, the entry US$ 0.2 billion, found in the row US and the column Japan in the 'raw matrix' is calculated as the share of Japan in total US FDI assets (2.5/124.3) times total US FDI income receipts (US$ 8.7 billion; see Table 5.1).

In stage 6, the entire WAM for 1970 was estimated in the second phase of the mathematical reconciliation procedure. This involves an estimation based on the adjusted marginal row and column totals de-

Table 5.1 Stages in the construction of the matrix for FDI income, 1970 (in US$ billions)

	US	Japan	EU	OOECD	CMEA	MOE	OB	DB	PB	ROW	Multi	Total
Stage 1: Raw marginal totals												
column	0.9	0.1	2.1	1.6	0.0	2.8	0.5	0.5	2.4	0.4	0.0	11.2
row	8.2	0.1	3.7	0.5	0.0	0.0	0.0	0.0	0.0	0.1	0.0	12.6
*Stages 2–3**												
Stage 4: Adjusted marginal totals												
column	0.8	0.1	1.9	1.4	0.0	6.1	0.3	0.5	1.6	0.5	0.0	13.3
row	8.7	0.1	3.8	0.5	0.0	0.0	0.0	0.0	0.0	0.1	0.0	13.3
Stage 5: Matrix for FDI stocks 1975												
US	0.0	3.4	12.4	13.9	0.0	0.5	0.0	0.0	0.6	1.0	0.0	31.9
Japan	2.5	0.0	0.5	0.4	0.0	0.0	0.0	0.0	0.1	0.1	0.0	3.6
EU	34.2	2.0	29.6	8.0	0.0	0.4	0.0	0.0	0.7	2.4	0.0	77.3
OOECD	45.7	1.3	21.2	4.0	0.0	0.9	0.0	0.0	1.1	1.7	0.0	75.8
CMEA	0.0	0.0	0.0	0.0	0.0	0.0	0.0	0.0	0.0	0.0	0.0	0.0
MOE	6.0	2.1	0.3	0.8	0.0	0.0	0.0	0.0	0.0	0.0	0.0	9.2
OB	5.8	0.9	5.4	0.0	0.0	0.0	0.0	0.0	0.0	0.0	0.0	12.1
DB	6.7	3.4	1.3	0.0	0.0	0.0	0.0	.0	0.4	0.3	0.0	12.2
PB	20.9	2.7	9.6	11.8	0.0	0.0	0.0	0.1	0.7	0.2	0.0	46.1
ROW	2.5	0.3	5.9	5.8	0.0	0.0	0.0	0.0	0.0	0.1	0.0	14.8
Multi	0.0	0.0	0.0	0.0	0.0	0.0	0.0	0.0	0.0	0.0	0.0	0.0
Total	124.3	16.1	86.2	44.7	0.0	1.9	0.1	0.1	3.6	5.9	0.0	282.9

* Due to data constraints, no adjustments were made in stages 2 and 3. See text.

(Continued)

	US	Japan	EU	OOECD	CMEA	MOE	OB	DB	PB	ROW	Multi	Total**
Stage 5: Raw matrix for FDI income												
US	0.0	0.2	2.4	3.2	0.0	0.4	0.4	0.5	1.5	0.2	0.0	8.7
Japan	0.0	0.0	0.0	0.0	0.0	0.0	0.0	0.0	0.0	0.0	0.0	0.1
EU	0.5	0.0	1.3	0.9	0.0	0.0	0.2	0.1	0.4	0.3	0.0	3.8
OOECD	0.2	0.0	0.1	0.0	0.0	0.0	0.0	0.0	0.1	0.1	0.0	0.5
CMEA	0.0	0.0	0.0	0.0	0.0	0.0	0.0	0.0	0.0	0.0	0.0	0.0
MOE	0.0	0.0	0.0	0.0	0.0	0.0	0.0	0.0	0.0	0.0	0.0	0.0
OB	0.0	0.0	0.0	0.0	0.0	0.0	0.0	0.0	0.0	0.0	0.0	0.0
DB	0.0	0.0	0.0	0.0	0.0	0.0	0.0	0.0	0.0	0.0	0.0	0.0
PB	0.0	0.0	0.0	0.0	0.0	0.0	0.0	0.0	0.0	0.0	0.0	0.0
ROW	0.0	0.0	0.1	0.0	0.0	0.0	0.0	0.0	0.0	0.0	0.0	0.1
Multi	0.0	0.0	0.0	0.0	0.0	0.0	0.0	0.0	0.0	0.0	0.0	0.0
Total	0.8	0.2	3.9	4.2	0.0	0.5	0.7	0.6	2.1	0.5	0.0	13.3
Stage 6: Reconciled matrix for FDI income												
US	0.0	0.1	0.6	0.4	0.0	6.2	0.1	0.4	0.9	0.2	0.0	8.8
Japan	0.0	0.0	0.0	0.0	0.0	0.0	0.0	0.0	0.0	0.0	0.0	0.1
EU	0.6	0.0	1.2	0.9	0.0	0.0	0.2	0.1	0.5	0.3	0.0	3.8
OOECD	0.2	0.0	0.1	0.0	0.0	0.0	0.0	0.0	0.1	0.1	0.0	0.5
CMEA	0.0	0.0	0.0	0.0	0.0	0.0	0.0	0.0	0.0	0.0	0.0	0.0
MOE	0.0	0.0	0.0	0.0	0.0	0.0	0.0	0.0	0.0	0.0	0.0	0.0
OB	0.0	0.0	0.0	0.0	0.0	0.0	0.0	0.0	0.0	0.0	0.0	0.0
DB	0.0	0.0	0.0	0.0	0.0	0.0	0.0	0.0	0.0	0.0	0.0	0.0
PB	0.0	0.0	0.0	0.0	0.0	0.0	0.0	0.0	0.0	0.0	0.0	0.0
ROW	0.0	0.0	0.1	0.0	0.0	0.0	0.0	0.0	0.0	0.0	0.0	0.1
Multi	0.0	0.0	0.0	0.0	0.0	0.0	0.0	0.0	0.0	0.0	0.0	0.0
Total	0.8	0.1	1.9	1.4	0.0	6.2	0.3	0.5	1.6	0.5	0.0	13.4

** 'Total' column figures for stage 5 (raw matrix for FDI income) are row totals of adjusted marginals derived in stage 4.

(Continued)

Table 5.1 (Continued)

	US	Japan	EU	OOECD	CMEA	MOE	OB	DB	PB	ROW	Multi
Matrix of reliabilities											
US	0.1	1	1	1	0.1	2	2	2	2	2	0.1
Japan	1	0.1	1	1	0.1	2	2	2	2	2	0.1
EU	1	1	1	1	0.1	2	2	2	2	2	0.1
OOECD	1	1	1	1	0.1	2	2	2	2	2	0.1
CMEA	0.1	0.1	0.1	0.1	0.1	0.1	0.1	0.1	0.1	0.1	0.1
MOE	2	2	2	2	0.1	4	4	4	4	4	0.1
OB	2	2	2	2	0.1	4	4	4	4	4	0.1
DB	2	2	2	2	0.1	4	4	4	4	4	0.1
PB	2	2	2	2	0.1	4	4	4	4	4	0.1
ROW	2	2	2	2	0.1	4	4	4	4	4	0.1
Multi	0.1	0.1	0.1	0.1	0.1	0.1	0.1	0.1	0.1	0.1	0.1
Degree of reliability											
Raw marginal totals:											
· column	3	3	3	3	3	3	3	3	3	3	1
· row	4	4	4	4	4	4	4	4	4	4	1
Adjusted marginal totals											
· column	1	1	1	1	1	1	1	1	1	1	1
· row	1	1	1	1	1	1	1	1	1	1	1

rived in stage 4, the 'raw matrix' derived in stage 5, and various degrees of reliabilities for the interior of the matrix and the marginal totals. The 'matrix of reliabilities' in Table 5.1 gives the reliabilities per cell of the matrix, and for the marginal totals. In stage 2 the latter were estimated in relation to the marginal totals for other variables, and later, in stage 6, in relation to the relative reliability of the interior of the matrix. As set out in the previous chapter, FDI income is less reliable than trade flows and nonfactor services, but more reliable than other capital flows. In stage 6, the 'adjusted marginal totals' are highly reliable. For the non-zero entries in the interior of the matrix, degrees of reliabilities have been assigned to the cells according to data availability. Thus there are four blocs in the matrix, of which the intra-OECD bloc is considered as the most reliable bloc because it has the greatest data availability. However, this does not necessarily mean that adjustments in this bloc are small. For example, the estimate for US income from the EU is US$ 2.4 billion in the 'raw matrix', but only US$ 0.6 billion in the reconciled matrix. In spite of its high relative reliability, the value for this cell was forced down by the column total for EU payments of only US$ 1.9 billion.

The computation of EU other investment income received from the US, 1985

Again in constructing the matrix for other investment income (DIC) for 1985, and the entry for EU investment income from the US in 1985, the final outcome is a fusion of various categories of information, in this case: (1) total EU other investment income from the BOP, referred to as 'raw data, first estimate', (2) total EU other investment estimated from total EU stocks of foreign assets, referred to as 'raw data, second estimate', (3) total US other investment payments, also 'raw data' from the BOP, (4) origin and destination information, which in this particular cell mainly stems from US data on the geographical distribution of foreign liabilities, (5) the accounting constraints in the WAM, and (6) the assessed relative reliability of the various data sources used in the WAM. In principle, every single cell in the complete WAM may affect any other cell, but some cells have a more direct impact on a particular cell than others.

To get a better understanding of how these categories of information work together in the construction process, let us first look at the 'raw

Table 5.2 *The computation of EU's OCA income from the US and the accounting constraints in the WAM, 1985 (in US$ billions)*

Stage 1: Raw aggregates

EU totals	Current Account					GDI	GNS	Total
	MER	NFS	DFC	DIC	TRA			
receipts	641.7	179.9	14.3	127.2	33.6	485.6		1482.4
reliability	1	2	3	4	3	2		
payments	632.1	150.6	14.3	132.9	44.7		511.5	1488.2
reliability	1	2	4	5	3		4	
	Capital Account					GDI	GNS	Total
	OCA	FDI	RES					
inflows	165.7	18.6					511.5	695.7
reliability	5	3					4	
outflows	175.8	23.9	-1.2			485.6		684.1
reliability	4	4	2			2		
World totals	MER	NFS	DFC	DIC	TRA	OCA	FDI	RES
receipts	1921.7	446.7	54.2	269.4	99.0	408.2	62.3	
payments	1921.7	450.7	43.2	315.6	102.9	62.4	331.0	18.2

(Continued)

Stage 3: Second estimates								
EU totals	Current Account					GDI	GNS	Total
	MER	NFS	DFC	DIC	TRA			
receipts				110.8				
reliability				4				
World totals	MER	NFS	DFC	DIC	TRA	OCA	FDI	RES
receipts				308.4				
reliability				5				
Stage 4: Reconciled row and column totals								
EU totals	Current Account					GDI	GNS	Total
	MER	NFS	DFC	DIC	TRA			
receipts	641.8	180.6	12.7	152.8	35.7	479.6		1503.2
payments	632.1	150.1	16.7	125.9	40.8		537.5	1503.2
	Capital Account					GDI	GNS	Total
	OCA	FDI	RES					
inflows	157.7	18.4					537.5	713.5
outflows	211.4	24.0	-1.4			479.6		713.5
World totals	MER	NFS	DFC	DIC	TRA	OCA	FDI	RES
receipts = payments	1921.7	450.3	44.1	308.9	99.8	394.8	62.5	0.0

(Continued)

Table 5.2 *(Continued)*

Stage 5: The raw matrix: EU's receipts and payments

	US	Japan	EU	OOECD	CMEA	MOE	OB	DB	PB	ROW	Multi	Total
EU income	15.3	10.0	60.0	14.0	2.0	2.9	2.2	3.0	17.8	0.0	2.2	129.4
reliability	2	2	3	3	4	4	1	1	1	4	1	
EU payments	5.0	4.3	60.0	18.9	0.0	7.3	2.9	1.0	2.0	0.1	0.0	101.5
reliability	2	2	3	3	4	4	4	4	4	4	4	

Stage 6: The reconciled matrix: EU's receipts and payments

	US	Japan	EU	OOECD	CMEA	MOE	OB	DB	PB	ROW	Multi	Total
EU income	16.9	5.7	77.5	22.5	4.6	0.2	2.2	3.0	17.9	0.0	2.2	152.8
EU payments	20.4	6.4	77.5	2.0	0.0	12.9	4.2	0.6	1.7	0.2	0.0	125.9

marginal totals' for DIC in Table 5.2, which show a gap between total world incomings and outgoings of US$ 46.2 billion. Given this discrepancy we would expect an upward adjustment for receipts and/or a downward adjustment for payments. But the equality between other investment income receipts and payments is only one of many accounting constraints. On the 'national level' – in this case the EU group level – the following accounting constraints must be satisfied:

$$\textit{Total current account incomings} + \textit{GDI} = \textit{Total current account outgoings} + \textit{GNS} \quad (5.1)$$

$$\textit{Total capital outflows} + \textit{changes in reserves} + \textit{GDI} = \textit{Total capital inflows} + \textit{GNS} \quad (5.2)$$

Deducting the second from the first equation gives the balance of payments equation which states that

$$\textit{Total current account incomings} - \textit{total current account outgoings} = \textit{Total capital outflows} + \textit{changes in reserves less capital inflows} \quad (5.3)$$

Under the heading 'Raw data: EU totals', Table 5.2 gives the figures for the EU in 1985 for these equations, disaggregated into five current account categories and two capital account categories, plus the degree of reliability assigned to each type of transaction. To achieve consistency in equation (5.1), there are of course many options. One would be an increase in one or more categories of current account receipts and/or GDI, another would be a decrease in one or more categories of current account payments and/or GNS. In equation (5.2) there is a smaller discrepancy, which tends to put downward pressure on capital inflows and GNS and upward pressure on capital outflows, RES and GDI. The mathematical reconciliation procedure is an iterative method that achieves consistency by searching for a solution that is as close to the initial values as possible, allowing the figures to vary according to their relative reliabilities. Thus, if only these two constraints had to be satisfied, there would be upward adjustments for current account receipts, GDI and capital account inflows, and downward adjustments for current account payments, GNS and capital inflows. Given the assigned reliabilities, the largest adjustments would be found for DIC payments and OCA capital inflows (degree 5), adjustments for DFC payments (degree

4) would be half the size of adjustments for DIC payments, and the smallest adjustments would be for MER (degree 1).

Introducing global constraints however, alters the solution because these constraints may push the adjustments in other directions. For example, the EU accounting constraints put upward pressure on DFC receipts but the world total for DFC receipts is larger than total payments. Thus the global constraints explain the lower figure for EU DFC receipts in the 'reconciled data: EU totals' in Table 5.2. The reconciled world total for DIC is closer to the initial input for payments than for receipts, which were considered less reliable than payments. The EU has absorbed a large share of the adjustment, in fact, the upward adjustment for DIC was larger than necessary for the gap in EU's equation (5.1) to close, resulting in a larger total for equation (5.1) than in the 'raw data'. This could happen partly because of the enormous discrepancy in DIC, but also because the EU is large. Obviously, given a similar degree of reliability, larger figures will tend to absorb larger parts of discrepancies than smaller figures. Similarly, countries or country groups with relatively consistent statistics will absorb a small part of the global discrepancies. Japan is a clear example of both of these tendencies: Japan is a relatively small 'group' in the WAM and Japanese statistics show very small discrepancies in equations (5.1) and (5.2) and in all four reconciled WAMs, the adjustments for Japan were quite small.

Finally, the interior for the matrix is first estimated on the basis of national data sources, and then reconciled in the mathematical reconciliation procedure. The estimates in the 'raw matrix' are too low to fit the accounting constraints of the WAM, but only a small part of the upward adjustment is attributed to EU investment income from the US which rises from US$ 15.3 billion to US$ 16.9 billion. This is due to the assigned degree of reliability, but even more so to the total for the US investment income payments, which allows limited room for change. A large adjustment is made in the account of the EU itself to compensate for the underestimation for intra-EU investment which occurs because many EU countries do not publish financial data by origin and destination.

Table 5.3 Discrepancies in the adjusted estimates for 1980 (in US$ billions)

(1) Discrepancies at the country group level

	'Ex'	'Im'	GNS	GDI	DAS	DLI	RES	D1	D2
US	335.2	350.5	431.5	436.1	79.2	59.3	-7.0	-10.8	-26.9
Japan	164.5	180.3	327.3	343.6	26.2	45.1	-5.0	0.5	13.9
EU	1054.1	1114.0	671.6	714.1	239.0	277.2	1.0	-17.4	39.2
OOECD	277.4	300.5	198.1	217.4	48.8	53.6	-3.5	-3.9	1.2
CMEA	198.8	208.9	177.5	184.6	0.6	6.8	0.4	-2.9	6.6
MOEs	260.7	141.0	209.3	95.6	50.9	-9.3	-2.4	6.0	-62.6
OBs	124.0	132.1	63.2	70.8	1.5	11.8	2.2	-0.6	12.5
DBs	82.2	86.2	155.1	164.6	0.7	8.8	-3.7	5.5	4.4
PBs	228.9	253.9	240.7	250.0	9.6	18.4	-8.7	-15.6	0.1
ROW	111.7	106.3	75.8	73.9	4.6	7.1	-0.9	3.5	1.5
Multi	5.0	5.0	0.0	0.0	8.7	8.7	0.0	0.0	0.0
Total	2842.5	2878.7	2550.1	2550.7	469.8	487.5	-27.6	-35.7	-10.1

'Ex' : total current account incomings
'Im' : total current account outgoings
GNS : gross national saving
GDI : gross domestic investment
DAS : total net changes in assets
DLI : total net changes in liabilities
RES : net changes in reserves
D1 : discrepancy between ('Ex' – 'Im') and (GNS – GDI)
D2 : discrepancy between (DAS + DLI - RES) and (GNS - GDI)

(Continued)

Table 5.3 (Continued)

(2) Discrepancies at the global level

Current account		Capital account	
Merchandise trade	0.0	Foreign direct investment	-7.5
Nonfactor services	-15.8	Other capital	25.2
Foreign direct investment income	4.3	Net changes in reserves	-27.7
Investment income other capital	-18.2		
Unrequited transfers	-6.7		
Total current account	-36.3	Total capital account	-10.0

5.3 Discrepancies, Reliabilities and the Reconciliation Procedure

To indicate of the size of the discrepancies that have been solved in the mathematical reconciliation procedure and the sensitivity of the method given the assumptions about the reliability of the data for the WAM for 1980, the discrepancies at the country group level for 1980, which are derived from equations (5.1) and (5.2) in the previous section are provided in Table 5.3. Column D1 in Table 5.3 gives the discrepancy in equation (5.1); column D2 gives the discrepancy in equation (5.2). These figures refer to the discrepancies in the raw data after they have been manually adjusted, i.e. in the end of construction stage 2. The table shows that the discrepancies for the US, Major Oil Exporters and Private Borrowers are relatively large. (This was also true in 1970, 1975 and 1985). Table 5.3 also gives the global discrepancies for 1980, i.e. a large discrepancy for nonfactor services – a relatively large category on the current account – and for investment income related to OCA and flows of OCA. Due to the adjustments made in stage 2, the discrepancies on the global current account and capital account are smaller than in the BOP (see Table 3.1). This does not hold for 1970 and 1975 when the global trade balance surplus on the current account compensates for global deficits on other current account transactions in the BOP. Table 5.3 shows that in 1980 there was only a small difference (US$ 0.5 billion) between world investment and world saving. This means that the adjustment required to balance world investment and world savings is equally small.

In the reconciliation procedure, five different degrees of reliability are assigned to the different transactions based on the data analysis in Chapter 3. As trade matrices are not altered in the reconciliation procedure, the highest degree of reliability ('degree 1') has been assigned to merchandise trade while nonfactor services figures are considered as less reliable than those for merchandise trade ('degree 2'). The recording of financial flows is considered less reliable than the recording of trade flows, and unrequited transfers and FDI figures are considered more reliable than OCA figures. For FDI, the figures for net changes in assets are considered more reliable than those for net changes in liabilities; for OCA this is the converse. For FDI, income credits figures are considered more reliable than those for debits; for OCA this is the converse. This leads to the following schedule for financial flows:

1. The figures for unrequited transfers and foreign direct investment income and changes in assets are considered the most reliable financial flows ('degree 3').
2. Less reliable are the figures for payments and net changes in liabilities for direct investment and other capital ('degree 4').
3. An exception is made for LDCs: because of the availability of matrix interiors that are consistent with net changes in liabilities and interest payments a high degree of reliability ('degree 1') has been assigned to these entries. In this case, the relative reliability compared with other financial variables has been decisive for assessing the degree of reliability.
4. The lowest degree of reliability has been assigned to interest income and net changes in assets for other capital ('degree 5').
5. Gross domestic investment recording is considered as fairly reliable ('degree 2'), while gross national saving, usually a residual in national accounts, is less reliable ('degree 4').

Table 5.4 gives the difference between the results of stage 2 and stage 3 of the reconciliation procedure, in three scenarios. In other words, it compares the data input with the data output of the mathematical reconciliation procedure for the row and column totals. A negative entry in Table 5.4 indicates that the value in the reconciled WAM is higher than in the manually adjusted WAM. The first scenario corresponds to the degrees of reliability in the RWAMs. To obtain an indication of the sensitivity of the method for different degrees of reliability, two other sets of degrees of reliabilities have been assigned to the data. The second and third scenarios summarize the results of this exercise. In the second scenario there is less variation in degrees of reliability than in the first scenario. Degree 1 has been used for merchandise trade and LDC debt data and degree 2 for nonfactor services, gross domestic investment, transfers, foreign direct investment income and net changes in assets and other capital income payments and net changes in liabilities. Degree 3 has been assigned to gross national savings, foreign direct investment payments and net changes in liabilities. In scenario 3, entries are either reliable (merchandise trade and LDC debt data) or not

Table 5.4 Degree of reliability in the mathematical reconciliation procedure (in US$ billions)

Scenario 1: Large variation in degrees of reliability

	'Exports'	'Imports'	GNS	GDI	DAS	DLI
US	-9.8	2.8	-1.6	0.2	21.4	-4.7
Japan	-0.1	0.2	-0.7	0.2	-0.1	0.1
EU	-12.1	11.1	-4.9	0.9	-3.6	-1.0
OOECD	-2.4	1.7	-0.2	0.1	12.6	-4.3
CMEA	-1.3	1.5	0.2	0.1	0.0	-0.6
MOE	4.9	-0.9	-0.1	0.0	-51.6	0.1
OB	3.6	-0.6	3.4	-1.5	-0.3	0.1
DB	0.5	-0.8	-3.3	0.9	-0.0	0.0
PB	-11.7	2.7	0.9	-0.5	4.2	-1.0
ROW	5.6	-4.2	4.9	-1.3	-6.5	5.2
Multi	0.0	0.0	0.0	0.0	-0.0	-0.0
Total	-22.8	13.5	-1.4	-0.9	-23.9	-6.1

Scenario 2: Medium variation in degrees of reliability

	'Exports'	'Imports'	GNS	GDI	DAS	DLI
US	-10.2	4.4	-3.3	0.5	18.6	-5.0
Japan	-0.1	0.2	-0.6	0.2	-0.2	0.2
EU	-16.9	11.5	-8.9	2.0	-7.1	0.7
OOECD	-4.7	4.1	-3.8	1.1	9.0	-3.1
CMEA	-1.6	1.7	-0.3	0.2	0.0	-0.1
MOE	4.1	-8.8	6.4	-0.4	-44.3	0.4
OB	3.0	-1.5	3.6	-1.6	0.0	0.0
DB	0.5	-0.9	-3.2	0.9	0.0	0.0
PB	-8.0	8.4	-0.7	0.0	1.1	-1.0
ROW	11.4	-5.4	10.4	-2.8	-1.5	1.2
Multi	0.0	0.0	0.0	0.0	0.0	0.0
Total	-22.5	13.7	-0.4	0.1	-24.4	-6.7

(Continued)

(all other categories).

Table 5.4 shows that the three scenarios lead to different results, but the differences are not alarmingly large. The differences between the

Table 5.4 (Continued)

Scenario 3: Small variation in degrees of reliability

	'Exports'	'Imports'	GNS	GDI	DAS	DLI
US	-10.2	9.6	-2.8	6.2	11.8	-6.5
Japan	-0.1	0.3	0.5	1.3	-0.1	0.4
EU	-14.8	16.7	-13.1	1.0	-3.8	7.1
OOECD	-6.2	6.3	-6.8	1.8	3.6	-4.8
CMEA	-1.6	1.7	-0.8	-0.4	0.0	0.0
MOE	3.7	-21.7	17.9	-1.4	-31.6	0.5
OB	3.0	-1.6	2.0	-3.3	0.0	0.0
DB	0.6	-0.8	-2.8	1.2	0.0	0.0
PB	-7.4	10.1	-7.3	-5.4	0.4	-0.4
ROW	11.8	-5.5	12.9	-0.8	-0.4	1.4
Multi	0.0	0.0	0.0	0.0	0.0	0.0
Total	-21.2	15.1	-0.3	0.2	-20.1	-2.3

'Exports' : total current account incomings
'Imports' : total current account outgoings
DAS : total net changes in assets
DLI : total net changes in liabilities

three scenarios are larger for the groups that showed large inconsistencies at the country group level. In particular, for Major Oil Exporters and the US, the results are relatively sensitive for the assessed degrees of reliability. With the increase in variation in degrees of reliability, a larger share of the adjustments takes place in capital flows, while the share in adjustment decreases for domestic transactions and current account incomings. De Jong et al. (1993a) performed a similar sensitivity analysis of different assumptions about data source reliability in the mathematical reconciliation procedure for WAMs. The WAMs in their study are constructed for different years and different classifications, but they also concluded that the degree in variation did not matter much: little sensitivity of the results was observed whether the relative reliabilities were set at 1:8 or 2:4. This is an indication of the robustness of the WAM balancing method.

5.4 Interpreting the Reconciled World Accounting Matrices

The allocation of discrepancies in the reconciled WAMs

Table 5.5 gives the difference between the RWAMs and the BOP for the different categories of balance of payments transactions: a positive number in the table indicates that the value for the transaction is larger in the RWAMs than in the BOP. 'Current account net' is the difference between total current account receipts ('in') and payments ('out'). This difference represents the world current account discrepancy in the BOP. Similarly, the difference between total inflows and outflows on the world capital account is equal to the world capital account discrepancy in the BOP. It follows from the accounting identities implicit in the RWAMs that both global net changes in reserves and net errors and omissions are equal to zero in the RWAMs. Therefore, the values in the table for these categories represent the global discrepancies on these accounts in the BOP.

Tables 5.6 and 5.7 present a disaggregation of Table 5.5. From Table 5.6 it is immediately clear that, in absolute terms, differences between the RWAMs and the BOP on the *current account* are much larger for merchandise trade than for the other categories. As demonstrated in Chapter 3, this can largely be explained by a difference in country coverage, in particular for CMEA countries. This is reflected in Table 5.6 which gives the difference between the RWAMs and the BOP by country group and by type of current account transaction. This table shows that about 50 per cent of the difference in exports is accounted for by the CMEA; the EU and Official Borrowers each account for 10 to 20 per cent of the difference in both imports and exports, and the Major Oil Exporters account for 10 to 20 per cent of the difference in exports. Nonfactor services have increased considerably in the RWAMs, in particular for current account incomings. This is due to the relatively large adjustment for income earned by the 'missing fleet', and to the adjustments made for CMEA countries that are not recorded in the BOP. Investment income is split into income related to foreign direct investment (FDI) and other capital (OCA). The Tables 5.5 and 5.6 show large differences for investment income receipts related to OCA in 1980 and 1985. According to Table 5.6, the difference in 1980 can almost entirely be attributed to the US and Private Borrowers, while in

Table 5.5 *The difference between RWAM and BOP by transaction (in US$ billions)*

	1970		1975		1980		1985	
	receipts	paym'ts	receipts	paym'ts	receipts	paym'ts	receipts	paym'ts
Current account								
Merchandise trade	54.2	62.3	140.0	160.6	327.0	331.6	261.6	248.9
Nonfactor services	10.7	4.6	27.6	14.5	61.0	22.4	55.6	30.5
FDI income	0.8	2.1	-2.6	2.0	-1.2	3.1	-10.1	0.8
OCA income	3.0	-0.4	4.9	-0.2	20.0	1.3	44.3	-9.8
Transfers	1.5	-2.0	3.2	-4.2	3.5	-3.1	13.7	11.1
Total current acct.	70.2	66.6	173.1	172.7	410.3	355.3	365.1	281.7
Current account net	3.6		0.4		55.0		83.4	
Capital account								
FDI	1.3	-0.6	3.5	-1.9	5.6	-1.8	15.1	0.2
OCA	-6.9	7.0	-3.5	3.8	-10.6	52.7	-16.1	72.7
Changes in reserves	10.7		7.7		27.7		9.1	
Total capital acct.	5.1	6.4	7.8	1.9	23.0	50.9	8.1	72.9
Capital account net	-1.3		5.9		-27.8		-64.8	
Errors and omissions	-2.3		-6.2		-27.2		-18.6	

Note: Columns may not tally due to rounding.

1985 the EU and the US largely accounted for the difference.

Table 5.7 gives a disaggregation of Table 5.5 by country group and type of capital account transaction. As discussed earlier, global discrepancy in OCA is relatively large. Consequently, the largest adjustments on the capital account balances have been allocated to OCA flows. The adjustments are particularly large for net changes in assets in 1980 (US$ 52.7 billion) and 1985 (US$ 72.7 billion). Table 5.7 shows that the substantial increases in net changes of assets for Major Oil Exporters in 1975, 1980 and 1985, and for the EU in 1985, are the main sources for this difference. In 1980, the RWAM shows a large upward adjustment in OCA inflows for the US that is related to the elimination of the large errors and omissions. A possible explanation of this upward adjustment may be capital flight from LDCs. On the accounts for flows of FDI, the adjustments are much smaller than for OCA and largely consist of increases in net inward flows of the US and the EU.

Table 5.6 *Differences between RWAM and BOP on the current account (in US$ billions)*

	1970		1975		1980		1985	
	receipts	paym'ts	receipts	paym'ts	receipts	paym'ts	receipts	paym'ts
Merchandise trade								
US	1.0	1.5	1.1	5.3	-9.1	8.3	-2.4	-6.9
Japan	0.6	1.4	1.6	3.5	5.7	11.0	6.3	-2.7
EU	4.8	9.5	17.3	23.7	42.1	63.5	26.2	24.5
OOECD	-0.1	2.1	-0.4	4.8	1.7	10.9	-13.2	-11.5
CMEA	31.4	33.0	71.4	84.8	128.2	130.8	132.8	127.8
MOE	4.4	0.7	13.9	-5.0	69.4	16.2	48.3	25.7
OB	7.1	9.6	21.8	31.7	46.6	48.1	29.4	57.7
DB	1.0	0.9	4.3	3.8	12.7	10.2	-4.6	-7.8
PB	0.2	0.4	-1.4	0.2	-4.0	-3.7	0.2	3.2
ROW	3.7	3.3	10.4	7.8	33.7	36.3	38.7	38.8
Multi	0.0	0.0	0.0	0.0	0.0	0.0	0.0	0.0
Total	54.2	62.3	140.0	160.6	327.0	331.6	261.6	248.9
Nonfactor services								
US	-0.2	-0.1	-0.3	0.3	0.6	-0.5	0.2	-0.2
Japan	0.0	-0.1	0.0	-0.0	0.0	-0.1	0.0	-0.1
EU	0.4	-0.4	-8.4	6.7	4.5	-3.5	0.7	-0.5
OOECD	0.3	-0.2	-0.3	0.3	0.6	-0.6	0.0	-0.0
CMEA	7.4	6.1	22.7	10.5	32.0	30.6	30.3	32.6
MOE	0.2	0.1	1.0	0.4	2.1	0.4	1.6	4.0
OB	0.9	-0.6	5.1	-2.8	3.6	1.0	11.8	-7.1
DB	0.2	0.2	1.2	0.4	2.8	0.3	1.8	0.7
PB	0.9	-0.3	3.7	-1.0	9.5	-6.0	4.5	0.4
ROW	0.5	0.0	2.8	-0.2	5.2	0.8	4.6	0.7
Multi	0.0	0.0	0.0	0.0	0.0	0.0	0.0	0.0
Total	10.7	4.6	27.6	14.5	61.0	22.4	55.6	30.5
FDI income								
US	0.6	0.0	-2.1	0.2	-0.8	0.2	-8.3	0.1
Japan	0.0	0.0	0.0	0.0	0.0	0.0	-0.1	0.0
EU	0.2	-0.2	-0.4	0.8	-0.4	1.4	-1.6	0.5
OOECD	0.0	-0.2	0.0	0.3	0.0	0.1	-0.1	0.1
CMEA	0.0	0.0	0.0	0.0	0.0	0.0	0.0	0.0
MOE	0.0	3.4	0.0	0.7	0.0	0.9	0.0	0.0
OB	0.0	-0.2	0.0	-0.2	0.0	0.1	0.0	0.0
DB	0.0	0.1	0.0	0.6	0.0	0.6	0.0	0.0
PB	0.0	-0.9	0.0	-0.5	0.0	0.3	0.0	0.1
ROW	0.0	0.1	0.0	0.1	0.0	0.2	0.0	0.0
Multi	0.0	0.0	0.0	0.0	0.0	0.0	0.0	0.0
Total	0.8	2.1	-2.6	2.0	-1.2	3.1	-10.1	0.8

Table 5.6 (Continued)

	1970		1975		1980		1985	
	receipts	paym'ts	receipts	paym'ts	receipts	paym'ts	receipts	paym'ts
OCA income								
US	0.7	0.0	2.1	-0.7	12.7	-2.8	13.1	-3.4
Japan	0.0	0.0	0.6	-0.2	0.0	0.0	1.2	-0.2
EU	2.5	-0.6	-3.1	0.8	-0.9	0.2	25.6	-7.0
OOECD	0.1	-0.1	0.9	-0.3	1.2	-0.7	0.6	-0.3
CMEA	0.0	0.0	0.0	0.0	0.0	-0.3	0.0	0.4
MOE	0.0	0.0	0.0	0.0	0.0	0.0	0.0	0.1
OB	0.0	0.0	1.1	-0.3	-1.6	0.3	4.2	-0.1
DB	0.0	0.0	-0.1	0.1	-0.2	1.7	-1.4	-0.3
PB	0.0	0.0	2.8	-0.9	7.6	-2.2	-2.8	-7.2
ROW	-0.7	0.0	-0.2	0.6	-1.2	2.8	-1.0	3.5
Multi	0.4	0.2	0.8	0.8	2.3	2.3	4.8	4.8
Total	3.0	-0.4	4.9	-0.2	20.0	1.3	44.3	-9.8
Transfers income								
US	0.0	-0.4	0.0	-0.3	0.0	-0.2	0.0	-0.7
Japan	0.0	0.0	0.0	0.0	0.0	0.0	0.0	0.0
EU	0.7	-1.7	2.0	-4.8	2.6	-5.2	2.1	-4.0
OOECD	0.1	-0.1	0.1	-0.2	0.1	-0.1	0.1	-0.1
CMEA	0.4	0.0	0.2	0.0	0.0	0.0	0.0	1.3
MOE	0.0	0.0	0.0	-0.2	0.0	-0.1	0.0	1.8
OB	0.6	-0.1	0.0	-0.2	0.0	0.0	0.1	-0.1
DD	-0.1	0.0	0.0	0.0	0.0	0.0	0.0	0.0
PB	0.0	0.0	0.0	0.0	0.0	-0.2	0.0	0.0
ROW	-0.3	0.0	-0.7	0.0	-1.8	0.0	-1.5	0.0
Multi	0.1	0.3	1.6	1.6	2.7	2.7	12.9	12.9
Total	1.5	-2.0	3.2	-4.2	3.5	-3.1	13.7	11.1

In a balance of payments statement, the discrepancy between the current account balance and the capital account balance (including net changes in reserves) is recorded on the account for net errors and omissions. In the RWAMs, this statistical difference no longer exists; it has been allocated to both current and capital account transactions because it may arise from errors and omissions on both accounts (see Chapter 3). As shown in Chapter 3 (see Table 3.2), net errors and omissions are large for some country groups, and the adjustments that are required to eliminate this discrepancy may therefore have a substantial impact on

Table 5.7 *Differences between RWAM and BOP on the capital account (in US$ billions)*

	1970		1975		1980		1985	
	receipts	paym'ts	receipts	paym'ts	receipts	paym'ts	receipts	paym'ts
FDI								
US	0.1	-0.4	0.2	-1.5	2.4	-0.8	5.6	0.0
Japan	0.0	0.0	0.0	-0.1	0.0	0.0	0.2	0.0
EU	0.9	-0.2	1.8	-0.4	2.7	-1.0	4.2	0.1
OOECD	0.2	0.0	0.2	0.0	0.1	-0.1	0.6	0.1
CMEA	0.0	0.0	0.0	0.0	0.0	0.0	0.0	0.0
MOE	0.0	0.0	0.0	0.0	0.0	0.0	0.2	0.0
OB	0.0	0.0	0.1	0.0	-0.1	0.0	2.5	0.0
DB	0.0	0.0	-0.2	0.0	0.0	0.0	0.3	0.0
PB	0.2	0.0	1.6	0.0	0.8	0.0	1.4	0.0
ROW	0.0	0.0	0.0	0.0	0.0	0.0	0.2	0.0
Multi	0.0	0.0	0.0	0.0	0.0	0.0	0.0	0.0
Total	1.3	-0.6	3.7	-1.9	5.9	-1.8	15.1	0.2
OCA								
US	-0.6	1.9	6.5	-1.4	17.7	-2.2	-2.7	0.1
Japan	0.1	-0.7	0.2	-0.2	0.0	0.0	-0.4	5.5
EU	-2.8	6.3	3.0	-12.7	1.0	-2.9	-8.0	35.6
OOECD	0.4	-1.4	3.7	-6.0	4.5	-13.2	-2.1	2.4
CMEA	0.0	0.0	0.6	-0.2	0.7	0.0	-0.1	0.1
MOE	-0.7	0.1	0.0	24.3	-0.1	56.1	-0.1	21.5
OB	-0.2	0.0	-1.4	-0.6	0.3	0.5	-0.9	-3.8
DB	-0.2	0.0	-0.7	0.2	-4.1	0.1	-4.8	0.4
PB	-1.9	-0.3	-13.8	-2.4	-34.0	-0.8	-8.4	2.1
ROW	-1.9	0.2	-5.2	-0.9	-5.2	6.5	0.0	-2.7
Multi	0.8	0.8	3.6	3.6	8.7	8.7	11.5	11.5
Total	-6.9	7.0	-3.5	3.8	-10.6	52.7	-16.1	72.7

the balances of both current and capital account. This problem is most serious for the US which had large positive errors and omissions in 1980 and 1985. One possible cause for positive errors and omissions would be underestimation of current account receipts or capital inflows; alternatively, current account payments or capital outflows may be overestimated. In 1980 the errors and omissions for the US in BOP were US$ 25 billion. As a result of the balancing method, in the RWAM two thirds of this discrepancy have been allocated to capital inflows, while the US$ 18.5 billion discrepancy in 1985 has almost entirely been allocated to investment income.

Finally, GNS and GDI have been adjusted in order to accommodate the accounting constraints in the WAM: by definition, the difference between GNS and GDI equals the current account balance and the capital account balance (including net changes in reserves). Large adjustments were made to fill the many gaps in data coverage, in particular for CMEA, Major Oil Exporters and Official Borrowers, in the major source, the *World Tables* of the World Bank. In the mathematical reconciliation procedure, sizeable adjustments have been made for GNS, which has allowed more variation than GDI. The adjustments were largest for the US and Private Borrowers. For the US, downward adjustments for GNS were about US$ 15 billion in 1975 and 1985, and US$ 28 billion in 1980. Private Borrowers saw an increase in GNS of US$ 6 billion (1975), 15 billion (1980) and 7 billion (1985).

Generally, net balances are the relatively small differences between two large gross estimates. Therefore, if an equally large but offsetting adjustment is made for both incomings and outgoings, the net balance is not affected, while small adjustments in opposite directions may lead to large shifts in balances. As illustrated in Table 5.6, the increases in gross flows on the current account in the RWAMs have been largest for the CMEA countries. Since the increases in incomings and outgoings were of the same size, the large adjustments for the CMEA have not had much effect on the world current account discrepancy in the BOP.[1] For Major Oil Exporters, adjustments in the RWAMs are smaller than for the CMEA, but the increases in current account incomings considerably exceeded those in outgoings. Consequently, the current account positions for Major Oil Exporters have undergone large shifts.

Table 5.8 gives (1) the current accounts calculated from the BOP; and (2) the reconciled current accounts in the RWAMs, both in current values and expressed as percentages of GNP. These show only one shift from positive to negative or vice versa: the deficit of US$ 6.8 billion for Major Oil Exporters in 1985 in BOP has changed to a surplus of US$ 11.5 billion in 1985 in the RWAMs. Obviously, the deficit on the global current account in the BOP demands a net increase in global current account incomings in the RWAMs. Table 5.8 shows large increases for the EU, Major Oil Exporters and Private Borrowers in particular, and in 1985 also for the US and Japan. These increases

Table 5.8 *Current account balances in BOP and in RWAM (in US$ billions)*

	Current account balances in current values				Current account balances as a percentage of regional GNP			
	1970	1975	1980	1985	1970	1975	1980	1985
BOP								
US	2.3	18.1	1.9	-114.9	0.2	1.1	0.1	-2.9
Japan	2.0	-0.6	-10.7	48.7	1.0	-0.1	-1.0	3.6
EU	2.5	-0.1	-39.5	18.6	0.4	0.0	-1.3	0.7
OOECD	-0.7	-9.8	-14.2	-5.2	-0.3	-2.0	-1.7	-0.6
CMEA	0.0	-0.8	-6.4	0.2	0.0	-0.2	-1.0	0.0
MOE	0.2	28.1	65.2	-6.8	0.9	17.4	15.5	-1.6
OB	-1.9	-6.9	-11.2	-12.2	-1.6	-3.6	-3.2	-3.0
DB	-1.2	-6.9	-8.0	-20.3	-0.8	-2.3	-1.4	-3.6
PB	-4.4	-16.7	-32.6	3.8	-2.5	-4.0	-3.3	0.4
ROW	-2.4	-4.7	0.5	4.6	-5.6	-4.7	0.3	2.5
Multi	0.0	0.0	0.0	0.0	0.0	0.0	0.0	0.0
World	-3.6	-0.3	-55.0	-83.4	-0.1	0.0	-0.5	-0.7
World*	17.6	92.7	190.2	235.3				
RWAM								
US	3.4	14.3	0.4	-101.1	0.3	0.9	0.0	-2.5
Japan	1.3	-1.6	-15.7	59.0	0.6	-0.3	-1.5	4.4
EU	4.5	-19.9	-46.9	58.0	0.6	-1.3	-1.5	2.3
OOECD	-2.5	-14.3	-20.0	-5.9	-1.2	-2.9	-2.4	-0.7
CMEA	0.0	-1.8	-7.3	1.0	0.0	-0.5	-1.2	0.1
MOE	0.7	47.0	118.4	11.5	2.7	29.1	28.2	2.7
OB	-1.8	-7.1	-12.1	-17.4	-1.6	-3.7	-3.5	-4.3
DB	-1.2	-6.4	-5.3	-17.2	-0.8	-2.1	-0.9	-3.0
PB	-2.3	-9.0	-7.0	9.4	-1.3	-2.1	-0.7	1.1
ROW	-2.1	-1.2	-4.5	2.7	-4.8	-1.2	-2.1	1.5
Multi	0.0	0.0	0.0	0.0	0.0	0.0	0.0	0.0
World	0.0	0.0	0.0	0.0	0.0	0.0	0.0	0.0
World*	19.8	122.6	237.6	283.2				

Notes: World* is the world total in absolute value.

are larger than necessary for the world current account discrepancy to be equal to zero. Especially in 1975 and 1980, the increase in net current account incomings for Major Oil Exporters and Private Borrowers is (partially) compensated for by decreases in net current account incomings for industrialized countries.

Expressed as a percentage of world GNP, the world current account discrepancy in the BOP was higher in 1980 and 1985 than in 1970 and 1975. It is clear from the table that the allocation of the world current account discrepancy over the country groups has increased rather than decreased global imbalances: current account imbalances as a percentage of GNP are larger, with Diversified Borrowers, Private Borrowers (all years) and the US (1985) as major exceptions. As a measure of 'global imbalance', the sum of absolute values of current account deficits/surpluses shows a tendency for global imbalances to increase. The increase is stronger in the RWAMs than in BOP. If, as suggested in the RWAMs, imbalances are larger than is usually perceived, international capital markets have played a role in global financing that is even larger than is generally assumed.

An obvious conclusion is that the differences between the RWAMs and the BOP are quite large. The question is then: are they large enough to make a difference for the interpretation of economic problems? One of the principal findings in the IMF report on the world current account discrepancy is that 'the negative discrepancy in the world current account is not concentrated in any individual country or grouping of countries to such an extent that the interpretation of basic problems has been distorted' (IMF 1987: 108). This conclusion is not quite confirmed in the RWAMs, where the adjustments are disproportionate for some country groups and do not always move in the same direction for all the country groups. Disproportionate adjustments were made in particular for major oil exporters. As a consequence of these adjustments the 'oil-shocks' as expressed in terms of current account surpluses doubled in 1975 and 1980 compared with the BOP. For LDCs there has been a tendency for larger current account deficits for Official Borrowers, while Private Borrowers' net current account incomings were significantly higher in the RWAMs than in the BOP.

The large deficit on the 1985 US current account

The large deficits on the current account for the US that have been recorded since 1982 have drawn much attention. In the context of the large world current account discrepancy in the 1980s, the question is whether a part of this deficit can be ascribed to an overstatement of the large US deficit. One of the positions in the debate on this issue is that the US, being a large country, is likely to account for a large share of the world current account discrepancy. Proportional distribution of the world current account discrepancy results in a reduction of the US deficit by US$ 10 to 20 billion (see for example Wallich 1984: 18).

Cline (1989) has followed a 'weighted proportional' approach to allocate the world current account discrepancy to individual countries. The weights are derived from the same IMF report (1987) that, based on a wide range of methods, attributed the world current account discrepancy in 1983 to the major regions in the world. The report allocated 31 per cent of the world current account discrepancy to Industrial Countries, 28 per cent to oil exporters in the Middle East and 41 per cent to developing countries. Within the groups, these shares in world current account discrepancy are allocated according to the share of each country in total trade turnover (imports plus exports). His adjustments lead to small increases in current account receipts for the US: US$ 1.8 billion in 1980 and US$ 4 billion in 1985.

The large US current account deficits not only coincide with the large world current account discrepancy, but also with large net errors and omissions on the US BOP. The errors and omissions are often associated with unrecorded capital inflows (see for example Bach 1983). This leads to the following paradox: if US capital inflows are underestimated, then the net US investment position is much worse than the reported figures suggest. Investment income is estimated in the US statistics by applying a relevant interest rate to the recorded amounts of assets and liabilities. As a result of the alleged overestimation of the net US investment position, the US net investment income would be overstated, and the discrepancy on this global account would be even larger. This line of argument is put forward by Marris (1987). He argues that a positive adjustment for transport receipts, based on the 'proportionality position' would be more or less cancelled out by the overstatement of US investment income. Therefore, the US current account is neither underestimated nor overestimated.

A possible answer to the apparent paradox is found in Ulan and Dewald (1989). They argue that the revaluations for the US investment position made by the balance of payments compilers are inadequate because they do not reflect effects of market prices on important components of US investments abroad and foreign investment in the US. They conclude that the US net international investment position tends to be larger than the official measures suggest when inflation-adjusted estimates of market values of international investments are taken into account. Revaluation increases the value of US holdings abroad more than it increases the value of investment in the US. Thus, net investment income would be underestimated and consequently the US current account deficit would be overestimated by substantial amounts. Another reservation against Marris' argument is that investment income paid on unrecorded capital inflows is not likely to return to the countries of origin of the initial capital outflows.

In the RWAMs, the US current account positions in 1970, 1975 and 1980 do not differ dramatically from those in the BOP but in 1985, the deficit is US$ 13.8 billion smaller than in the BOP. In the RWAMs, this adjustment is not only consistent with a balanced global current account, but also with the other world and national accounting constraints. For example, the 1985 US current account deficit in the RWAMs is much closer to the difference between GDI and GNS as reported in the World Tables than the estimate from the BOP.

5.5 Concluding Remarks

The purpose of this chapter has been to clarify what happens to the data in the construction process. Generally, the adjustments made in the RWAMs are not distributed proportionally over the country groups. This is due to 'manual' adjustments made in the first construction stage for specific types of transactions and specific countries, and the differences in the assigned degree of reliability for different types of transactions. The largest 'disproportionate' adjustments are made for Major Oil Exporters. As a consequence, the surpluses of the current account balances for Major Oil Exporters were about twice the reported balances in BOP in 1975 and 1980. For Private Borrowers a considerable upwards adjustment for investment income receipts increased the Private Borrowers' current account incomings, while the Official Borrowers' large current account deficits in BOP were even larger in the RWAMs.

The disproportionate adjustments stress the relevance of the method, since they mean that the picture of the world economy changes when the discrepancies are allocated over the various country groups. Yet, the picture of the world economic structure that emerges from the construction method seems to be a plausible basis for economic analysis.

6 Global Linkages in the Reconciled WAMs

6.1 Introduction

The reconciled world accounting matrices (RWAMs) provide a 'one-page summary' of the world economy for 1970, 1975, 1980 and 1985. The structure of the world economy in the RWAMs reveals: (1) the relative importance of categories of transactions and country groups in the world economy, (2) the pattern of directional flows, and (3) the trade and financial balances between pairs of country groups. The first of these three aspects can also be studied using regular international macroeconomic statistics. For the second and the third aspect, and for the study of global macroeconomic linkages, the WAM is particularly useful, which is why this chapter mainly concerns global linkages in trade and finance *between* the country groups of the RWAMs. The emphasis is on global linkages in 1985, the latest available year. The analysis focuses on the three groups of LDCs in the RWAMs: (1) Official Borrowers, (2) Diversified Borrowers, and (3) Private Borrowers.[1] The matrices are presented in current US dollars and the discussion in this chapter is thus focused on value.

The analyses of transaction type and the geographical composition of international transactions are based on the row and column totals of the matrices in the RWAMs. This type of information can also be drawn from the usual international data sources and the main patterns have been often discussed in other studies. Of course, the results from the RWAMs may differ from the results of other studies because of the adjustments made for the large data discrepancies in the data sources.

Directional trade flows have been described in other studies, but for financial transactions this type of descriptive analysis has to date focused on single categories, for example aid flows (see for example Das 1986), or Japanese finance in the US (see for example Matsukawa 1987). In the RWAMs, however, we have complete trade and financial matrices, which enable us to study the link between the directional patterns of trade and finance. This link is studied on two levels. Firstly, a direct comparison is made between the directional flows: if country group X has strong trade links with country group Y, does it also have strong financial links with group Y? Secondly, the link is studied by examining pairwise current and capital account balances: if country group X has a current account deficit with country group Y, does it have a capital account surplus with group Y? If there is a link between pairwise capital and current account balances this may be interpreted as a reflection of market imperfections, because if goods and capital markets were 'perfect' no such link would exist.

6.2 The Distribution of International Transactions

The world economy by transaction type

The world totals for international current and capital account transactions as a percentage of world GNP are given in Table 6.1. Clearly, in a balance of payments context, in 1985 merchandise trade was by far the largest category. Investment income, although increasingly important, is relatively small compared to merchandise trade and nonfactor services. The five main categories of current account transactions in the RWAMs are merchandise trade, nonfactor services, investment income related to FDI, investment income related to OCA and transfers. The largest category, merchandise trade, is further subdivided into four categories: SITC 0 – 1 (food, beverages and tobacco), SITC 2 + 4 (crude materials, animal and vegetable oils, etc.), SITC 3 (mineral fuels, lubricants and related materials) and SITC 5 – 9 (manufactures). Of these, trade in manufactures is the most significant.

International capital flows have also grown greatly since 1970, but the extent to which they have grown depends very much on how they are defined. It is often observed (see for example Bergsten 1988) that the increase in capital flows was many times the increase in trade. Such observations, however, are based on changes in gross capital flows, while capital flows in the RWAMs are defined as net changes in liabilities and in assets. In our definition capital flows are closely related to

Table 6.1 International transactions as a percentage of world GNP

	1970	1975	1980	1985
Current account				
Merchandise trade, of which:	11.3	15.8	18.8	16.0
SITC 0 – 1	1.5	1.8	1.8	1.4
SITC 2 + 4	1.2	1.3	1.3	1.0
SITC 3	1.0	3.0	4.3	3.0
SITC 5 – 9	7.6	9.7	11.4	10.6
Nonfactor services	2.9	3.7	4.1	3.7
Investment income FDI	0.5	0.4	0.5	0.4
Investment income OCA	0.6	1.0	2.0	2.6
Transfers	0.5	0.7	0.8	0.8
Total current account	15.7	21.6	26.2	23.5
Capital account				
FDI	0.4	0.5	0.5	0.5
OCA	1.2	2.0	4.2	3.3
Total capital account	1.6	2.5	4.7	3.8

the imbalances in current account transactions. Thus defined, world capital flows are smaller than world trade flows: for example, in 1985 world trade was US$ 2,000 billion and world capital flows US$ 500 billion. We also see that world capital flows were larger in 1980 than in 1985 due to the larger current account imbalances in 1980.

The geographical distribution of international transactions

The relative positions of the country groups as international transactors in the world economy can be calculated directly from the four core tables presented in the previous chapter. Table 6.2 presents these calculations as shares for the country groups in global current account transactions and capital account transactions. Some striking figures in the table are the large shares for industrialized countries in total international capital flows, particularly in 1985. Industrialized countries accounted for about 70 per cent of world current account transactions, and for about 90 per cent of world capital account transactions. We also see huge

Table 6.2 *The geographical distribution of international transactions (shares as a percentage of world totals)*

Current Account

	Receipts				Payments			
	1970	1975	1980	1985	1970	1975	1980	1985
US	15	13	12	13	15	12	12	17
Japan	5	6	6	8	5	6	6	6
EU	38	36	37	36	37	38	39	34
OOECD	13	11	10	11	13	12	10	11
CMEA	9	9	7	7	9	9	7	7
MOE	3	8	9	5	3	4	5	4
OB	5	5	4	4	5	6	5	5
DB	2	3	3	4	3	3	3	4
PB	6	7	8	8	6	8	9	8
ROW	3	3	4	4	4	3	4	3
Multi	0	0	0	1	0	0	0	1
Total	100	100	100	100	100	100	100	100
IC	71	68	65	69	70	68	67	68
LDC	13	15	15	16	14	17	17	17

Capital Account

	Inflows				Outflows			
	1970	1975	1980	1985	1970	1975	1980	1985
US	12	12	13	28	28	21	12	6
Japan	5	3	9	12	6	2	5	25
EU	51	45	56	38	55	34	49	52
OOECD	15	18	12	11	7	6	7	9
CMEA	0	1	2	0	0	0	0	0
MOE	0	0	-2	0	0	31	21	3
OB	4	5	2	3	0	0	0	0
DB	3	4	2	3	0	1	0	1
PB	7	9	4	1	1	0	1	3
ROW	0	0	0	0	2	1	2	0
Multi	2	3	2	3	2	3	2	3
Total	100	100	100	100	100	100	100	100
IC	83	78	90	90	93	63	73	92
LDC	14	18	8	7	1	1	1	4

Note: Columns may not tally due to rounding.

capital outflows from Major Oil Exporters associated with the recycling of the oil surpluses in 1980 and 1985.

Comparing the four years, the clearest shift evident from Table 6.2 is found on the US capital account, which shows that the US has changed from a capital exporter into a capital importing country.[2] Furthermore, the RWAMs reveal that LDCs increased their share in global current account transactions, but were not included in the trend for internationalization of capital markets. Table 6.2 shows some clear differences between the groups of LDCs. Firstly, the increase in the share in world current account incomings for LDCs comes on account of Diversified and Private Borrowers, while the share for Official Borrowers stagnated. Secondly, there is a clear drop in the share in world capital inflows between 1970/75 and 1985 for Private Borrowers whereas the shares for Official and Diversified Borrowers slightly increased. Thirdly, capital outflows from LDCs, often referred to as 'capital flight', were substantial for Private Borrowers, as reflected in the 3 per cent share in world capital outflows for Private Borrowers in 1985, whereas the same share for Diversified Borrowers and Official Borrowers remained very close to zero.

To link the structure by type of transaction to the geographical distribution of international transactions, a coefficient a is applied to the total current account incomings for Official Borrowers, Diversified Borrowers and Private Borrowers in transaction i (q_i); this coefficient is defined as:

$$a = S_i / S \qquad (6.1)$$

where:

- q_i : the value of country group X's total current account incomings or capital inflows in category i
- S_i : the share of country group X in world current account incomings or capital inflows in category i
- S : the share of country group X in total world current account incomings or capital inflows

Table 6.3 gives the values for a for current account incomings and capital account inflows for LDCs. The table shows the relative importance of different types of transaction on the current account and the capital account for Official, Diversified and Private Borrowers. If $a = 1$, the

Table 6.3 *Changes in the type of international transaction of LDCs: α*

	Official Borrowers				Diversified Borrowers				Private Borrowers			
	1970	1975	1980	1985	1970	1975	1980	1985	1970	1975	1980	1985
Current account (receipts)												
Merchandise trade, of which:	1.1	1.0	1.0	0.8	1.0	1.0	1.1	1.1	1.0	1.0	1.0	1.1
SITC 0 – 1	2.7	2.9	2.7	3.2	2.9	2.3	2.2	2.2	2.0	1.5	1.3	1.2
SITC 2 + 4	2.1	2.0	1.9	1.9	2.8	2.5	2.3	1.9	2.2	1.8	1.7	1.7
SITC 3	1.1	1.3	1.3	1.7	0.7	1.5	1.4	1.7	3.0	2.2	1.9	2.0
SITC 5 – 9	0.5	0.4	0.5	0.4	0.4	0.4	0.5	0.6	0.3	0.4	0.5	0.6
Nonfactor services	0.7	1.0	0.9	1.4	1.0	0.9	0.9	1.2	1.2	1.2	1.1	1.0
Investment income FDI	0.0	0.0	0.0	0.1	0.1	0.1	0.1	0.2	0.0	0.0	1.0	1.0
Investment income OCA	0.3	0.6	0.1	0.5	0.5	0.2	0.2	0.2	0.5	1.5	1.2	1.4
Transfers	3.5	3.4	5.1	5.1	2.9	2.9	2.2	1.7	1.4	0.7	0.5	0.5
Capital account (net changes in liabilities)												
FDI	0.3	0.4	1.1	2.1	0.7	1.2	1.4	2.2	1.7	2.9	4.1	10.7
Official flows	10.6	11.6	22.7	15.2	9.9	5.0	17.2	10.1	3.2	3.0	5.1	15.7
Private flows	0.3	0.0	0.0	0.2	0.2	0.5	0.2	0.3	0.5	0.3	0.4	-1.3

share of a country group X in the world total for category i is equal to the group's share in total world current or capital transactions. If $a > 1$, category i is a relatively important category for country group X and vice versa. In other words, if $a > 1$, country group X has a larger share in the world total of a specific transaction than we would expect on the basis of country groups relative size. For example, for Official Borrowers we would expect a high value for a for official transfers. In fact, in the table we see that it is 5.1 in both 1980 and 1985. This means that Official Borrowers receive a portion of global official transfers that is five times larger than it would receive if all official transfers were distributed evenly over the world. i.e. every country group would receive a similar share in its world current account incomings.

In general, we see high values for a for merchandise trade – with the exception of trade in manufactures – and for official flows. For Official Borrowers, the values for a for transfers were already large in 1970/75, and even larger in 1980/85, while for Diversified and Private Borrowers the relative importance of transfers declined. Thus Official Borrowers have become increasingly dependent on official transfers as a source of current account incomings, as opposed to other categories, of which the main one – merchandise trade – showed a decline. For Private Borrowers transfers are a very small category in 1985, but investment income now has an a larger than one.

On the capital account, there is much more variation in the values for a. As expected, we see high values for official flows. Interestingly, for FDI the values are also larger than one, while private flows are of little importance in a global context. In general, the values for a suggest that the world current account is characterized by substantial differences among LDCs, while the world capital account is characterized by substantial differences between LDCs and the rest of the world.

The directional flows of international transactions

With the origin and destination matrices we can see the interactions between countries in international trade and finance. As we have seen in Chapter 1, these matrices are only relevant if there are asymmetries in the origin and destination of transactions; otherwise we could just distribute the transactions proportionally over the groups and the matrix would not provide any additional information. Hence the key question is: is trade and finance distributed evenly over the country groups or is there a tendency for some groups to interact with some at the expense of others? To measure the degree of linkage between country group X and the other country groups j in transactions in i, the linkage coefficient β for q_{ij} has been defined as:[3]

$$\beta = S_{ij} / S_i \tag{6.2}$$

where:

- q_{ij} : the value of country group X's exports in transactions in i to country group j
- S_{ij} : the share of country group X in world exports in i to country group j
- S_i : the share of country group X in world exports in i

The linkage coefficient may be applied to both trade and financial flows. For financial flows, the equivalent concept to exports (i.e. 'sales of goods') can be interpreted as 'sales of liabilities', i.e capital imports. Thus, for financial flows the linkage coefficient is the ratio between the share of country X in total capital outflows in financial instrument i from country j and the share of country X in the world total for capital exports in financial instrument i. When country group X has a share in j's market for commodity or financial instrument i equal to its share in the world market for i, then $\beta = 1$.[4] If country group X is totally excluded from the market for i in j, for example when there is complete credit rationing in type of loan i, then $\beta = 0$. If the value for β is larger than 1, this is referred to as a positive bias in trade or financial flows between country X and country j; similarly, there is a negative bias in trade or financial flows when the value for β is smaller than 1.

Thus the linkage coefficient β expresses the degree to which trade and finance of one country group are biased towards (or away from) another country group. A simple numerical example might help. Suppose that Private Borrowers receive US$ 15 billion in FDI from the US (q_{ij}) while total US outflows in FDI are US$ 50 billion. Then, $S_{ij} = 15/50 = 0.3$. Total world flows in FDI are US$ 100 billion of which Private Borrowers receive US$ 20 billion, i.e. a share (S_i) of 0.2. In this case the linkage coefficient ($\beta = 0.3/0.2$) is larger than one and there is 'positive linkage'; in other words, Private Borrowers receive more than their proportionate share of FDI from the US. It seems that Private Borrowers are relatively competitive in attracting FDI from the US.

Table 6.4 Global linkage in current account transactions (1985): β

	US	Japan	EU	OOECD	CMEA	MOE	OB	DB	PB
US	0.0	2.0	0.7	2.3	0.2	0.7	1.0	1.3	2.1
Japan	2.2	0.0	0.4	0.7	0.3	1.3	1.2	2.8	1.3
EU	0.6	0.3	1.6	1.1	0.4	1.2	0.7	0.6	0.7
OOECD	2.3	1.0	0.8	0.8	0.5	0.5	0.6	0.6	0.6
CMEA	0.1	0.2	0.5	0.6	8.4	0.4	1.5	0.7	0.2
MOE	0.3	3.3	0.9	0.2	0.2	1.1	2.0	1.4	1.9
OB	1.1	1.1	0.8	0.5	1.5	2.5	1.4	0.5	0.6
DB	0.8	4.0	0.5	0.4	0.6	1.7	1.4	0.6	1.2
PB	2.0	1.5	0.7	0.4	0.3	0.7	1.5	1.0	1.4

Table 6.4 gives the linkage coefficients for current account transactions in 1985. A first observation is that biases indeed exist: there is great variation in the values for β. Another observation is the remarkable symmetry in the table. For example, the β's for the US and Japan are close to 2, both from Japan to the US and the other way round. Linkage between Japan and the EU, on the other hand, is low, the β's are approximately 0.4. We do not see these symmetrical patterns in international capital account transactions, as can be observed from Table 6.5. In this table, capital account transactions are split into FDI and OCA for the presentation of β, because of the large differences between these two categories in the values for β. A conceptual difficulty is the interpretation of the coefficient when (net) flows are negative. For example, for Private Borrowers in 1985 S_i has a value of -0.006. In the same year, Private Borrowers received a large share of total US capital outflows (S_{ij} = 0.41), which we interpret as a sign of relative competitiveness in attracting capital from the US. Yet the value for β is large but negative. This implies that when we get a value for β that is negative or very large it is rather meaningless on its own and it is necessary to consider β in connection with the matrix for flows it was calculated from. Another solution to this problem would be to look at stocks instead of flows, but then of course we measure linkage over a longer period, and no longer look at bias in balance of payments financing in a particular year.

Table 6.6, which gives some more detail on global linkage for LDCs in other years for total merchandise trade and total capital flows, shows

Table 6.5 Global linkage in capital account transactions (1985): β

	US	Japan	EU	OOECD	MOE	OB	DB	PB
FDI								
US	0.0	0.8	1.1	2.3	1.8	1.4	0.0	1.6
Japan	2.3	0.0	0.7	0.4	0.0	0.1	0.1	0.0
EU	1.6	0.4	1.0	0.6	0.8	0.0	0.0	0.7
OOECD	0.2	1.7	0.9	0.9	2.1	9.4	21.0	0.5
MOE	2.0	2.7	0.3	0.3	0.0	0.2	0.1	0.2
OB	0.9	2.4	1.3	0.0	0.0	0.3	0.0	0.1
DB	2.4	2.6	0.1	0.0	0.0	0.4	1.6	0.7
PB	2.1	0.6	1.5	1.1	0.0	0.2	0.3	0.7
OCA								
US	0.0	1.4	0.8	0.1	3.0	3.8	3.7	3.7
Japan	1.3	0.0	1.7	0.3	0.0	0.0	0.0	0.1
EU	0.0	1.0	1.1	2.2	-0.1	0.0	0.0	0.0
OOECD	3.2	1.4	0.9	0.3	1.7	0.0	0.0	0.1
CMEA	-41.4	1.6	2.4	3.4	0.0	0.0	0.0	0.0
MOE	-40.7	7.7	-0.2	-0.4	0.0	0.0	0.0	0.0
OB	3.5	0.5	0.4	0.3	1.7	0.0	0.0	0.0
DB	-1.9	1.7	0.4	-1.2	1.0	0.0	0.0	0.0
PB	-73.3	0.9	5.8	5.0	7.1	0.0	0.0	0.0

that the bias in trade and financial flows is in many instances clear and substantial. There is for example a strong positive bias for merchandise exports of Diversified Borrowers to Japan and for Diversified Borrowers' capital inflows from Japan. Official Borrowers and Private Borrowers are more focused on the US, both for trade and finance. In 1985, the US is the only country (group) with positive total capital flows to Private Borrowers, resulting in a very high value for β.

Finally, to measure the degree of bias for the world as a whole, a weighted average for β has been calculated using the shares in world trade or capital as weights for each cell in the matrices. For trade, the measure has been 1.7 in each year of the period. For finance, the value for this measure was less stable, varying from 1.8 (1970) to 2.2 (1980 and 1985) and 3.4 (1980). Thus the degree of bias in world financial flows has been significantly higher than for trade in the four benchmark years. This implies that the 'geographical distortion' in financial markets is larger than in trade markets. Shifts in the directional patterns

Table 6.6 *Linkage coefficients for LDCs trade and finance: β*

		US	Japan	EU	OOECD	CMEA	MOE	OB	DB	PB	ROW	Multi
Trade flows												
1970	OB	1.4	1.4	0.9	0.4	1.3	1.5	1.8	0.8	0.5	0.7	..
	DB	1.1	3.0	0.8	0.4	0.7	1.1	0.9	0.5	1.8	2.0	..
	PB	1.9	1.8	0.9	0.5	0.3	0.2	1.2	0.9	1.7	0.5	..
1975	OB	2.2	1.1	0.8	0.4	1.2	1.4	1.3	0.8	0.5	0.7	..
	DB	1.4	4.1	0.5	0.3	0.5	0.7	1.1	0.6	1.5	2.2	..
	PB	2.5	1.4	0.8	0.5	0.3	0.5	1.4	1.1	1.2	0.9	..
1980	OB	1.6	1.3	0.8	0.4	1.2	1.0	1.7	0.8	0.5	1.3	..
	DB	1.2	4.2	0.5	0.4	0.7	0.8	0.9	0.7	1.4	1.9	..
	PB	2.4	1.2	0.7	0.5	0.4	0.6	1.4	1.2	1.3	0.7	..
1985	OB	1.3	1.2	0.9	0.3	1.6	1.3	1.6	0.6	0.8	0.7	..
	DB	0.8	4.0	0.5	0.3	0.6	1.5	1.2	0.6	1.5	3.1	..
	PB	1.9	1.5	0.7	0.4	0.3	0.8	1.3	1.0	1.6	0.9	..
Capital flows												
1970	OB	1.5	0.7	0.5	1.6	..	0.0	0.1	0.0	0.0	0.0	7.9
	DB	1.4	3.7	0.4	1.0	..	1.2	0.2	-0.2	0.2	0.0	7.5
	PB	1.1	0.8	0.8	1.5	..	-0.5	0.1	-0.5	0.2	0.0	5.8
1975	OB	0.5	1.5	0.5	0.6	8.8	1.4	0.0	0.0	0.0	0.0	7.9
	DB	1.5	10.1	0.4	0.6	26.9	0.1	0.0	0.1	0.9	0.1	6.7
	PB	2.0	2.8	0.8	1.0	-3.0	0.0	0.0	0.2	0.8	0.0	4.7
1980	OB	1.6	1.6	0.4	0.4	31.5	0.4	0.0	0.0	0.0	0.0	21.6
	DB	0.8	2.9	0.5	1.1	21.5	0.5	0.0	0.0	0.3	0.1	16.1
	PB	1.4	3.0	0.8	2.0	0.7	0.0	0.0	0.0	0.3	0.0	6.2
1985	OB	2.2	0.7	0.6	0.2	13.0	1.4	0.0	0.0	0.0	0.0	11.9
	DB	2.9	1.7	0.3	-0.7	-0.9	0.8	0.0	0.8	0.0	0.1	11.6
	PB	27.8	-0.1	-1.2	-5.4	-12.8	-3.8	0.0	0.6	0.2	0.1	24.2

in finance are generally much larger than those in trade patterns, indicating that stability in directional trade patterns is higher than that in international financial patterns.

The geographical balances

The patterns of trade and finance by origin and destination may give a completely different picture than trade and financial balances between pairs of country groups, because although trade and financial flows between country groups may be large, on balance they may be small, or vice versa. The main question is thus whether there is a 'match' between current and capital account balances for pairs of country groups. For example, if Diversified Borrowers have a trade deficit with Japan, is this deficit matched by a surplus on the Diversified Borrowers' capital account with Japan, or is this deficit financed by other country groups? Tied aid may, for example, tend to increase the degree of 'match', because it implies that finance from country group X is used to finance exports from country group X.

To measure the 'degree of match' for each pair of countries the ratio γ_j has been defined for country group X that links X's current account imbalances with other country groups *j* to X's capital account imbalances with another country group *j*:

$$\gamma_j = f_j / (-x_j) \qquad (6.3)$$

where:

f_j : capital account balance of country group X with country group *j*

x_j : current account balance of country group X with country group *j*

The ratio will have a value of one when matching is complete: i.e. the current account imbalance between two country groups is entirely financed by the (net) creditor country group. When the net financial flow exceeds the current account imbalance, $\gamma_j > 1$, while $\gamma_j < 1$ if the imbalance is incompletely financed. The value for γ_j is negative if the flows are the 'wrong' way around and infinite when X's current account balance with country *j* is zero.

Table 6.7 gives the current and capital account balances for the three groups of LDCs with the other country groups *j* and the corresponding

Table 6.7 *Current and capital account balances of LDCs with other country groups:* γ_j

		US	Japan	EU	OOECD	CMEA	MOE	OB	DB	PB	ROW	Multi	Total
1970													
OB	Current acct.	-0.1	-0.8	-0.4	-0.6	0.2	-0.2	0.0	-0.1	-1.2	-0.3	-0.1	-3.7
	Capital acct.	1.3	0.0	1.6	0.3	0.0	0.2	0.0	0.0	0.0	0.0	0.4	3.8
	γ_j	22.1	0.0	3.9	0.5	-0.2	-0.2	..	0.0	0.0	0.0	3.2	1.0
DB	Current acct.	-0.9	-0.6	-0.9	-0.5	0.0	0.0	0.1	0.0	0.5	0.5	-0.1	-1.9
	Capital acct.	0.8	0.4	0.6	0.1	0.0	0.2	0.0	0.0	0.0	0.0	0.3	2.3
	γ_j	0.9	0.6	0.6	0.2	0.6	-6.6	0.0	..	0.0	0.0	3.8	1.2
PB	Current acct.	-1.8	-0.7	-0.3	-0.4	0.4	-0.6	1.2	-0.5	0.0	0.0	-0.2	-2.9
	Capital acct.	1.1	0.1	1.6	0.4	0.1	0.1	0.0	0.0	0.0	0.0	0.4	3.8
	γ_j	0.6	0.1	6.2	1.1	-0.2	0.3	0.0	0.0	..	0.0	2.1	1.3
1975													
OB	Current acct.	4.5	-3.9	-1.2	-2.2	0.4	-4.6	0.0	-0.7	-4.2	-0.7	-0.2	-12.6
	Capital acct.	1.3	0.3	0.7	0.6	0.1	7.9	0.0	0.2	-0.1	0.0	2.2	13.0
	γ_j	-0.3	0.1	0.6	0.3	-0.2	1.7	..	0.2	-0.0	0.0	12.7	1.0
DB	Current acct.	-2.1	0.4	-5.9	-1.9	-0.6	-1.1	0.7	0.0	0.5	1.3	-0.2	-8.9
	Capital acct.	1.2	0.9	1.7	0.3	0.2	0.1	-0.2	0.0	0.8	0.0	1.4	6.5
	γ_j	0.6	-2.2	0.3	0.2	0.3	0.1	0.2	..	-1.8	0.0	7.4	0.7
PB	Current acct.	-2.4	-3.7	-2.9	0.8	1.3	-6.6	4.2	-0.5	0.0	0.7	-0.4	-9.6
	Capital acct.	5.3	0.7	2.9	1.2	-0.0	0.1	0.1	-0.8	0.0	0.0	1.5	11.0
	γ_j	2.2	0.2	1.0	-1.6	0.0	0.0	0.0	-1.8	..	0.0	3.5	1.1

(Continued)

Table 6.7 *(Continued)*

		US	Japan	EU	OOECD	CMEA	MOE	OB	DB	PB	ROW	Multi	Total
1980													
OB	Current acct.	5.1	-0.8	-8.0	-3.7	-0.6	-10.3	0.0	-1.1	-11.1	1.8	-0.5	-29.2
	Capital acct.	3.0	0.8	9.3	0.7	0.4	6.5	0.0	0.0	0.0	0.0	6.0	26.7
	γ_j	-0.6	1.0	1.2	0.2	0.7	0.6	..	0.0	0.0	0.0	12.1	0.9
DB	Current acct.	-6.9	7.0	-6.5	-3.7	-0.3	-4.7	1.1	0.0	1.2	3.5	-0.7	-10.1
	Capital acct.	1.1	1.4	2.6	0.6	0.2	4.1	0.0	0.0	0.0	0.0	2.8	12.8
	γ_j	0.2	-0.2	0.4	0.2	0.8	0.9	-0.0	..	0.0	0.0	4.1	1.3
PB	Current acct.	13.1	-4.2	-10.1	-0.6	5.3	-19.9	11.1	-1.2	0.0	0.4	-1.1	-7.2
	Capital acct.	0.9	1.0	4.5	-0.1	0.0	2.0	0.0	0.0	0.0	0.0	2.3	10.5
	γ_j	-0.1	0.2	0.4	-0.2	0.0	0.1	0.0	0.0	..	0.0	2.0	1.5
1985													
OB	Current acct.	4.1	-5.8	-3.0	-5.2	-2.3	-8.3	0.0	-4.2	-10.7	-1.2	-1.0	-37.6
	Capital acct.	5.2	2.9	6.4	2.2	1.3	8.8	0.0	0.0	0.2	-0.1	10.6	37.4
	γ_j	-1.3	0.5	2.1	0.4	0.6	1.1	..	0.0	0.0	-0.1	10.6	1.0
DB	Current acct.	-5.6	-2.2	-12.0	-4.1	-1.4	-2.5	4.2	0.0	-0.1	2.9	-1.6	-22.5
	Capital acct.	0.2	5.7	3.0	-1.1	0.0	2.4	0.0	0.0	0.2	-0.1	6.1	16.4
	γ_j	0.0	2.5	0.3	-0.3	0.0	1.0	0.0	..	2.0	0.0	3.7	0.7
PB	Current acct.	16.5	-3.2	-1.9	-3.3	1.5	-13.9	10.7	0.1	0.0	3.3	-2.2	7.5
	Capital acct.	-4.5	-0.4	-2.9	-2.4	-0.2	1.0	-0.2	-0.2	0.0	-0.3	4.2	-5.9
	γ_j	0.3	-0.1	-1.5	-0.7	0.1	0.1	0.0	2.0	..	0.1	1.9	0.8

Note: Columns many not tally due to rounding.

values for γ_j. In a balance of payments statement, transfers are registered on the current account, but the role they play in the economies of LDCs is similar to the role of capital inflows since they are used to finance deficits on the trade account. Therefore, in this exercise, transfers have been moved from the current account to the capital account and the current account balances do not match those implicit in Tables A5.1 to A5.4. Thus defined, the current accounts of Official Borrowers, Diversified and Private Borrowers were in deficit in the four RWAM-years, except for Private Borrowers in 1985. If γ_j in the 'total' column is smaller than one, the current account deficit has partly been financed by a decrease in reserves, while a value larger than one implies an increase in reserves.

With few exceptions, the total current account deficits of Official Borrowers, Diversified Borrowers and Private Borrowers consist of pairwise deficits with all country groups *j*. The major exceptions are (1) sizeable current account surpluses with the US for Official Borrowers (1975) and Official Borrowers and Private Borrowers (1980, 1985); (2) a large current account surplus for Diversified Borrowers with Japan in 1980. Except for Private Borrowers in 1985 and intra-LDC capital balances, pairwise capital accounts of LDCs have been in surplus.

In the coefficient γ_j the pairwise balances are connected. Firstly, in the current account surpluses of Official, Diversified and Private Borrowers, which coincide with capital account surpluses, the flows are inverted and it is more the fact that the value for γ_j is negative that is significant than the actual value of the coefficient. The major examples of negative values for γ_j that follow from surpluses on both the current and the capital account are found for Official Borrowers' balances with the US in 1975, 1980 and 1985, for Diversified Borrowers' balances with Japan in 1975 and 1980, and for Private Borrowers and the US in 1980.

Secondly, the combination of current account deficits with capital account surpluses is clearly the most common pattern, but there is great variation in the value for γ_j. For Official Borrowers, the surpluses on the capital balance with the EU tend to be much larger than is necessary to cover the deficits on the current account. Thus, a part of Official Borrowers' capital surpluses with the EU is used to finance deficits with other industrialized countries. For Diversified Borrowers, the shift in the role for Japan in financing the current account deficits is remarkable. In 1970, all groups of industrialized countries financed at least a part of their own current account surpluses with Diversified Borrowers; in 1985 Japan's value for γ_j was 2.5, thus Japan supplied the lion's share of the Diversified Borrowers' current account deficit with the rest of the world. For Private Borrowers the US has been a major net source of foreign finance, thus financing the gaps between Private Borrowers and the other industrialized countries. Thirdly, the combination of deficits on both the current and the capital account leads to negative values for γ_j. This was the common pattern for Private Borrowers in 1985. Finally, a fourth combination is possible: a surplus on the current account and a deficit on the capital account. In 1985, balances between Private Borrowers and the US have a 'degree of match' of 0.3, but in this match Private Borrowers finance 30 per cent of the US deficit with Private Borrowers.

6.3 Some Implications of Biases in International Trade and Finance

These linkage coefficients indicate sizeable geographical biases in patterns of international trade and finance. Both for trade and finance, country (groups) often receive disproportionate shares from other country (groups) while pairwise current account deficits rarely mirror pairwise capital account surpluses. This means that it is worthwhile and interesting to construct and investigate origin and destination matrices, and, eventually, to include these matrices in a global model which takes these biases and links into account. Next arises the question as to the economic interpretation and the policy relevance of these biases. What is the economic meaning of a particular value for α? For example, Official Borrowers have a value for α for SITC $0-1$ of 3.2, which implies that Official Borrowers exports are strongly concentrated in a slowly growing export category so that their export performance is likely to lag behind world export growth. Their very high value for α for transfers and official flows means that Official Borrowers are highly dependent on donor preferences. Japan's striking values for β indicate that preferences of Japanese importers and investors are biased strongly towards Diversified Borrowers. Thus for Diversified Borrowers growth in Japanese capital exports and trade imports is highly relevant, and if Japan reduces its capital exports or trade imports, Diversified Borrowers are likely to face balance of payments difficulties. Economic growth in Japan will, other things being equal, lead to a more than average positive effect on Diversified Borrowers' export performance. Links with the US are positive for each of the LDC groupings, in particular for Private Borrowers. Thus US import increases would tend to be relatively favourable for LDCs. For the EU we see only negative values for β, both for trade and finance. For Official Borrowers the positive links with CMEA stand out. These indicate that Official Borrowers were particularly sensitive to recent changes in the former CMEA countries which led to a cut in both trade export opportunities and capital outflows from this region. On top of this, Official Borrowers were biased towards Major Oil Exporters, a country group that has strongly diminished its aid efforts since 1985.

In the discussion of current account deficits it is sometimes argued that – in the current international monetary setting – deficits do not matter as long as they can be financed easily. The ease of financing a deficit is not only related to differences in expected real rates of return, but also to the degree to which foreign investors are willing to maintain or increase their portfolio share in a particular type of foreign asset. Also, a persistent current account deficit may lead to an accumulation of foreign debt which could at some point undermine market confidence and lead to financing problems.

With reference to the oil price shocks in 1974 and 1979, an obvious and simple assumption would be that countries that ran current account deficits due to the higher oil prices would stand a smaller chance of running into balance of payments problems as long as they received a substantial share of the capital exports associated with the current account surpluses of oil exporting countries. Table 6.8 gives, for 1975 and 1980, the 'pairwise' balances for Major Oil Exporters with the other country groups and the corresponding values for γ_j.[5] Major Oil Exporters had large surpluses on the current account almost in every instance. Diversified and Private Borrowers in both years and Official Borrowers in 1980 could not finance their current account deficits with Major Oil Exporters using capital surpluses from Major Oil Exporters. This in contrast with the more favourable values for γ for the Other OECD Countries and the EU, and to a lesser extent Japan and the US. Looking at the values for β for trade flows, it is clear that Diversified Borrowers and Private Borrowers are not strongly linked with Major

Table 6.8 MOEs 'pairwise' balance of payments positions (in US$ billions) and γ_j

	Current account			Capital account			γ_j
	receipts	paym'ts	balance	inflows	outflows	balance	
1975 MOE							
US	6.9	10.2	-3.3	0.7	2.1	-1.4	-0.42
Japan	19.3	5.2	14.1	0.3	0.0	0.3	-0.02
EU	42.7	21.2	21.5	0.0	8.4	-28.4	1.32
OOECD	7.4	2.6	4.8	0.0	10.9	-10.9	2.25
CMEA	2.9	1.1	1.8	0.0	0.0	0.0	0.00
MOE	2.5	2.5	0.0	-0.9	-0.9	0.0	...
OB	7.0	7.1	-0.1	0.0	3.1	-3.1	-26.86
DB	1.7	0.6	1.1	0.0	0.1	-0.1	0.09
PB	7.9	1.2	6.6	0.0	0.1	-0.1	0.01
ROW	1.2	0.8	0.4	0.0	0.0	0.0	0.00
Multi	0.0	0.0	0.0	0.0	0.0	0.0	0.00
Total	99.4	52.4	47.0	0.2	43.8	-43.7	0.93
1980 MOE							
US	36.5	20.1	16.4	-3.5	12.5	-16.0	0.98
Japan	51.2	15.0	36.2	-0.7	32.1	-32.8	0.91
EU	90.6	62.6	28.0	-0.5	32.8	-33.3	1.19
OOECD	16.2	8.2	8.0	0.0	32.4	-32.4	4.05
CMEA	5.4	3.2	2.2	0.0	0.0	0.0	0.00
MOE	8.4	8.4	0.0	-4.7	-4.7	0.0	0.00
OB	14.2	9.4	4.8	0.0	1.0	-1.0	0.21
DB	7.0	5.4	1.6	0.0	0.9	-0.9	0.58
PB	25.0	7.0	18.0	0.0	0.0	0.0	0.00
ROW	6.1	2.8	3.3	0.0	0.0	0.0	0.00
Multi	0.0	0.0	0.0	0.0	0.0	0.0	0.00
Total	260.6	142.2	118.4	-9.5	107.0	-116.5	0.98

Note: Columns and rows may not tally due to rounding.

Oil Exporters. Only a relatively small share of their exports goes to this country group. This suggests that Diversified Borrowers and Private Borrowers had little opportunity to compensate their higher import values (on account of the oil price rise), with higher exports to Major Oil Exporters. Especially Private Borrowers in 1980 (with a high, US$ 18.0 billion deficit on the current account with Major Oil Exporters and a negligible share in Major Oil Exporters capital exports) must have had some difficulty in financing the current account deficit.

Chapter 1 briefly looked at what might happen when Japan decides to close its current account balance in the most recent RWAM (1985) by increasing its imports by US$ 59 billion, keeping the shares in Japan's geographical distribution in international trade and finance constant. Table 6.9 summarizes the results.

The point is that there is a difference in preferences between current and capital account transactions, that may lead to large imbalances in the world economy. Column three in Table 6.9 gives the – sometimes large – differences between the shares in trade incomings and capital inflows. This difference may be considered as yet another 'bilateral' linkage coefficient in trade and finance, which looks at the links between country (groups) from another perspective. Due to the biases in trade and finance, a shift in Japan's propensity to import may have enormous consequences for the balance of payments financing requirements in other countries. For example, column (4) of the table shows that the EU needs an extra US$ 15.9 billion in international reserves, while Major Oil Exporters and Private Borrowers receive US$ 8.2 and 7.5 billion in additional foreign reserves.

The next example sheds some light on what may happen if the major donors of the Official Borrowers double their official disbursements to this group of mainly low income countries that have almost no access to private finance. Official Borrowers are assumed to use these funds entirely to increase their imports from other countries; this corresponds to the 'orthodox view' on the effects of aid on growth, as expressed in the two-gap model (Chenery & Strout 1966), where aid leads to a one for one increase in imports. These donors are also assumed to increase their imports according to the market shares of their trading partners in 1985; column (1) in Table 6.10 gives the additional disbursements from the major donors, and column (2) shows how the increase in Official Borrowers' imports is distributed over the country groups. The EU is the largest beneficiary in this case, since it provides a smaller share of aid than it receives in the form of extra export income. This may help to explain why the EU countries are inclined to increase their aid disbursements. The US, Japan and Major Oil Exporters are the main 'losers' due to the asymmetry in the links between trade and finance. Perhaps there is a relation between this asymmetry and the tendency for

Table 6.9 *What happens when Japan closes its current account deficit by an increase in imports (in US$ billions)*

	Share in world exports to Japan	Share in capital exports from Japan	Linkage coefficient δ	Add'l change in external reserves
US	25.6	36.0	-10.4	-6.1
EU	10.0	37.0	-27.0	-15.9
OOECD	11.1	15.9	-4.8	-2.8
CMEA	1.2	0.5	0.7	0.4
MOE	15.9	1.9	13.9	8.2
OB	4.4	2.3	2.1	1.2
DB	13.9	5.0	8.8	5.2
PB	12.6	-0.1	12.7	7.5
ROW	4.8	0.1	4.7	2.8
Multi	0.6	1.3	-0.7	-0.4

Note: Due to increased exports to Japan and decreased capital imports from Japan.

these countries to decrease their aid donations. But this leaves us to question why Japan would increase its aid disbursements to LDCs. Perhaps the increase in aid flows from Japan is connected to the increase in FDI, where aid flows support the FDI flows.

In the 'next round', interest payments from Official Borrowers to their major donors should increase. If Official Borrowers use the additional funds to increase their productive capacity, they may be able, in due course, to increase their exports. If, on the other hand, Official Borrowers do not use the funds to finance imports, but spend the money on debt reduction, there will be no changes in capital and current balances, because the increase in capital inflows into Official Borrowers is then offset by in increase in capital outflows from Official Borrowers.

Finally, the large US current account deficits in 1980 and 1985, the statistical aspects of which were discussed in the previous chapter, illustrate the role of deficits in facilitating exports of Private Borrowers and the financing of LDC deficits. Is it true that the US borrowed from industrialized countries in order to import from Private Borrowers and to lend to LDCs? To answer these questions we need the pairwise cur-

Table 6.10 What happens when aid disbursements to OBs double (in US$ billions)

	Added disbursements to OBs	Added exports to OBs	Change in BoP finance requirem't
US	4.4	2.7	-1.7
Japan	1.5	0.9	-0.6
EU	3.1	3.4	0.3
Other OECD (OOECD)	0.6	0.4	-0.2
CMEA	1.3	1.6	0.3
Major Oil Exporters	1.0	0.6	-0.4
LDCs: Official Borrowers	0.0	1.2	1.2
LDCs: Diversified Borrowers	0.0	0.3	0.3
LDCs: Private Borrowers	0.0	0.7	0.7
Total	11.9	11.9	0.0

rent and capital account balances of the US.

Firstly, as Table 6.11 shows there is a 'nice' match between the large US current account deficit with Japan and the US capital account surplus with Japan. Apparently, as indicated by the value for γ_j, Japan financed about 90 per cent of its own current account surplus with the US. By contrast, the Other OECD Countries also had a large surplus with the US but only financed one third of it. The EU, meanwhile, combined a relatively small surplus with the US with a relatively large deficit on the capital account. Thus the EU was the most important source of foreign finance for the US in 1985. In addition, the US ran surpluses on the current account with Diversified Borrowers and on both the current account and the capital account with Major Oil Exporters. Where did this foreign inflow go to? As already mentioned, a large part – US$ 16.4 billion – went to the Other OECD Countries. Another substantial amount (US$ 9.2 billion) went to Official Borrowers to finance US deficits on both the current and the capital account. The relations between the US and Private Borrowers are quite similar to those with the Other OECD Countries: the US clearly was a large source of export incomings for Private Borrowers, and on balance there is a large deficit of the US with Private Borrowers. In spite of the rather large inflows into the US from Private Borrowers, only about one third of this deficit

Table 6.11 The 'pairwise' international balances of the US in 1985

	Current account			Capital account			γ_j
	receipts	payments	balance	inflows	outflows	balance	
Japan	43.0	84.0	-41.0	40.7	2.1	38.6	0.9
EU	90.3	102.6	-12.3	55.1	7.9	47.2	3.8
OOECD	3.3	118.3	-115.0	12.3	3.7	8.6	0.3
CMEA	4.3	2.4	1.9	0.0	-1.4	1.4	-0.8
MOE	11.4	7.4	4.0	9.5	-0.3	9.8	-2.4
OB	16.9	21.9	-5.0	-2.2	1.9	-4.1	-0.8
DB	19.0	13.5	5.5	2.1	2.3	-0.2	0.0
PB	61.7	77.9	-16.2	12.2	7.9	4.3	0.3
ROW	24.1	35.0	-10.9	0.0	0.2	-0.2	0.0
Multi	1.0	2.9	-1.9	0.0	2.5	-2.5	-1.3
Total	275.0	465.9	-190.9	129.7	26.8	102.9	1.0

is financed by Private Borrowers. Thus we see a mixed pattern of rather complex linkages, and no clear differences between US linkages with LDCs and industrialized countries in general.

6.4 Concluding Remarks

One of the conclusions to emerge from this descriptive analysis of global linkages is that LDCs have increased their shares in global current account transactions, but have hardly participated in the 'globalization' of international capital flows: their shares in global capital inflows decreased sharply between 1975 and 1985, while their share in global capital outflows remained low.

A central feature of the analysis in this chapter is the measurement of the extent to which pairwise flows of trade and finance are biased: flows are not distributed proportionally over the country groups. The fact that bias exists implies that we cannot see the world as one big marketplace, where goods and financial assets are traded irrespective of the country (group) of origin or destination. Some country (groups) seem to have strong linkages in current account transactions, which are often symmetrical, i.e. if country (group) X imports a more than proportionate share from country (group) Y, this is matched by a more than proportionate flow in the opposite direction.

Both trade and financial flows are clearly biased, while biases in trade and finance between the same pair of country groups may differ considerably. The existence of biases in international markets can be explained by imperfections in commodity and capital markets. For example, in spite of the trend towards deregulation in international trade and finance, there are still barriers to trade and legal restrictions that affect the directional patterns of international flows. Also geographical distance and transaction costs, regional and historical ties or asymmetric information, or simply the product mix available for exports, may explain a deviation from the 'norm' where international transactions are distributed proportionally over the country groups. Taking these factors into account, one would expect a positive linkage for countries that belong to one regional bloc, like the EU. Indeed, on the current account there was (e.g. in 1985) positive intra-EU linkage. On the capital account however, intra-EU linkage does not deviate from the norm. Perhaps geographical distance and historical and economic ties play a larger role in trade than in finance. However, measured by a weighted average for β, both the degree of bias and the volatility were much higher for financial flows than for trade flows. This points to the opposite case where 'geographical distortion' in finance is relatively large.

Next pairwise current and capital account balances were examined to establish if there is a 'match' between the two. The most common pattern for LDCs is pairwise current account deficits and capital surpluses. A clear example of the opposite was the Private Borrowers' current account surplus with the US, in combination with a capital account deficit in 1985. In the other years, the US has been a major source of net capital inflows for Private Borrowers. The EU, that was shown to have weak linkages in directional flows with LDCs, financed more than its proportionate share of current account deficits with Official Borrowers. For Diversified Borrowers this role was played by Japan. A major conclusion is that there has been a shift away from the US towards the EU and Japan as a major source of foreign finance for LDCs.

Using the pairwise balances we also looked at the US current account deficit in 1985 to see where it originated and who financed it. The US current account deficit was found to consist of deficits with the other industrialized countries, Official and Private Borrowers. Except for Official Borrowers, they all contributed to finance it, but a major role was played by the EU, which financed nearly four times its own current account surplus with the US. Thus also in the financing of current account balances there are clear biases.

7 Constant Market Share Analysis

7.1 Introduction

The previous chapter describes shifts in exports, capital flows and stocks of international debt and significant changes in the world economy. It shows that factors of origin and destination seem to matter and that patterns of trade and finance are clearly biased. A next question is how to distinguish the relevant policy aspects, i.e. the aspects that policy-makers may be able to influence as opposed to aspects that are beyond their control. A suitable method to study this question is constant market share (CMS) analysis. This method has proven useful for the analysis of exports, but is new in the analysis of financial variables.

The purpose of CMS analysis is to ascribe the increase in exports of a given country to four components: (1) an increase in world exports, (2) the commodity composition, (3) the market distribution and (4) increased competitiveness. By decomposing the increase of a country's exports into these four effects, CMS provides insight into the extent to which a country's exports are concentrated in commodities and markets that can be considered as growing relatively slowly or rapidly and what the nature of the actual expansion has been, i.e. whether the expansion matches the country's export shares or reflects a shift in the country's export shares. If the country's export shares are larger, this may be interpreted as an increase in competitiveness. For policy-makers this is important information because it indicates the direction of desired policy action. If a country's exports are declining because of a decrease in competitiveness, policy-makers may want to adjust their economies in order to promote competitiveness. If a country's exports are concentrated in slowly growing markets and products, policy-makers may wish to bend their export patterns into more favourable directions, but this may not be easy and will probably take a long time.

In regional economics, CMS analysis, also known as 'shift and share' analysis, has been used since the early 1940s (see Creamer 1943). Tyszinski (1951) was the first to apply the technique to export growth. Since then, CMS analysis has been widely used for the analysis of export growth. For example Gerards and Jager (1980) investigated why Dutch exports lagged behind world exports in the period 1973–79, using CMS analysis because it includes structural factors as well as competitiveness; usually, the latter takes a central part in the analysis of export growth. They found no decrease in competitiveness, but did find that changes in structural factors caused the Dutch exports to lag behind world exports. For instance, in 1973 and 1974 the relatively slow growth in Dutch exports was explained by the country's concentration on slowly growing markets (in the EU).

In order to apply CMS analysis to financial matrices the matrices are considered to describe international sales and purchases of financial liabilities or assets. As in the case of the linkage coefficient in the previous chapter, sales of financial liabilities (i.e. capital inflows) are treated as sales of export products: the increase in capital inflows is decomposed to establish if the increase corresponds to the country's share in the world total at the start of the period, or whether it is due to an increase in its share in world finance.

7.2 Constant Market Share Analysis

This section shows how in CMS analysis[1] the decomposition of a change in flows or stocks into the four effects is derived for a given country group. The following symbols are used:[2]

A: Merchandise trade

A_{ij} = share of country X in world exports of type i to country j;
A_i = share of country X in world exports of type i;
A_j = share of country X in world exports to country j;
A = share of country X in world exports;
m_{ij} = value of country X's exports of type i to country j;
M_{ij} = value of world exports of type i to country j;
$M_i \equiv \sum_j M_{ij}$ or the value of world exports of type i;
$M_j \equiv \sum_i M_{ij}$ or the value of world exports to country j;

$$m \equiv \sum_i \sum_j m_{ij} \text{ or the value of country X's exports}$$
$$M \equiv \sum_i \sum_j M_{ij} \text{ or the value of world exports.}$$

Identity (7.1) describes the change in exports in product *i* from country X to country *j*:

$$\Delta m_{ij} \equiv \Delta(A_{ij} \cdot M_{ij}) \equiv A_{ij} \cdot \Delta M_{ij} + M_{ij} \cdot \Delta A_{ij} \cdot \Delta M_{ij} \cdot \Delta A_{ij} \quad (7.1)$$

Summed over all products *i* and countries *j*, the change in total exports of country X are:

$$\Delta m \equiv \Delta \sum_i \sum_j m_{ij} \equiv \sum_i \sum_j \Delta m_{ij} \equiv$$
$$\sum_i \sum_j A_{ij} \cdot \Delta M_{ij} + \sum_i \sum_j (M_{ij} + \Delta M_{ij}) \cdot \Delta A_{ij} \quad (7.2)$$

Extension of this identity with

$$\left[A \cdot \Delta M + \sum_i A_i \cdot \Delta M_i\right] \text{ and } -\left[A \cdot \Delta M + \sum_i A_i \cdot \Delta M_i\right]$$

gives:

$$\Delta m \equiv A \cdot \Delta M + \left[\sum_i A_i \cdot \Delta M_i - A \cdot \Delta M\right]$$
$$+ \left[\sum_i \sum_j A_{ij} \cdot \Delta M_{ij} - \sum_i A_i \cdot \Delta M_i\right]$$
$$+ \sum_i \sum_j (M_{ij} + \Delta M_{ij}) \cdot \Delta A_{ij} \quad (7.3)$$

This identity is then decomposed into four components of the change in country X's exports:

World effect:

$$A \cdot \Delta M$$

Composition effect:

$$\left[\sum_i A_i \cdot \Delta M_i - A \cdot \Delta M\right]$$

Since $\Delta M \equiv \Delta \sum_i M_i \equiv \sum_i \Delta M_i$, this term can be rewritten as:

$$\sum_i (A_i - A) \cdot \Delta M_i$$

Market effect:

$$\left[\sum_i \sum_j A_{ij} \cdot \Delta M_{ij} - \sum_i A_i \cdot \Delta M_i \right]$$

Since $M_i \equiv \sum_j M_{ij}$, this term can be rewritten as:

$$\sum_i \sum_j (A_{ij} - A_i) \cdot \Delta M_{ij}$$

Competition effect and interaction effect:

$$\sum_i \sum_j (M_{ij} + \Delta M_{ij}) \cdot \Delta A_{ij} \equiv \sum_i \sum_j M_{ij} \cdot \Delta A_{ij} + \sum_i \sum_j \Delta M_{ij} \cdot \Delta A_{ij}$$

B: Capital inflows (exports of financial liabilities)

B_{ij} = share of country X in world capital inflows of type *i* from country *j*;
B_i = share of country X in world capital inflows of type *i*;
B_j = share of country X in world capital inflows from country *j*;
B = share of country X in world capital inflows;
f_{ij} = value of country X's capital inflows of type *i* from country *j*;
F_{ij} = value of world capital inflows of type i from country *j*;
$F_i \equiv \sum_j F_{ij}$ or the value of world capital inflows of type *i*;
$F_j \equiv \sum_i F_{ij}$ or the value of world capital inflows from country *j*;
$f \equiv \sum_i \sum_j f_{ij}$ or the value of country X's capital inflows;
$F \equiv \sum_i \sum_j F_{ij}$ or the value of world capital inflows.

As for merchandise exports, we may decompose this identity into four components that sum up the change in country X's capital inflows:

World effect:

$$B \cdot \Delta F$$

Composition effect:

$$\sum_i (B_i - B) \cdot \Delta F_i$$

Market effect:

$$\sum_i \sum_j (B_{ij} - B_i) \cdot \Delta F_{ij}$$

Competition effect and interaction effect:

$$\sum_i \sum_j F_{ij} \cdot \Delta B_{ij} + \sum_i \sum_j \Delta F_{ij} \cdot \Delta B_{ij}$$

C: Stocks of foreign debt (accumulated exports of financial liabilities)

C_{ij} = share of country X in world debt stocks of type *i* from country *j*;
C_i = share of country X in world debt stocks of type *i*;
C_j = share of country X in world debt stocks from country *j*;
C = share of country X in world debt stocks;
d_{ij} = value of country X's debt stocks of type *i* from country *j*;
D_{ij} = value of world debt stocks of type *i* from country *j*;
$D_i \equiv \sum_j D_{ij}$ or the value of world debt stocks of type *i*;
$D_j \equiv \sum_i D_{ij}$ or the value of world debt stocks from country *j*;
$d \equiv \sum_i \sum_j d_{ij}$ or the value of country X's debt stocks;
$D \equiv \sum_i \sum_j D_{ij}$ or the value of world debt stocks.

For debt stocks the four effects are:

World effect:

$$C \cdot \Delta D$$

Composition effect:

$$\sum_i (C_i - C) \cdot \Delta D_i$$

Market effect:

$$\sum_i \sum_j (C_{ij} - C_i) \cdot \Delta D_{ij}$$

Competition effect and interaction effect:

$$\sum_i \sum_j D_{ij} \cdot \Delta C_{ij} + \sum_i \sum_j \Delta D_{ij} \cdot \Delta C_{ij}$$

The calculation of the market, competition and interaction effects is problematic for capital flows because they are defined in net terms. If, for example, country (group) X receives a large positive net flow from country (group) Y, while total capital exports from Y are small and negative, the result would be a large negative market effect for X. To avoid this type of odd result, the treatment of capital flows in the CMS analysis is different from trade and stocks. Firstly, the market, competition and interaction effect have been calculated from the matrix for total capital flows. In this 'two-level' analysis, there is no type-of-loan effect.[3] The calculation of the market, competition and interaction effect from the matrices for total capital flows gives results that are consistent, i.e. the positive/negative signs are 'right' and more stable than the calculations from the disaggregated matrices because the negative net flows are netted out. However, because the results for the net capital flows remain rather shaky, another variation of the CMS analysis has also been calculated, taking advantage of the availability of the matrices for new disbursements for LDCs. In this variation, LDCs comprise the 'world' standard or point of reference; the shifts in shares of Official Borrowers, Diversified Borrowers and Private Borrowers in new loans to LDCs are compared.

7.3 Interpreting the Four Effects

The sum of the first three effects ('structural term') represents the change in merchandise exports, capital inflows or stock of foreign debt if country X maintains its shares in each flow or stock. The world effect gives the change for country X which would have resulted if country X had maintained its share in the world total. The composition and the market effect follow from the country's favourable or unfavourable concentration on products or markets. The composition effect will be positive if country X's merchandise exports or capital inflows are concentrated on high-growth export products or liabilities and negative if country X has concentrated on slowly-growing export products or foreign liabilities. The market effect refers to origin and destination matrices: it will be positive if country X's merchandise exports or capital inflows are concentrated on high-growth markets and negative if country X had concentrated on slowly-growing markets. The fourth effect, the 'competitiveness term', is a residual: it can be derived as the difference between the total change in country X's exports (Δm) and the structural term. It represents the change in country X's exports that follows from shifts in country X's shares in world trade. If there is no competitiveness effect, the country has maintained constant market shares in its export markets. The competitiveness term may be split into the competition and the interaction effect. Changes in relative competitiveness are identified by the competition effect ($\Sigma\Sigma M_{ij} \cdot \Delta A_{ij}$), which reflects shifts in country X's market shares. The competition effect is commonly associated with changes in relative prices.[4] The interaction effect ($\Sigma\Sigma\Delta M_{ij} \cdot \Delta A_{ij}$), emerges when both world trade and country X's share in world trade have changed over the period.

These four effects have different implications for policy-makers. The part of the change in exports that can be ascribed to the world effect is mostly exogenous: it is a factor policy-makers cannot change. The market effect and the composition effect are endogenous as well as exogenous, but the underlying factors are slow to change. If a country's merchandise exports are concentrated on slow-growth export products, the country may wish to shift towards products with higher export growth, like industrial products, but this is a slow process. A country may wish to attract more private capital (increase its exports of private liabilities), but as we have seen in Chapter 2, some countries simply have no access to these markets. Also for official capital flows LDCs are largely dependent on the preferences of the donor countries and there is little room for LDCs to shift to donors with high growth in aid disbursements. If a country wishes to shift towards more favourable merchandise export markets, there may be barriers to access these markets as in the case of the Common Agricultural Policy of the EU. The competition effect may be considered as largely endogenous, as competitiveness may be stimulated by devaluation or investments in human capital or infrastructure. The interaction effect has a large element of luck attached to it: it is the 'bingo-effect', which occurs when everything points into the right direction.

The interpretation of the CMS effects for the financial matrices is similar to the interpretation of the effects for export growth but needs some further clarification. The world effect for capital flows represents the change in country X's sales of financial liabilities which would result if country X maintained its share in world capital flows. For stocks, it represents the change in stock which would result if the country maintained its share in world debt. The composition effect follows from concentration on types of financial instruments with fast-(or slowly-) growing use. The market effect follows from concentration on lending countries with fast or slow growing capital exports.

The competition effect can be seen to reflect changes in the 'competitiveness' of the borrowing country in selling its liabilities. It cannot be associated with changes in relative prices as simply as in the case of merchandise exports: interest rates, stock market prices and/or asset values would provide an equivalent to price in commodity markets, but interest rates and asset prices do not always clear international capital markets. The term 'credit rationing' characterizes the situation where some borrowing countries have access to commercial funding and others do not. In the definition of Stiglitz and Weiss (1981: 394–5), there is credit rationing when (1) some applicants receive loans and others do not, while the rejected applicants would not receive a loan even if they offered to pay a higher interest rate, and (2) there are groups of potential borrowers who are unable to obtain loans at any interest rate, even though with a larger supply of credit, they would. Therefore, shifts in the competition effect might best be seen as shifts in the lenders' appreciation of the repayment capacity of the borrowing country. It is therefore labelled the 'creditworthiness' effect. This effect provides potentially important information to policy-makers and investors, in LDCs as well as in industrialized countries.

Thus the parallel of the competition effect for merchandise exports would be the creditworthiness effect for foreign loans which reflects elements such as the attractiveness of bonds, the repayment capacity of loans, the perceived profitability of foreign direct investments, the possibility of nationalization or moratoria, or revaluations of outstanding loans. Where trade flows consist of objective items like cars, coffee or computers, a foreign investment represents a subjective view of the future which is based on the discounted present value of the investment. An investment involves risk and uncertainty; the perception of the assessed risk and uncertainty attached to an investment can change rapidly, and with it the perceived creditworthiness will change. In LDCs uncertainty is greater, there is less information about the economic situation, which makes it more difficult for LDCs to sell their liabilities. The creditworthiness effect is a potential measure of what the market perceives, which may be useful in situations where interest rates and asset prices do not clear international capital markets.

Repayment capacity is likely to be less important in the allocation of official flows than in commercial borrowing; usually humanitarian motives and the donor's political and commercial interests related to merchandise export or FDI are seen as the main motivations for official loans to LDCs (see, for example, Maizels & Nissanke 1984). The revealed priorities of aid donors are here reflected in the competitive index. However, in the 1980s the link between allocation of official finance and repayment capacity has become tighter and conditionality has increased for both multilateral and bilateral lending to LDCs. Countries only receive new loans when they have reached agreement on repayment of outstanding obligations, and this necessarily includes an element of perceived repayment capacity, although the nature of the relationship between financial flows and lending is not so straight forward.

The financial flow matrices in the WAM have net changes in assets in the columns and net changes in liabilities in the rows. If repayments are larger than new disbursements, the entries on the rows become negative which may lead to odd results, since negative shares have no obvious meaning. For the application of CMS analysis, it would have been more convenient to have separate matrices for disbursements and repayments. In the case of LDCs, however, an argument can be made for the use of net changes in liabilities since new disbursements, especially in the 1980s, have often been used to finance repayments.

Partly to overcome the problem of the negative entries, but also as an additional source of information in itself, CMS analysis has in this chapter also been applied to the matrices for stocks of financial liabilities, using the net changes in stocks as a proxy for cumulative changes in flows. As discussed in the previous chapter, patterns in financial flows are less stable than trade flows. Thus, the limited number of years for which RWAMs have been constructed is more problematic for financial flows than for trade flows. Stocks incorporate information for a longer period and their periodic changes are therefore likely to be more representative for the trends that have occurred in the 1970–85 period than financial flows. The competition effect for stocks also adds another element to the analysis: it may be seen to include a portfolio preference motive. Lenders may wish to hold and adapt certain shares of their total assets in certain parts of the world in order to spread risks and interests optimally.

Negative entries form a practical problem specific to the application of CMS analysis to financial flows, but as Richardson (1971) has shown, the technique is subject to a number of other problems. The conclusions drawn from the analysis may be different when (a) another time period is selected, (b) the calculations are in current or in constant prices, (c) another 'world' standard is defined, (d) the level of commodity disaggregation and country groupings is changed, or (e) the market effect is calculated before the composition effect, instead of after the composition effect as in equation (7.3).

The possibilities for assessing the sensitivity for these problems in applying CMS analysis to RWAMs are rather limited. In this case, the shortest time period possible in the RWAMs (five years) has been selected. As trade shares are more stable over time than financial shares, the results of the analyses of financial transactions are sensitive to a specifically selected time period, and it would therefore be desirable to have a longer series of RWAMs than is available for this study. The addition of CMS analysis for stocks matrices can reduce the influence of the time element. The calculations are based on current prices, because this study considers trade and finance in a balance of payments context. Because exports and capital inflows are considered primarily as sources of foreign exchange used to finance imports, changes in the nominal value of exports are more relevant than changes in the real value. In nearly all calculations, the whole world has been used as 'world' standard, even when LDCs are clearly not competing with the whole world, as in the case of official finance. For capital flows, some calculations have been made using LDCs as a point of reference, which is the appropriate standard for official finance. An alternative option would have been to consider the CMS effects for the three groups of LDCs using only competing exports as a standard, but the selection of more restricted standard of reference countries is a difficult problem for trade and non-official capital flows that require considerable additional information. Thus the maximum level of disaggregation in the RWAMs has been used: four categories of merchandise trade and three types of foreign lending, ten country (groups) and one institutional sector (multilateral banks).

7.4 The Results

The results of the CMS analysis are presented in Table 7.1 (the 'core' table), Tables 7.2 and A7.1 which present disaggregations of the results in Table 7.1, and Table 7.3, which presents CMS results for LDCs, with LDCs themselves as a point of reference. The tables decompose the changes in trade and foreign finance for three groups of LDCs: Official Borrowers, Diversified Borrowers and Private Borrowers (see Chapter 2 for an explanation of this classification). The three periods examined are 1970–75, 1975–80 and 1980–85 for trade and capital flows, and 1975–80 and 1980–85 for foreign debt.

Table 7.1, the 'core' table, decomposes the changes in trade and net changes in flows and stocks of liabilities and shows how the changes in (A) merchandise exports, (B) capital inflows and (C) foreign debt have been decomposed into the world effect, the composition effect, the market effect, the competition effect and the interaction effect. A brief glance at this table shows an interesting difference between the country groups: where the Official Borrowers saw a continuous decrease in their competitiveness for merchandise trade, for the other two groups the competitiveness effect was the largest factor explaining their good export performance. This leads to some interesting questions. Did these countries have access to private finance because of their good export performance, or was it the other way around? Did foreign flows enable them to adjust their economies, thereby improving their competitiveness, or were they forced to adjust because they had to meet the relatively tight conditions attached to private finance?

The composition effect in Table 7.1 has been disaggregated into the four trade categories and the three types of foreign finance in Table 7.2. Table A7.1 which gives the geographical distribution of the market effect by category of trade and foreign finance, shows how the market effect is disaggregated by country group (in the columns) and by product (in the rows). The next sections will discuss the world effect (section

Table 7.1 *Constant market share analysis: core table (in US$ billions)*

	Official Borrowers			Diversified Borrowers			Private Borrowers		
	1970–75	1975–80	1980–85	1970–75	1975–80	1980–85	1970–75	1975–80	1980–85
*Constant market share analysis of LDC exports of merchandise trade**									
Export increase	24.4	43.3	-19.8	16.1	39.7	7.2	39.5	115.1	9.8
World effect	29.7	53.0	-5.3	13.0	30.2	-3.9	33.3	75.2	-10.8
Commodity effect	-0.6	-2.8	-3.7	-1.5	-0.6	-3.9	9.1	5.5	-10.9
Market effect	2.2	1.7	-0.3	0.9	1.6	-0.4	1.1	4.7	4.8
Competition effect	-2.2	-3.0	-9.3	0.6	3.9	18.4	-0.1	13.0	31.0
Interaction effect	-4.7	-5.6	-1.3	3.1	4.7	-3.0	-3.9	16.7	-4.3
Constant market share analysis of LDC capital inflows									
Increase in capital inflows**	5.3	4.4	3.3	3.3	3.9	5.2	7.5	8.2	-14.4
World flows effect	3.9	19.0	-1.2	3.0	12.7	-0.9	6.9	28.8	-2.0
Loan type effect	0.8	-11.9	1.7	0.4	-3.7	1.1	-0.6	-11.7	2.6
Market effect	-0.9	-3.4	3.8	0.8	2.8	5.1	-3.8	-1.6	10.6
Competition effect	-0.2	-3.2	7.7	0.9	-2.3	6.8	1.3	-5.9	-3.9
Interaction effect	2.4	-8.2	-6.9	-1.3	-9.4	-5.7	3.1	-13.0	-19.0
Constant market share analysis of LDC debt									
Increase in debt		62.5	65.6		69.3	55.7		274.5	171.4
World debt effect		99.3	55.4		90.1	56.3		194.0	181.2
Debt type effect		-27.7	26.9		-11.7	9.6		-45.6	-6.3
Market effect		2.0	-5.0		-4.1	7.2		-7.4	10.5
Competition effect		-5.5	-6.1		0.0	-10.5		49.3	10.6
Interaction effect		-5.7	-5.6		-5.0	-6.9		84.2	-24.6

* Columns may not tally due to rounding.

** Unlike the tables for trade and debt, the market, competition and interaction effects for capital flows have been calculated in a 'two-level' analysis; therefore the sum of the four effects does not add up to the total increase in capital flows.

7.5), the composition effect (section 7.6), the market effect (section 7.7) and the competition effect (section 7.8).

7.5 The World Effect

In the world effect, total growth in world trade, capital flows or stocks is multiplied by country X's share of the world total. It is hence large in periods of high trade growth (periods 1 and 2) and negative for trade and capital flows in the third period. The size of the world effect for a particular group depends on the share of the group in the world total at the beginning of each period. The world effect measures the increase that would result if the country group maintained its share in the world total; if growth in the country group is equal to world growth, the effect is equal to the increase in exports of the same country group. Thus the difference between the world effect and actual export growth measures the extent to which growth in a country group is faster or slower than world growth. Whatever the size of the effect, it is clear that LDCs can hardly influence growth in world trade or capital flows and hence the effect is largely exogenous.

Table 7.1 shows some dramatic changes in the merchandise exports of Official Borrowers. The figures indicate that their trade growth clearly lagged behind world growth: in period 1 and 2 the export increase is smaller than the world effect and in period 3 the export decrease is much larger than the decrease on account of the world effect. For both Diversified Borrowers and Private Borrowers the story is quite different: they both experienced export growth larger than could be expected from their world effect; in the third period their exports even increased in spite of the negative world effect. In other words: they have a larger share in the total.

While the share of LDCs in world trade has remained relatively stable over the past decades, the shares of individual countries have varied greatly. It has often been observed (Sampson 1990: 324) that for the majority of LDCs who rely on commodity exports for the bulk of their export earnings, their share in world exports has consistently and dramatically declined. The CMS results for the world trade effect suggest that these countries are primarily found among the Official Borrowers. This tendency is also observed by Page (1990) who concludes that countries that rely on official flows as the principal source of foreign finance suffer from persistently declining terms of trade, in some cases aggravated by sluggish export volumes.

Regarding capital flows and debt stocks, the most striking figures in Table 7.1 are the high world effects in 1975–80 for capital inflows. The actual increases in capital inflows are much smaller than the increases predicted by the world effect. This holds in particular for Official Borrowers for which the world effect was nearly fivefold the increase in actual inflows. In the third period there is a clear difference between the Private Borrowers and the other two groups: Official Borrowers and Diversified Borrowers saw an increase in inflows in spite of the negative world effect, while Private Borrowers' capital inflows declined by seven times the world debt effect. However, for Private Borrowers in the same period, the gap between the world effect and the increase in debt is small. As (net) capital flows may change violently from year to year, it is perhaps wiser to look at the debt figures.

Trends in foreign debt of LDCs are usually discussed in the context of trends in macroeconomic variables of LDCs (e.g. Das 1986, World Bank, World Debt Tables), such as shifts in debt service ratios or debt to GNP ratios. CMS analysis places these trends in foreign finance to LDCs in a world perspective: it relates the patterns in LDCs to world patterns. It shows that the three groups of LDCs had similar experiences in the 1970s, growth in capital flows was relatively fast in the first period, and relatively slow in the second. But in the third period Official Borrowers and Diversified Borrowers received a relatively large share of foreign finance, while Private Borrowers' inflows were negative and the increase in external indebtedness relatively small. The divergence in patterns may well be a result of the debt crisis, which caused private flows to LDCs to end abruptly, an effect which was of course most severely felt by the Private Borrowers. The following sections examine whether the differences and similarities can be explained by the composition of foreign finance and shifts in creditworthiness.

7.6 The Composition Effect

The composition effect for merchandise trade

The composition effect depends on the commodity composition of the country (group) in question and on the growth in trade in each category. Thus the composition effect for trade is a 'commodity effect'. Country (groups) that are concentrated in categories showing rapid growth will have positive effects, and country (groups) that are concentrated on categories with slow or negative growth will have negative effects.

According to Table 7.1, the commodity effect has been persistently negative for Official Borrowers and Diversified Borrowers. The size of the effect however, is, if anything, surprisingly small. One would expect larger negative commodity effects for countries that are primarily exporters of primary products. However, for Official Borrowers in the third period it accounted for nearly one fifth of the export decrease and for Private Borrowers it neutralized a large part of the export increase achieved by an increase in competitiveness. The composition effect is to a large extent exogenous to the countries involved, since an unfavourable commodity composition is very difficult to change except very slowly.

Table 7.2, which disaggregates the commodity effect for total trade into commodity effects for the four trade categories, shows that in the first two periods the effects are positive for all trade categories except manufactures, while in the third period the commodity effects for all categories are negative; for trade in food, raw materials and fuels this is due to the decline in world trade values, but for manufactures the relatively small share in trade in manufactures causes the negative effect. Due to the large shifts in the value for trade in fuels, the commodity effect for Private Borrowers was dominated by the commodity effect for this trade category. Thus Private Borrowers suffered from their concentration on fuels, while none of the groups could benefit from the increase in exports of manufactures given their relatively small shares. This implies that there are important exogenous factors in LDC's export structures which cannot be affected by domestic policy changes, at least not in the short run.

The composition effect for capital flows and debt stocks

While the composition effect for trade depends on commodity composition and the growth rates of trade categories, the composition effect for finance is determined by the composition of foreign finance by loan type and by the growth rates of loan types. Thus the composition effect for finance is a 'loan type effect' (for flows) or a 'debt type effect' (for stocks). The loan type effect is closely linked to the country classification of LDCs: Official Borrowers are by definition largely dependent

Table 7.2 Composition effect by category (in US$ billions)

	Official Borrowers			Diversified Borrowers			Private Borrowers		
	1970–75	1975–80	1980–85	1970–75	1975–80	1980–85	1970–75	1975–80	1980–85
Commodity effect by trade category									
SITC 0–1 (food)	5.3	7.8	-1.4	2.6	3.0	-0.7	3.6	2.8	-0.4
SITC 2+4 (crude materials)	1.7	3.3	-0.7	1.3	2.7	-0.8	2.3	3.6	-1.1
SITC 3 (fuels)	0.8	4.3	-1.2	-0.9	4.2	-1.5	15.6	24.4	-8.5
SITC 5–9 (manufactures)	-8.4	-18.2	-0.4	-4.4	-10.6	-0.9	-12.4	-25.2	-0.9
Total	-0.6	-2.8	-3.7	-1.5	-0.6	-3.9	9.1	5.5	-10.9
Loan type effect by category									
Foreign direct investment	-0.4	-0.8	0.0	-0.1	0.2	0.1	0.7	3.9	1.1
Official flows	3.3	5.4	0.2	2.4	1.3	0.1	1.2	1.3	0.1
Other private flows	-2.2	-16.5	1.5	-1.8	-5.2	0.9	-2.6	-16.9	1.3
Total	0.8	-11.9	1.7	0.4	-3.7	1.1	-0.6	-11.7	2.6
Debt type effect by category									
Foreign direct investment		-1.1	-1.0		-0.2	0.9		12.9	3.8
Official debt		35.4	58.2		14.2	28.0		14.9	7.0
Other private debt		-61.9	-30.4		-25.7	-19.3		-73.5	-17.1
Total		-27.7	26.9		-11.7	9.6		-45.6	-6.3

Note: Columns may not tally due to rounding.

on official finance and Private Borrowers on private finance. Thus the loan type effect for official loans that follows from the term $(B_i - B)$ is likely to be larger for Official Borrowers than for Private Borrowers; if official flows rise rapidly, Official Borrowers will have the largest positive loan type effect. Table 7.1 shows relatively small loan type effects for periods 1 and 3. In the second period, large negative effects appear in other private flows, a category which rose strongly in these years, but compared to the world standard, it is a relatively small source of foreign finance for LDCs. The debt type effect reflects this pattern in period 2, but an echo of the events which took place in 1975–80 is still visible in the large debt type effects in the third period.

Table 7.2, which decomposes the type-of-loan and the type-of-debt effect into three categories, shows that in general the trends are quite similar for the three groups. An exception is FDI, which made a positive contribution to Private Borrowers' capital inflows. Apparently, either countries with access to private OCA flows are also more capable (or willing) to attract FDI, or countries that have attracted FDI have easy access to private OCA flows through the operations of multinational enterprises. Given the concentration on FDI, Private Borrowers are likely to have benefited more from the upsurge in FDI which took place after the RWAM period.

As expected, there are large effects for Official Borrowers' official flows, especially in the debt type effect. These effects follow directly from the classification. They are largely exogenous, since Official Borrowers have by definition limited access to private markets. What we see in the third period, is that the debt type effect explains a large share of the increase in foreign debt for Official Borrowers. This suggests that adjustment problems faced by Official Borrowers after the debt crisis were met by a substantial increase in foreign official debt, which we do not observe for the other two groups. In other words, the adjustment burden related to the debt crisis and the decrease in foreign capital flows fell more heavily on the Diversified and Private Borrowers than on the Official Borrowers.

For private flows, the loan type effect is negative in period 1 and 2 but becomes positive in period 3 due to a *decrease* in the value of world private flows between 1980 and 1985 that coincides with negative values for $(B_i - B)$. Thus in the third period the relatively small shares lead to a positive effect for private flows. Generally, the composition effects are dominated by large swings in the effects for private flows. This illustrates the problem of volatility: private flows are unpredictable, hence concentration on private flows make countries more vulnerable to sudden shifts in the availability of these exogenously-determined and unpredictable flows.

7.7 The Market Effect

The market effect for merchandise trade

The market effect depends on the market composition of the country group in question and on the import growth of its trading partners. Countries that are concentrated on trading partners with fast import growth will have positive effects and countries that are concentrated on trading partners with slow import growth will have negative effects. Table 7.1 shows that the market effects tend to be of the same order of magnitude as the total commodity effect. Table A7.1 disaggregates the market effect by trading partner and commodity category, to reveal some interesting patterns which are netted out in the 'core' table. The most striking figures are the positive market effects with the US for Official Borrowers and Private Borrowers in periods 1 and 2. In the third period, the largest share of growth in world trade originated in the US, but the import increase is largely explained by the increase in imports of manufactures, while the imports of fuels dropped significantly.

For Official Borrowers, whose positive market effect with the US was based on fuel exports in the earlier period, this resulted in a negative market effect with the US. Private Borrowers have positive links with the US in exports of manufactures that counter the negative effect on account of fuels, but reduce the market effect with the US to a negligible amount.

Another sizable positive effect is the large market effect for Diversified Borrowers with Japan in period 2 because of trade in fuels. In period 3, Japan left the fast growers, and experienced negative growth for trade in fuels which is consistent with the negative market effect for Diversified Borrowers. There are large negative effects in periods 1 and 2 resulting from trade with the EU, since the EU has a large bias for intra-EU trade. In the third period, EU trade growth was negative. Therefore, the negative bias in EU imports from LDCs led to positive market effects. For Private Borrowers, which as a group have the largest negative bias for EU imports, this largely explains the positive effect in the third period. Outside the CMEA area, Official Borrowers form the only group that has positive links with the CMEA; there is a strong bias towards Official Borrowers in CMEA imports in period 1 and 2.

Thus although the size of the total market effects in this exercise is not impressive, the totals disguise some sizable effects at a more disaggregated level. To some extent, market effects are exogenous and hard to change for the exporting countries, especially if they are based on restricted access to markets. As we have seen, market effects are potentially large. Improved market access to the large and mostly rapidly growing markets in industrialized countries, as gained in the Uruguay Round, may therefore make a substantial difference in the export performance of LDCs.

The market effect for capital flows and debt stocks

The market effects for capital flows and stocks follows from the market distribution: countries that are concentrated on partner countries with rapidly (or slowly) growing capital exports will have positive (negative) effects. The calculation of the market effect requires matrices by origin and destination. As explained in the previous chapters, these matrices in the RWAMs are less reliable than the trade matrices due to the many gaps and data problems for directional flows and stocks of foreign finance. Thus the CMS results from the market effect should be interpreted with greater caution than those for merchandise trade.

Table 7.1 shows that the trend has been an increase in the market effect for LDCs. A major shift in the sources of growth in capital exports has been from the US and Major Oil Exporters towards Japan; contrary to world trends, the capital exports of Japan sharply increased in period 3.

Can this shift explain the trend in LDCs' market effects? As set out in Section 7.2, Table A7.1 presents 'two-level' results for flows and 'three-level' results for stocks. Given the sensitivity of CMS analysis to changes in the level of aggregation, it is useful to check if the results from a 'two-level' analysis are likely to differ from results from a 'three-level' analysis, i.e. by comparing the 'three-level' results for stocks (as presented in the tables) with 'two-level' results for stocks. This comparison indicates that although the value for the total market effect may differ significantly, the geographical distribution of the total market effect is similar for the two approaches. For example, if 80 per cent of Private Borrowers' market effect for stocks in the 'two-level' analysis comes on account of Japan, in the 'three-level' analysis about 80 per cent of Private Borrowers' market effect is also accounted for by Japan. This is a reassuring conclusion, as it confirms the validity of the method, and in turn allows the examination of the market effect for capital flows to focus on the interpretation of the geographical distribution of the market effect.

Table A7.1 shows that in the first period, for each of the three groups a small but positive market effect follows from capital flows from the US. In the second period, capital inflows from Japan have an enormous positive impact on the Diversified Borrowers' market effect, but the effect with Japan is also positive for the other groups. For Private Borrowers, both the Japan and the US account for sizeable shares in the market effect. In period 3, market effects are substantial, especially for Private Borrowers. The major geographical source for each of the groups is Japan; the positive market effect results from a combination of positive links with Japan and fast growing capital exports from this country.

Table 7.3 gives the results for the intra-LDC variant that has LDCs as a point of reference, and not the whole world as in the other tables. A first observation is that the 'world' effect is large. The world effect, as we have seen earlier, is exogenous to LDCs, since they have little influence over growth in world capital flows. The market effects are relatively small, indicating that the differences among LDCs are much smaller than the differences between LDCs and the rest of the world. Compared to the whole world, Private Borrowers had a large market effect in period 3 (see Table 7.1), but compared to other LDCs, this effect was small.

Finally, the CMS results for stocks (see section C of Table A7.1) offer a third perspective on the effect of market composition on growth in external debt of LDCs. The most spectacular figure here is the enormous market effect for Private and Diversified Borrowers in period 3 on account of private debt issued in Japan. Other substantial effects are found for Private Borrowers in growth in private debt issued in the US.

Table 7.3 *Constant market share analysis with LDCs as a point of reference (in US$ billions)*

	Official Borrowers			Diversified Borrowers			Private Borrowers		
	1970–75	1975–80	1980–85	1970–75	1975–80	1980–85	1970–75	1975–80	1980–85
Increase in disbursements	6.5	6.4	6.2	4.6	8.0	11.3	7.5	8.2	-5.8
World flows effect	5.9	11.0	2.5	4.7	8.1	2.4	6.9	28.8	6.8
Loan type effect	-0.1	-1.2	0.1	0.0	0.8	-0.2	-0.6	-11.7	0.1
Market effect	0.5	-1.6	0.5	0.0	0.9	0.5	-3.8	-1.6	-1.0
Competition effect	-0.2	-1.3	3.5	0.1	0.1	6.9	1.3	-5.9	-10.4
Interaction effect	0.5	-0.1	-0.4	-0.2	-1.8	1.8	3.1	-13.0	-1.4

Note: Columns may not tally due to rounding.

7.8 Competitiveness in International Markets

The sum of the world effect, the composition effect and the market effect reflects the change in exports which would result if a country (group) maintained its export shares in the disaggregated flows or stocks. The residual changes in trade flows, capital flows or stocks are identified by the competitiveness term. For the analysis in this chapter, the competitiveness term has been split into a competition effect and an interaction effect. The competition effect ($\Sigma\Sigma Q_{ij} \cdot \Delta S_{ij}$) relates the increase in the share of a flow to the initial world total. The interaction effect ($\Sigma\Sigma\Delta Q_{ij} \cdot \Delta S_{ij}$) relates the increase in the share to the increase in the world total over the period.

The competition effect, which reflects changes in a country's market shares, is generally interpreted as a measure for change in relative competitiveness. If a country has increased its share in a particular market, its competitiveness is assumed to have increased. The interaction effect combines changes in the volume of a particular market with shifts in the shares in these markets. If trade increases are combined with increased shares in particular markets, a country experiences an export boom. For financial flows and stocks, the competition effect is labelled 'creditworthiness' effect. For capital flows, a positive competition effect may be interpreted as a reflection of increased creditworthiness, which enabled a country to increase its share in the world market. This shift in the share may be seen as a reflection of a shift in the portfolio preferences of lending countries, based on a perceived rise in the creditworthiness of a borrowing country.

Positive interaction effects stem from growing shares in growing markets. While LDCs can try to improve creditworthiness in order to gain a larger share of the pie, they cannot influence the size of the pie; an increase in the volume of the market itself lies beyond their control. Therefore we consider creditworthiness to some extent endogenous and the interaction effect exogenous. In effect, the interaction effect for capital flows is the equivalent of an export boom in merchandise trade.

Competitiveness in merchandise trade

Official Borrowers (as Table 7.1 shows) have clearly been uncompetitive in international export markets. Moreover, their luck has been bad, in the sense that they could not benefit from increasing shares in fast growing markets, as the negative interaction effects show. Their competitiveness showed a strong decrease throughout the period, and reached its lowest point in the third period, when over 50 per cent of the decrease in exports by Official Borrowers can be attributed to the competitiveness term. A disaggregation of the term shows that the loss in competitiveness is evenly distributed over the different categories. Thus there has been a persistent overall decline which came about in commodities as well as markets.

Quite contrary to this experience, the competitiveness of Diversified and Private Borrowers increased enormously, as we can see from the rise in the competition effect. In line with its nature, the interaction effect, which reached a peak for Private Borrowers in 1975–80, was erratic. An analysis of the Diversified Borrowers' increase in competitiveness shows that it was gained in trade in food, fuels and manufactures, in all (regional) markets. For Private Borrowers fuels played a large role, but in the course of the RWAM-period competitiveness was enforced by an improvement in the competition effect for manufactures, which largely materialized in the rapidly-growing markets of the US.

Competitiveness in international finance: the creditworthiness effect

Because calculating the creditworthiness term from net capital flows encounters problems similar to those that arise in calculating the market effect, the results for capital flows are also based on (1) a 'two-level' analysis for net flows with the world as the point of reference and (2) a 'three-level' analysis with LDCs as the point of reference. As for the market effect, a comparison of 'two-level' and 'three-level' results for stocks has shown that the size of the total competition and interaction effect may vary significantly in the two approaches, while the geographical patterns are similar.

Table 7.1 shows small creditworthiness effects for net capital flows in period 1. For Diversified and Private Borrowers the effect is positive; both groups managed to increase their shares in the capital flows from the US and Japan. The positive interaction effect of Private Borrowers partly originated in the US, the rest of it in the Major Oil Exporters. Also Official Borrowers had a positive interaction effect, or 'bingo-effect' originating from a shift towards Major Oil Exporters.

Period 2 shows the same pattern for each of the three groups: the creditworthiness effect is negative, explaining a substantial share of the gap between the world effect and the actual increase in their capital inflows. What becomes apparent here, is what we might refer to as the 'debt cycle': a period of generous lending, and perhaps over-optimism of lenders, is followed by a period of pessimism where countries are cut off from foreign loans (see for example Vos 1991). Moreover, as the LDC shares dropped, the markets grew; the declining shares of LDCs in the rapidly-growing markets of industrialized countries and major oil exporters, resulted in large negative interaction effects.

In period 3, official and diversified borrowers increased their shares in the markets of the US, the EU and major oil exporters, an increase which resulted in large competition effects. Private borrowers' shares in all markets except the US decreased sharply. Apparently, there was a sharp decline in perceived creditworthiness in all markets, except the US. However, the US capital exports decreased in this period, and therefore the large increase in creditworthiness in the US was almost entirely countered by a decrease on account of the interaction effect. None of the groups of LDCs benefited from growth in Japanese capital exports. On the contrary, the sizeable negative interaction effects point at shifts towards country groups with negative growth.

For stocks, the competitiveness term for Official Borrowers and Diversified Borrowers is negative but relatively small, ranging from 5 to 10 per cent of the total change in indebtedness. Apparently these countries ranked low on the portfolio preference scales of foreign investors. Private Borrowers' shares in private assets – both FDI and other capital (OCA) – of industrialized countries increased considerably in period 2. The increases in Private Borrowers' shares in the fast-growing assets of industrialized countries resulted in enormous interaction effects with industrialized countries. In period 3, Private Borrowers' share in US assets continued to increase substantially but their shares in other markets dropped; hence there was an overall decrease in both the creditworthiness and interaction effects. Also, changes in the perceived creditworthiness were not spread evenly over the creditor countries.

Finally, the 'three-level' results for new loans with LDCs as a point of reference show an increase in creditworthiness for Official Borrowers and Diversified Borrowers, while creditworthiness for Private Borrowers declined. This decline in Private Borrowers' perceived creditworthiness is largely accounted for by a drop in the share of new loans from Japan and the EU, while both Official Borrowers and Diversified Borrowers increased their shares in these loans.

7.9 Concluding Remarks

The results of the CMS analysis have some interesting policy implications. For trade, the key issues are market access and competitiveness. Concentration on – or access to – fast-growing markets may give a substantial boost to a country's export performance. In the coming years, the extent to which the Uruguay Round can resolve the problem of restricted market access, will become clearer. In the meantime it is clear that export success depends as much on markets as on domestic reform. Competitiveness is a domestic factor influenced by product quality and price, so improvement in competitiveness would require investment in modern plants, infrastructure and human skills to promote product quality, while devaluation makes export prices more competitive.

Lack of competitiveness is a problem for Official Borrowers, and this explains the poor trade performance of this group. Apparently the large official aid flow, a large part of which was aimed at investments in infrastructure, industry and human capital, could not counter the declining trend in competitiveness. It seems that Official Borrowers in particular need open markets – to help them integrate in the world economy – rather than more foreign aid. Meanwhile, Diversified and Private Borrowers have increased their exports through improved competitiveness. Since the world effect, and to a lesser extent also the market and the commodity effect, is exogenous, countries that have to adjust will do this through the competition effect.

Trends in capital flows are dominated by the market effect. A major shift during the RWAM period was from the US towards Japan. Changes in the origin of the investor, each with portfolio preferences for particular countries, matters more than local conditions, so any improvement may need some concurrent action to reduce risk to creditor countries, e.g. Japan. Thus competition between LDCs for capital flows may not be the best way to encourage investment in LDCs as a whole; what is needed is rather a change in investment portfolio preferences in industrialized countries.

8 Summary and Conclusions

This study describes the reasoning and modalities underlying a set of world accounting matrices (WAMs) and demonstrates their use as an analytical tool. This final chapter summarizes its major findings and conclusions and indicates directions for further applications of the WAMs and WAM-related research.

8.1 Changes in the World Economy and International Macroeconomic Statistics

Since the 1970s, large changes in the world economy, and particularly the rapidly-changing patterns of international trade and finance, have made the links between trade and finance increasingly complex. As a consequence of the greater complexity, it has become increasingly difficult to produce reliable international macroeconomic statistics, and the quality and coverage of these statistics has deteriorated. Because of their inconsistency, these data sources may be highly misleading.

The current approach to the production of data on global macroeconomic statistics is directed at aspects of international trade and finance or national accounts. However, to combat the statistical problems, we need a systematic approach which integrates statistics for trade, finance and domestic saving and investment. This study proposes a world accounting matrix (WAM) which has been developed to meet the analytical and statistical requirements of the world economy.

The WAM is based on the concept that related variables should be placed in an integrated framework that makes the relationships between the variables explicit. The building blocks for the WAM are the national accounting identities. Summed over all countries they give us the familiar global identities like 'world exports are equal to world imports'.

In the WAM-framework, the accumulation balance holds a central position: it links the balances on the current and the capital account of the balance of payments to the balance of domestic saving and investment. The four main blocs of the WAM follow from the accumulation balance; they record the current account transactions, the capital account transactions, domestic saving and domestic investment. The system is supplemented by tables for stocks of external assets and liabilities and gross national products. A central assumption in this study is that origin and destination of international transactions are important enough to effort the construction of matrices that record the origin and destination of international trade and finance.

8.2 The Data Sources

Most of the data used to construct the WAM is drawn from the macroeconomic data sources published by international institutions. Clearly, the data requirements are enormous and for some cells of the matrices information is missing entirely. The major 'missing data' problem is the lack of financial data by origin and destination, in particular for financial flows among industrialized countries. For example, there is no systematic data source that tells us how much the EU has invested in Japan or vice versa; this type of data is available for LDCs because the LDC debt crisis created a need for systematic and consistent data on LDC debt.

One of the advantages of a worldwide, consistent data framework is that fragmentary information is systematically integrated and co-ordinated, allowing the best possible use of available information. To give a simple example, it is clear that if the US reports a loan to Italy, this is in principle equal to a loan from a US resident to an Italian resident. If Italy does not report loans by origin and destination, the Italian loans from the US can be estimated from the US reports, since they refer to the same cell in the matrix. Thus, although only one end of a transaction is reported, the other end is in principle also known.

8.3 The Construction Methodology

A first step in the construction method is to confront all these inconsistent and incomplete data in the WAM-framework. In some instances, mainly for variables that show large global inconsistencies, second estimates are calculated from related variables. For some missing or doubtful entries, additional information can be obtained from national sources. For example, reported investment income showing large global discrepancies is compared with calculated investment income estimated from reported stocks. Or, the interiors of the matrices for merchandise trade are used to estimate non-factor services – which represent another large data problem since this is nowhere reported – and then to derive their geographical network. Another element in the approach is to make adjustments for certain gaps and discrepancies based on a careful examination of the data sources and problems. Finally, the WAMs are reconciled in a mathematical procedure, which simultaneously reconciles a complete WAM.

In spite of huge gaps in the existing data sources, a series of reconciled WAMs can be (and has been) constructed. The construction of WAMs is feasible and these WAMs are to be considered as optimal given the limited available resources. However, the quality of the results depends greatly on the initial data input; we cannot expect miracles from the method, and the scope for improvement is large, if WAMs could be constructed along the same lines within a larger institutional setting and with greater resources.

8.4 The Analytical Results

This study is mainly about method, but is illustrated with a selection of analytical applications. Since the WAM is an accounting framework, analytical applications are limited as patterns can be observed and described but not explained. Thus, the contribution of the WAM to the analysis of patterns of trade and finance is to provide an initial exploration that may be seen as a necessary first step prior to modelling and explaining interactions between international trade and finance.

Comparison of the four WAMs gives some insight into the shifts in the structure of the world economy in these four benchmark years. They show that LDCs increased their share in world current account transactions, but were not included in the trend for internationalization of capital markets. The three groups of LDCs exhibit considerable differences in shifts in their current account transactions, while the shifts in capital account transactions are quite similar. Also, the geographical distribution of trade and finance is not proportional: there are clear 'biases' which imply that some country groups have larger shares in trade and finance of other country groups than can be predicted on the basis of their shares in world totals. For example, the EU imports a relatively small share of its total imports from LDCs, and exports a relatively small share of its total capital exports to LDCs. This asymmetry is also found in the financing of current account deficits. Investigating the current balances, we found that the US, Japan and the EU were all biased towards a particular group of LDCs, in the sense that they financed not only their own current account surplus with this group, but also the surpluses of others.

Constant market share analysis is a suitable tool for a more detailed analysis of the shifts in the shares of LDCs in world trade and finance. The novelty of the approach in this study is that this method, well-known in the analysis of export growth, is applied to capital flows and stocks. The financial matrices are interpreted as describing international sales and purchases of financial instruments. The most interesting aspect of this approach is that it decomposes the change in a country group's exports (or capital imports or debt stocks) into endogenous and exogenous components. From this perspective we looked at the LDC experience in 1970–85, but the technique can also be used to highlight the characteristics in a country's export or debt structure in relation to future export performance or availability of foreign finance.

8.5 Implications

Because the adjustments made in the reconciled WAMs are distributed disproportionally over the country groups, the inconsistencies in international macroeconomic statistics have implications for the interpretation of economic problems. The largest 'disproportionate' adjustments are made for the group of major oil exporters; the current account surpluses of this country group are much larger in the reconciled WAMs for 1975 and 1980 than reported by the IMF. This implies that this group is probably much richer in terms of foreign assets than is usually assumed. The US current account deficits, which have been extraordinarily large since 1983, were smaller in the reconciled WAMs than in the IMF reports. Transactions in the world economy are also distributed disproportionately over the country groups, and this gives the exercise an analytical ground. Not only is it worthwhile to construct matrices by origin and destination in order to contribute towards the solution of statistical problems, the matrices may also contribute to economic analysis.

8.6 Statistical Improvements and Further Research

It has been stressed throughout this study that the significant data problems for financial variables make the financial matrices the weakest part of the WAMs. Given the rapid changes in financial markets and the growing complexity in financial transactions, statistics will never be perfect. There is scope, however, for substantial improvements. For example, national sources offer much more information on the geographical origin and destination of international transactions than is incorporated in this study. Given the time-consuming nature of collecting data from national sources, it would be highly desirable if international organizations collect and harmonize these data. Obviously, since they do this for many other economic variables, they are well equipped for this type of work. Other problem areas in international financial statistics are the limited availability of data on gross financial flows, and the lack of consistency between stock and flow variables. If international organizations were to fill these gaps in the international macroeconomic statistics, they would not only improve their own statistics, they would provide the material with which high quality WAMs could be constructed.

In its best format, the WAM is set up as a flexible data system which allows for different aggregations of countries and transactions. It is then possible to construct WAMs for all sorts of different country classifications and aggregations of transactions, depending on the purpose of the exercise. Ideally, however, this work should also be carried out by the large international institutions themselves, because small teams are naturally limited and doing the job properly requires large resources.

This study has used a series of WAMs as a tool for the descriptive analysis of shifts in the patterns of trade and finance of LDCs. Vos (1992) was able to make use of these WAMs for multiplier analysis based on a simple demand-driven linear model for world trade and finance. De Jong and Vos (1994a & b) performed descriptive WAM-based analysis with their series of WAMs for 1985–90 (de Jong et al. 1993a & b). They focused on regionalization in trade and segmentation of international capital markets. They also studied FDI in relation to patterns in trade and (other) finance, to explore the way FDI should be incorporated in a global model. It appears that the possibilities for descriptive, exploratory data analysis with the WAM have been exhausted. We are ready for the next step, using the WAM as a database for a world model, where the behavioural equations of the model are built around the accounting constraints of the WAM. Hopefully, the insights from the exploratory WAM-based analysis will prove to be useful in the modelling stage.

Appendices

A2 Appendix to Chapter 2

Table A2.1 Country classification for the World Accounting Matrix

1	**US**		
2	**Japan**		
3	**EC**		
	Belgium	France	Netherlands
	Denmark	Ireland	Portugal
	Germany (FRG)	Italy	Spain
	Greece	Luxemburg	United Kingdom
4	**Other OECD (OOECD)**		
	Austria	Finland	Norway
	Australia	Iceland	Sweden
	Canada	New Zealand	Switzerland
5	**CMEA**		
	Albania	Germany (GDR)	Poland
	Bulgaria	Hungary	Romania
	Cuba	Korea (PDR)	USSR
	Czechoslovakia	Mongolia	Vietnam
6	**Major Oil Exporters (MOE)**		
	Bahrain	Kuwait	Saudi Arabia
	Brunei	Libya	Syria
	Iran	Oman	United Arab Emirates
	Iraq	Qatar	

(Continued)

Table A2.1 (Continued)

7	**Official Borrowers (OB)**		
	Bangladesh	Guyana	São Tomé
	Belize	Haiti	Senegal
	Botswana	Honduras	Seychelles
	Burkina Faso	India	Sierra Leone
	Burma	Jamaica	Solomon Islands
	Burundi	Jordan	Somalia
	Cape Verde	Lebanon	Sri Lanka
	Central Afric. Repub.	Lesotho	St. Vincent
	Chad	Liberia	Sudan
	Comoros	Madagascar	Swaziland
	Djibouti	Maldives	Tanzania
	Egypt	Malawi	Togo
	El Salvador	Mali	Uganda
	Equatorial Guinea	Malta	Vanuatu
	Ethiopia	Mauritania	Western Samoa
	Gambia	Mauritius	Yemen A.R.
	Ghana	Nepal	Yemen P.D.R.
	Grenada	Nicaragua	Zaire
	Guinea	Pakistan	Zambia
	Guinea Bissau	Rwanda	
8	**Diversified Borrowers (DB)**		
	Barbados	Costa Rica	Morocco
	Benin	Cyprus	Niger
	Bolivia	Dominican Rep.	Paraguay
	Cameroon	Fiji	Peru
	China	Guatemala	Thailand
	Colombia	Indonesia	Tunisia
	Congo	Kenya	Turkey
9	**Private Borrowers (PB)**		
	Algeria	Ivory Coast	Philippines
	Argentina	Korea Rep.	Papua New Guinea
	Bahamas	Malaysia	Trinidad
	Brazil	Mexico	Uruguay

(Continued)

Table A2.1 (Continued)

9	**Private Borrowers (PB)** (continued)		
	Chile	Nigeria	Venezuela
	Ecuador	Panama	Zimbabwe
	Gabon		
10	**Rest of the World (ROW)** (major countries)		
	Afghanistan	Israel	Singapore
	Angola	Kampuchea	South Africa
	Bermuda	Mozambique	Surinam
	Burma	Namibia	Taiwan
	Dominica	Netherlands Ant.	Yugoslavia
	Hong Kong		

Table A2.2 The ratio of official debt to total debt

	1970–75	1976–81	1982–87	1982–87*
Official Borrowers				
Average	77	86	86	77
Variation coefficient (%)	25	20	9	14
Bangladesh	97	99	97	92
Belize	100	94	81	70
Botswana	94	98	88	87
Burkina Faso	97	95	92	85
Burma	73	81	86	85
Burundi	79	86	95	90
Cape Verde	—	100	98	96
Central African Republic	60	62	89	84
Chad	65	74	78	71
Comoros	100	100	100	96
Djibouti	—	92	89	69
Egypt	71	84	79	68
El Salvador	37	60	83	77
Equatorial Guinea	100	92	86	78
Ethiopia	91	95	86	82
Gambia	100	90	83	72
Ghana	53	59	86	77
Grenada	37	73	91	86
Guinea	88	84	88	81
Guinea Bissau	—	76	75	65
Guyana	60	57	75	56
Haiti	76	88	85	75
Honduras	69	64	72	64
India	95	95	80	75
Jamaica	9	47	79	74
Jordan	89	78	70	53
Lebanon	99	89	72	67
Lesotho	92	90	90	88
Liberia	84	75	80	72
Madagascar	92	76	82	77

(Continued)

Table A2.2 (Continued)

	1970–75	1976–81	1982–87	1982–87*
Official Borrowers (continued)				
Maldives	100	100	88	61
Malawi	87	73	86	79
Mali	96	95	96	92
Malta	96	98	100	59
Mauritania	80	76	90	83
Mauritius	71	64	70	63
Nepal	90	100	97	90
Nicaragua	55	55	70	57
Pakistan	92	95	92	82
Rwanda	78	94	97	89
São Tomé	—	—	96	95
Senegal	55	57	86	76
Seychelles	100	100	90	87
Sierra Leone	58	62	77	67
Solomon Islands	—	100	87	80
Somalia	96	97	88	84
Sri Lanka	81	89	75	69
St. Vincent	78	87	97	92
Sudan	78	74	78	65
Swaziland	77	87	95	87
Tanzania	73	82	82	71
Togo	72	46	84	76
Uganda	82	78	89	84
Vanuatu	—	95	96	93
Western Samoa	—	73	95	91
Yemen A.R.	99	99	98	89
Yemen P.D.R.	100	100	100	94
Zaire	33	50	80	76
Zambia	32	60	80	65

(Continued)

Table A2.2 (Continued)

	1970–75	1976–81	1982–87	1982–87*
Diversified Borrowers				
Average	60	55	55	48
Variation coefficient (%)	35	18	16	21
Barbados	11	56	51	40
Benin	79	74	52	44
Bolivia	60	50	57	51
Cameroon	79	58	62	52
China	—	—	41	28
Colombia	67	56	46	37
Congo	77	59	41	35
Costa Rica	39	36	43	38
Cyprus	68	55	48	35
Dominican Republic	51	49	66	58
Fiji	58	67	58	55
Guatemala	50	59	66	60
Indonesia	64	51	50	43
Kenya	55	54	67	62
Morocco	76	51	66	62
Niger	94	60	61	56
Paraguay	72	60	59	54
Peru	17	34	40	33
Thailand	41	42	45	36
Tunisia	77	63	64	62
Turkey	91	70	61	51

(Continued)

Table A2.2 (Continued)

	1970–75	1976–81	1982–87	1982–87*
Private Borrowers				
Average	37	25	22	19
Variation coefficient (%)	34	39	47	42
Algeria	36	17	20	17
Argentina	14	13	10	8
Bahamas	44	15	12	10
Brazil	25	14	17	15
Chile	47	28	13	12
Ecuador	46	32	30	26
Gabon	40	24	37	28
Ivory Coast	46	28	30	27
Korea Republic	39	38	33	24
Malaysia	46	30	18	18
Mexico	18	11	11	10
Nigeria	61	42	22	19
Panama	40	28	34	26
Philippines	27	31	38	26
Papua New Guinea	11	26	24	22
Trinidad	47	42	31	26
Uruguay	45	28	17	14
Venezuela	28	7	2	2
Zimbabwe	33	18	38	31

* Including short-term debt.

A3 Appendix to Chapter 3 Data Sources for the WAM

Major Data Sources

Domestic transactions	*World Tables*, World Bank
Merchandise trade	*United Nations Trade Matrices System*, UNDIESA
International transport & travel	*Balance of Payments Statistics*, IMF
Foreign direct investment	*Balance of Payments Statistics*, IMF *Directory of Statistics of International Investment and Production*, Dunning & Cantwell (1987)
Other foreign capital	*Debtor Reporting System*, World Bank *Balance of Payments Statistics*, IMF National sources (see list below)
Unrequited transfers	*Balance of Payments Statistics*, IMF *Geographical Distribution of Financial Flows to Developing Countries*, OECD
Other current account	*Balance of Payments Statistics*, IMF
Net changes in reserves	*Balance of Payments Statistics*, IMF
Net errors & omissions	*Balance of Payments Statistics*, IMF
Interest rates, exchange rates	*International Financial Statistics*, IMF

Supplementary Data Sources

Domestic transactions	*National Accounts Statistics*, UN *DEC Analytical Database*, World Bank *World Development Report*, World Bank
Merchandise trade	*Direction of Trade Statistics*, IMF
Other foreign investment	*International Banking Statistics*, IMF *Banking Statistics*, BIS *Financing and External Debt of Developing Countries*, OECD Financial Market Trends, OECD

National Data Sources

United States	*Survey of Current Business*, Department of Commerce *Federal Reserve Bulletin*, Federal Reserve Bank
Japan	*Balance of Payments of Japan*, The Bank of Japan (in Matsukawa 1987)
Germany	*Statistische Beihefte zu den Monatsberichten der Deutsche Bundesbank*, Deutsche Bundesbank
France	*La Balance de Paiements de la France*, Banque de France
Canada	*System of National Accounts*, Statistics Canada
Italy	*Boletino Statistico*, Banca d'Italia
Netherlands	*Kwartaalbericht*, De Nederlandsche Bank N.V.
Belgium/Luxemburg	*Tijdschrift van de Nationale Bank van Belgie*, Nationale Bank van Belgie
United Kingdom	*Quarterly Bulletin of the Bank of England*, Bank of England
Switzerland	*Les Banques Suisses*, Banque Nationale Suisse

A4 Appendix to Chapter 4 The Mathematical Reconciliation Procedure

Stone's adjustment procedure can be formalized as follows:

'Consider a vector x^* (of type $v \cdot 1$) which contains unbiased estimates of the elements of another vector x of true values. Suppose that the elements of x are subject to m independent linear constraints, that is

$$Gx = h \qquad (A4.1)$$

where G, the constraint matrix, is of type $m \cdot v$ and rank m; and h, a vector of known constants, is of type $m \cdot 1$. Let V^*, or order v and rank greater than m, denote the variance matrix of the elements of x^*; and assume that any constraints satisfied by x^* are linearly dependent of (A4.1). Then the best linear unbiased estimator x^{**} of x is given by

$$x^{**} = x^* - V^*G'(GV^*G')^{-1}(Gx^* - h) \qquad (A4.2)$$

from which it can be seen that the elements of V^* need only be approximated up to a scalar multiplier, since any multiplier will disappear in the matrix product $V^*G'(GV^*G')^{-1}$. The variance matrix V^{**} of x^{**}, the vector of adjusted estimates, is given by

$$V^{**} = V^* - V^*G'(GV^*G')^{-1}GV^* \qquad (A4.3)$$

The variance matrix, V^*, of the final estimates which satisfy all the constraints differs from V^*, which relates to the initial estimates, in that it takes into account the constraints of the system as well as the initial impressions of the investigator' (Stone 1977: xxii).

The conceptual basis for the WAM is the following accounting identity (see Chapter 2):

$$\Sigma F_i = \Sigma (E_i - M_i - R_i - Tr_i) = \Sigma (S_i - I_i) = 0$$

The 'four major blocs' (current account, capital account, domestic saving and domestic investment) of the WAM follow from this accounting identity. As Table 2.5 and Tables A5.3–A5.6 show, the national and the global balances are captured as follows:

$$\begin{bmatrix} A & \hat{i} \\ \hat{s} & B \end{bmatrix} \tag{A4.4}$$

Where matrix A includes total transactions on the current account (E, M, R and Tr), matrix B total transactions on the capital account (F), matrix i is the diagonal matrix for GDI (I) and matrix s the diagonal matrix for GNS (S). The matrices A and B are the sum of submatrices for disaggregated current account and capital account transactions. For each submatrix X the constraints are:

$$\sum_i X_{ij} = x_{nj} \tag{A4.5}$$

$$\sum_j X_{ij} = x_{in} \tag{A4.6}$$

$$\sum_i x_{in} = \sum_j x_{nj} \tag{A4.7}$$

where x_{ij} is the ijth element of submatrix X and n is the number of country groups, and each submatrix X provides $2n + 1$ constraints.

Matrix W, the aggregate WAM, can be expressed in terms of its totals:

$$\sum_{i=1} a_{ij} + i_{ii} = w_{it} \qquad t = 2n + 1 \tag{A4.8}$$

$$s_{ii} + \sum_{i=1} b_{ij} = w_{(n+i)t} \tag{A4.9}$$

$$\sum_{j=1} a_{ij} + s_{jj} = w_{tj} \tag{A4.10}$$

$$i_{jj} + \sum_{j=1} b_{ij} = w_{t(n+j)} \tag{A4.11}$$

$$w_{it} = w_{ti} \qquad i = 1.2n \tag{A4.12}$$

Thus, the aggregate WAM provides $6n$ constraints.

A5 Appendix to Chapter 5

Table A5.1 *Raw matrices: 1970 current and capital accounts*

1970 Current Account

	US	Japan	EU	OOECD	CMEA	MOE	OB	DB	PB	ROW	Multi	Total
US	0.0	5.5	12.5	12.8	0.4	0.7	3.3	1.6	6.4	2.0	0.0	45.2
Japan	6.4	0.0	2.4	2.0	0.6	0.5	1.9	1.7	2.6	1.8	0.0	19.8
EU	10.3	1.5	62.6	17.7	4.4	1.9	6.6	2.6	5.7	4.7	0.0	118.0
OOECD	12.9	2.5	14.7	5.3	1.8	0.3	1.5	0.8	1.5	1.1	0.0	42.4
CMEA	0.3	0.6	3.8	1.5	23.1	0.3	2.0	0.6	0.3	0.7	0.0	33.2
MOE	0.3	2.1	7.3	0.8	0.2	0.3	0.6	0.1	0.6	0.4	0.0	12.6
OB	3.3	1.2	6.0	1.1	2.3	0.4	1.8	0.3	0.5	0.5	0.3	17.8
DB	1.2	1.1	2.4	0.5	0.6	0.1	0.4	0.1	0.8	0.6	0.1	7.8
PB	4.9	1.8	6.3	1.4	0.7	0.1	1.4	0.4	1.9	0.4	0.1	19.4
ROW	2.5	0.9	3.5	0.9	0.9	0.1	0.7	0.2	0.4	0.3	0.0	10.4
Multi	0.0	0.0	0.0	0.0	0.0	0.0	0.1	0.1	0.1	0.0	0.0	0.3
Column totals:												
Total allocated	42.0	17.1	121.4	44.0	34.9	4.6	20.4	8.5	20.9	12.4	0.5	326.8
Unallocated	22.7	5.3	46.5	15.6	7.3	5.0	4.2	2.8	8.3	3.5	0.4	121.6
Raw marginals	64.7	22.5	167.9	59.6	42.1	9.7	24.6	11.3	29.2	15.9	0.9	448.4
Row totals:												
Total allocated	45.2	19.8	118.0	42.4	33.2	12.6	17.8	7.8	19.4	10.4	0.3	326.8
Unallocated	21.8	3.9	49.3	13.7	7.3	1.2	3.1	2.8	6.0	4.4	0.6	114.1
Raw marginals	67.0	23.7	167.3	56.1	40.5	13.8	20.9	10.6	25.3	14.8	0.9	440.9

(Continued)

Table A5.1 (Continued)

1970 Capital Account

	US	Japan	EU	OOECD	CMEA	MOE	OB	DB	PB	ROW	Multi	Total
US	0.0	0.0	0.0	0.0	0.0	0.0	0.0	0.0	0.0	0.0	0.0	0.0
Japan	0.0	0.0	0.0	0.0	0.0	0.0	0.0	0.0	0.0	0.0	0.0	0.0
EU	0.0	0.0	0.0	0.0	0.0	0.0	0.0	0.0	0.0	0.0	0.0	0.0
OOECD	0.0	0.0	0.0	0.0	0.0	0.0	0.0	0.0	0.0	0.0	0.0	0.0
CMEA	0.0	0.0	0.0	0.0	0.0	0.0	0.0	0.0	0.0	0.0	0.0	0.0
MOE	0.0	0.0	0.0	0.0	0.0	0.0	0.0	0.0	0.0	0.0	0.0	0.0
OB	0.7	0.1	0.5	0.2	0.0	0.0	0.0	0.0	0.0	0.0	0.3	1.8
DB	0.5	0.2	0.3	0.1	0.0	0.0	0.0	0.0	0.0	0.0	0.2	1.3
PB	0.0	0.1	1.2	0.2	0.1	0.0	0.0	0.0	0.0	0.0	0.4	1.9
ROW	0.0	0.0	0.0	0.0	0.0	0.0	0.0	0.0	0.0	0.0	0.0	0.0
Multi	0.0	0.0	0.0	0.0	0.0	0.0	0.0	0.0	0.0	0.0	0.0	0.0
Column totals:												
Total allocated	1.2	0.4	2.0	0.5	0.1	0.0	0.0	0.0	0.0	0.0	0.8	5.1
Unallocated	10.8	4.3	6.4	4.8	4.2	4.3	4.4	4.4	4.4	4.4	3.5	55.7
Raw marginals	11.9	4.7	8.4	5.3	4.4	4.4	4.4	4.4	4.4	4.4	4.4	60.8
Row totals:												
Total allocated	0.0	0.0	0.0	0.0	0.0	0.0	1.8	1.3	1.9	0.0	0.0	5.1
Unallocated	6.4	5.1	9.7	7.3	5.0	5.2	3.3	4.0	4.4	5.3	4.9	60.7
Raw marginals	6.4	5.1	9.7	7.3	5.0	5.2	5.1	5.3	6.3	5.4	5.0	65.8

Table A5.2 Raw matrices: 1975 current and capital accounts

1975 Current Account

	US	Japan	EU	OOECD	CMEA	MOE	OB	DB	PB	ROW	Multi	Total
US	0.0	9.9	25.8	29.6	3.1	4.7	9.3	4.1	18.3	5.9	0.0	110.6
Japan	12.6	0.0	6.6	5.1	2.5	4.0	6.8	5.9	9.0	4.5	0.0	57.0
EU	20.0	3.1	165.1	40.8	16.4	11.7	17.0	8.7	19.9	10.6	0.0	313.2
OOECD	26.6	6.7	31.1	12.9	6.4	1.8	3.9	2.5	4.7	2.6	0.0	99.1
CMEA	0.8	1.5	11.7	4.9	53.0	0.8	4.4	1.6	0.9	2.0	0.0	81.6
MOE	6.5	16.6	38.8	5.6	2.8	1.5	6.7	1.6	7.5	1.1	0.0	88.5
OB	10.8	2.8	12.9	2.3	5.3	1.9	3.6	1.0	1.4	1.0	1.1	44.2
DB	4.0	5.7	4.9	1.0	1.3	0.5	1.7	0.5	2.5	1.9	0.2	24.2
PB	16.6	4.8	16.0	4.2	2.0	0.9	5.4	2.0	5.1	1.9	0.2	59.1
ROW	6.1	2.4	9.0	2.7	2.7	0.6	1.5	0.7	1.3	0.9	0.0	27.8
Multi	0.0	0.0	0.0	0.0	0.0	0.0	0.2	0.2	0.4	0.0	0.0	0.8
Column totals:												
Total allocated	104.1	53.4	321.9	109.1	95.5	28.3	60.3	28.8	71.0	32.3	1.5	906.2
Unallocated	39.7	19.2	135.4	38.2	20.7	23.1	9.0	8.3	22.0	8.4	0.9	324.9
Raw marginals	143.8	72.6	457.3	147.3	116.2	51.4	69.3	37.0	93.0	40.6	2.4	1231.0
Row totals:												
Total allocated	110.6	57.0	313.2	99.1	81.6	88.5	44.2	24.2	59.1	27.8	0.8	906.2
Unallocated	47.2	13.1	137.7	33.2	17.6	10.9	11.1	7.9	19.9	14.5	1.6	314.6
Raw marginals	157.7	70.2	450.9	132.3	99.2	99.4	55.2	32.1	79.0	42.3	2.4	1220.8

(Continued)

Table A5.2 (Continued)

1975 Capital Account

	US	Japan	EU	OOECD	CMEA	MOE	OB	DB	PB	ROW	Multi	Total
US	0.0	0.0	0.0	0.0	0.0	0.0	0.0	0.0	0.0	0.0	0.0	0.0
Japan	0.0	0.0	0.0	0.0	0.0	0.0	0.0	0.0	0.0	0.0	0.0	0.0
EU	0.0	0.0	0.0	0.0	0.0	0.0	0.0	0.0	0.0	0.0	0.0	0.0
OOECD	0.0	0.0	0.0	0.0	0.0	0.0	0.0	0.0	0.0	0.0	0.0	0.0
CMEA	0.0	0.0	0.0	0.0	0.0	0.0	0.0	0.0	0.0	0.0	0.0	0.0
MOE	0.0	0.0	0.0	0.0	0.0	0.0	0.0	0.0	0.0	0.0	0.0	0.0
OB	0.7	0.2	1.0	0.2	0.1	3.1	0.0	0.0	0.0	0.0	1.5	6.7
DB	1.3	0.8	0.5	0.2	0.2	0.1	0.0	0.0	0.0	0.0	0.8	3.8
PB	2.0	0.4	1.4	0.1	0.0	0.1	0.0	0.0	0.0	0.0	1.3	5.2
ROW	0.0	0.0	0.0	0.0	0.0	0.0	0.0	0.0	0.0	0.0	0.0	0.0
Multi	0.0	0.0	0.0	0.0	0.0	0.0	0.0	0.0	0.0	0.0	0.0	0.0
Column totals:												
Total allocated	4.0	1.3	2.9	0.5	0.2	3.3	0.0	0.0	0.0	0.0	3.6	15.7
Unallocated	35.0	1.9	54.3	13.4	0.1	16.3	0.4	0.7	3.1	1.0	0.0	126.2
Raw marginals	39.0	3.2	57.2	13.9	0.3	19.6	0.4	0.7	3.1	1.0	3.6	141.9
Row totals:												
Total allocated	0.0	0.0	0.0	0.0	0.0	0.0	6.7	3.8	5.2	0.0	0.0	15.8
Unallocated	16.0	3.7	56.3	20.8	1.2	0.2	0.4	1.3	4.2	6.0	3.6	113.7
Raw marginals	16.0	3.7	56.3	20.8	1.2	0.2	7.2	5.1	9.4	6.0	3.6	129.5

Note: Columns may not tally due to rounding.

Table A5.3 Raw matrices: 1980 current and capital accounts

1980 Current Account

	US	Japan	EU	OOECD	CMEA	MOE	OB	DB	PB	ROW	Multi	Total
US	0.0	21.5	55.7	51.1	4.5	8.1	12.9	12.0	48.2	13.3	0.0	227.3
Japan	33.1	0.0	18.5	10.6	4.3	12.0	8.8	13.0	22.9	13.5	0.0	136.7
EU	41.6	7.2	393.6	86.0	27.4	33.1	34.4	15.7	51.9	23.8	0.0	714.7
OOECD	51.4	12.1	74.8	22.7	12.6	6.0	6.8	5.5	12.0	6.0	0.0	209.9
CMEA	1.6	2.6	32.9	11.7	92.3	2.6	8.7	3.5	1.5	5.1	0.0	162.5
MOE	29.7	46.3	84.5	12.9	5.2	5.5	13.7	6.7	24.2	5.9	0.0	234.6
OB	18.0	7.6	30.4	4.7	8.3	5.2	7.7	2.0	3.7	4.7	1.7	94.0
DB	9.7	17.7	12.5	2.7	3.4	1.9	3.0	1.3	7.4	5.1	0.4	65.1
PB	53.4	14.4	45.5	9.8	5.9	4.1	13.0	6.0	17.5	5.0	0.2	174.8
ROW	21.8	6.9	24.6	9.0	4.5	2.4	3.2	2.0	4.6	3.5	0.3	82.8
Multi	0.0	0.0	0.0	0.0	0.0	0.0	0.5	0.7	1.2	0.0	0.0	2.3
Column totals:												
Total allocated	260.2	136.2	773.0	221.2	168.4	80.7	112.7	68.5	195.1	85.7	2.6	2104.3
Unallocated	90.4	44.1	340.9	79.3	40.5	60.3	19.5	17.7	58.8	20.6	2.4	774.5
Raw marginals	350.5	180.3	1114.0	300.5	208.9	141.0	132.1	86.2	253.9	106.3	5.0	2878.8
Row totals:												
Total allocated	227.2	136.6	714.7	209.9	162.5	234.5	93.9	65.0	174.7	82.9	2.3	2104.3
Unallocated	108.0	27.8	339.4	67.4	36.3	26.1	30.1	17.3	54.3	28.8	2.7	738.2
Raw marginals	335.2	164.5	1054.1	277.4	198.8	260.7	124.0	82.2	228.9	111.7	5.1	2842.5

(Continued)

Table A5.3 (Continued)

1980 Capital Account

	US	Japan	EU	OOECD	CMEA	MOE	OB	DB	PB	ROW	Multi	Total
US	0.0	0.0	0.0	0.0	0.0	0.0	0.0	0.0	0.0	0.0	0.0	0.0
Japan	0.0	0.0	0.0	0.0	0.0	0.0	0.0	0.0	0.0	0.0	0.0	0.0
EU	0.0	0.0	0.0	0.0	0.0	0.0	0.0	0.0	0.0	0.0	0.0	0.0
OOECD	0.0	0.0	0.0	0.0	0.0	0.0	0.0	0.0	0.0	0.0	0.0	0.0
CMEA	0.0	0.0	0.0	0.0	0.0	0.0	0.0	0.0	0.0	0.0	0.0	0.0
MOE	0.0	0.0	0.0	0.0	0.0	0.0	0.0	0.0	0.0	0.0	0.0	0.0
OB	2.3	0.8	1.2	0.3	0.5	1.0	0.0	0.0	0.0	0.0	4.3	10.3
DB	0.5	0.8	2.0	0.7	0.2	0.9	0.0	0.0	0.0	0.0	2.4	7.5
PB	-1.1	2.1	5.8	2.2	0.0	0.0	0.0	0.0	0.0	0.0	2.0	11.0
ROW	0.0	0.0	0.0	0.0	0.0	0.0	0.0	0.0	0.0	0.0	0.0	0.0
Multi	0.0	0.0	0.0	0.0	0.0	0.0	0.0	0.0	0.0	0.0	0.0	0.0
Column totals:												
Total allocated	1.6	3.7	9.0	3.2	0.7	1.9	0.0	0.0	0.0	0.0	8.7	28.8
Unallocated	77.5	22.5	230.0	45.6	-0.1	49.0	1.5	0.7	9.6	4.6	0.0	441.0
Raw marginals	79.2	26.2	239.0	48.8	0.6	50.9	1.5	0.7	9.6	4.6	8.7	469.8
Row totals:												
Total allocated	0.0	0.0	0.0	0.0	0.0	0.0	10.3	7.5	11.0	0.0	0.0	28.8
Unallocated	59.3	45.1	277.2	53.6	6.8	-9.3	1.5	1.3	7.4	7.1	8.7	458.7
Raw marginals	59.3	45.1	277.2	53.6	6.8	-9.3	11.8	8.8	18.4	7.1	8.7	487.5

Note: Columns may not tally due to rounding.

Table A5.4 *Raw matrices: 1985 current and capital accounts*

1985 Current Account

	US	Japan	EU	OOECD	CMEA	MOE	OB	DB	PB	ROW	Multi	Total
US	0.0	23.9	48.3	65.5	3.2	6.1	14.6	13.0	47.2	11.4	0.0	233.1
Japan	69.0	0.0	21.0	14.9	3.6	10.4	11.5	22.1	21.3	12.9	0.0	186.8
EU	65.1	8.0	352.9	78.8	20.7	25.2	33.7	20.3	42.9	17.1	0.0	664.7
OOECD	81.0	13.9	66.7	20.4	9.2	4.9	7.8	6.1	10.8	5.1	0.0	226.0
CMEA	2.0	1.7	29.2	10.6	97.4	2.7	12.8	4.5	2.6	1.9	0.0	165.3
MOE	3.2	24.4	28.3	2.3	1.9	4.3	12.3	7.0	18.7	4.8	0.0	107.3
OB	14.9	5.0	23.0	3.8	10.3	5.1	6.2	1.5	3.9	1.8	7.1	82.8
DB	10.3	17.1	12.3	2.8	3.2	4.2	5.3	1.7	7.4	8.4	2.1	74.8
PB	59.0	16.1	42.3	8.8	3.8	5.0	14.5	7.8	20.6	6.4	1.3	185.6
ROW	26.9	5.8	14.1	5.1	5.4	1.8	3.1	5.7	3.6	3.4	0.0	75.0
Multi	0.0	0.0	0.0	0.0	0.0	0.0	1.0	1.7	2.2	0.0	0.0	4.9
Column totals:												
Total allocated	331.5	115.8	638.4	212.9	158.9	69.8	122.8	91.4	181.2	73.2	10.5	2006.3
Unallocated	138.7	52.4	338.3	99.0	39.1	47.3	19.9	22.5	45.2	18.3	2.5	823.1
Raw marginals	470.2	168.2	976.7	311.9	197.9	117.1	142.7	113.9	226.4	91.5	12.9	2829.3
Row totals:												
Total allocated	233.1	186.8	664.7	226.0	165.3	107.3	82.8	74.8	185.6	75.0	4.9	2006.3
Unallocated	126.8	39.0	332.0	79.1	37.7	27.4	23.4	25.0	53.8	27.7	12.9	784.8
Raw marginals	359.8	225.8	996.8	305.0	203.0	134.7	106.2	99.8	239.4	102.8	17.7	2791.0

(Continued)

Table A5.4 (Continued)

1985 Capital Account

	US	Japan	EU	OOECD	CMEA	MOE	OB	DB	PB	ROW	Multi	Total
US	0.0	0.0	0.0	0.0	0.0	0.0	0.0	0.0	0.0	0.0	0.0	0.0
Japan	0.0	0.0	0.0	0.0	0.0	0.0	0.0	0.0	0.0	0.0	0.0	0.0
EU	0.0	0.0	0.0	0.0	0.0	0.0	0.0	0.0	0.0	0.0	0.0	0.0
OOECD	0.0	0.0	0.0	0.0	0.0	0.0	0.0	0.0	0.0	0.0	0.0	0.0
CMEA	0.0	0.0	0.0	0.0	0.0	0.0	0.0	0.0	0.0	0.0	0.0	0.0
MOE	0.0	0.0	0.0	0.0	0.0	0.0	0.0	0.0	0.0	0.0	0.0	0.0
OB	0.9	1.5	2.5	0.2	0.4	0.5	0.0	0.0	0.0	0.0	4.6	10.7
DB	-0.4	4.6	2.2	-0.9	0.0	0.3	0.0	0.0	0.0	0.0	4.1	9.9
PB	3.8	-0.5	-6.8	-0.8	-0.2	-0.5	0.0	0.0	0.0	0.0	2.9	-2.2
ROW	0.0	0.0	0.0	0.0	0.0	0.0	0.0	0.0	0.0	0.0	0.0	0.0
Multi	0.0	0.0	0.0	0.0	0.0	0.0	0.0	0.0	0.0	0.0	0.0	0.0
Column totals:												
Total allocated	4.2	5.6	-2.1	-1.5	0.1	0.4	0.0	0.0	0.0	0.0	11.6	18.3
Unallocated	22.5	102.0	201.8	41.7	1.1	-10.0	1.7	2.4	10.5	1.5	-0.1	375.1
Raw marginals	26.7	107.6	199.7	40.2	1.2	-9.7	1.7	2.4	10.5	1.5	11.5	393.4
Row totals:												
Total allocated	0.0	0.0	0.0	0.0	0.0	0.0	10.7	9.9	-2.2	0.0	0.0	18.3
Unallocated	132.7	54.7	184.2	52.3	1.6	2.1	2.3	5.0	7.3	-1.6	11.5	452.2
Raw marginals	132.7	54.7	184.2	52.3	1.6	2.1	13.0	14.9	5.1	-1.6	11.5	470.5

Note: Columns may not tally due to rounding.

Table A5.5 A reconciled WAM for 1970 (in US$ billions)

bloc CT : Current Account

	US	Japan	EU	OO-ECD	CMEA	MOE	OB	DB	PB	ROW	Multi	Total receipts
US	0.0	7.7	16.4	17.9	0.6	7.1	4.0	2.4	8.7	3.3	0.1	68.1
Japan	8.0	0.0	2.7	2.3	0.6	0.6	2.2	2.0	3.1	2.0	0.1	23.7
EU	19.2	2.1	93.2	23.8	4.6	2.9	7.1	3.7	8.1	6.1	0.2	171.1
OOECD	18.9	3.3	17.9	7.3	2.2	0.4	1.9	1.1	2.1	1.5	0.1	56.6
CMEA	0.3	0.8	5.5	2.0	27.9	0.4	2.5	0.8	0.4	0.9	0.0	41.3
MOE	0.3	2.2	8.0	0.8	0.2	0.4	0.7	0.1	0.6	0.4	0.0	13.8
OB	4.4	1.4	7.8	1.4	2.6	0.6	2.1	0.4	0.6	0.6	0.1	21.9
DB	1.7	1.5	3.0	0.6	0.7	0.3	0.5	0.1	1.0	0.7	0.1	10.3
PB	7.1	2.3	8.0	1.9	0.8	0.2	1.8	0.5	2.5	0.5	0.1	25.7
ROW	4.6	1.2	4.0	1.2	1.0	0.2	0.9	0.2	0.5	0.4	0.0	14.2
Multi	0.0	0.0	0.0	0.0	0.0	0.0	0.1	0.1	0.2	0.0	0.0	0.5
Total payments	64.7	22.4	166.6	59.1	41.3	13.1	23.7	11.5	28.0	16.3	0.5	447.3

bloc S: Gross National Savings

	US	Japan	EU	OO-ECD	CMEA	MOE	OB	DB	PB	ROW	Multi	Total S
US	124.6											124.6
Japan		78.0										78.0
EU			160.1									160.1
OOECD				47.6								47.6
CMEA					50.8							50.8
MOE						5.2						5.2
OB							17.0					17.0
DB								36.0				36.0
PB									34.5			34.5
ROW										10.4		10.4
Multi											0.0	0.0
Total S	124.6	78.0	160.1	47.6	50.8	5.2	17.0	36.0	34.5	10.4	0.0	564.3
CT+S	189.3	100.4	326.7	106.7	92.1	18.3	40.7	47.5	62.4	26.7	0.5	1011.6

Note: Figures may not tally due to rounding.

Table A5.5 (Continued)

bloc I : Gross Domestic Investment

	US	Japan	EU	OO-ECD	CMEA	MOE	OB	DB	PB	ROW	Multi	Total I	CT+I
US	121.2											121.2	189.3
Japan		76.7										76.6	100.4
EU			155.6									155.6	326.7
OOECD				50.1								50.1	106.7
CMEA					50.8							50.8	92.1
MOE						4.5						4.5	18.3
OB							18.8					18.8	40.7
DB								37.2				37.2	47.6
PB									36.7			36.7	62.4
ROW										12.6		12.6	26.7
Multi											0.0	0.0	0.5
Total I	121.2	76.6	155.6	50.1	50.8	4.5	18.8	37.2	36.7	12.6	0.0	564.3	1011.6

bloc F : Capital Account Transactions

	US	Japan	EU	OO-ECD	CMEA	MOE	OB	DB	PB	ROW	Multi	Total receipts	S+F
US	0.0	1.4	3.1	1.1	-0.1	0.0	0.0	-0.0	0.1	0.2	0.0	5.9	130.5
Japan	1.5	0.0	0.2	0.3	0.0	0.1	0.0	-0.0	0.1	0.2	0.0	2.3	80.3
EU	3.7	0.3	19.6	0.5	0.0	0.1	0.0	-0.0	0.1	0.2	0.0	24.4	184.5
OOECD	5.6	0.1	0.8	0.3	0.0	0.1	0.0	-0.0	0.1	0.2	0.0	7.1	54.7
CMEA	0.0	0.0	0.0	0.0	-0.0	0.0	0.0	0.0	0.0	0.0	0.0	0.0	50.8
MOE	0.1	0.0	0.0	0.0	0.0	-0.1	0.0	0.0	0.0	0.0	0.0	0.1	5.3
OB	0.9	0.1	0.5	0.2	0.0	-0.0	0.0	0.0	0.0	0.0	0.3	2.0	19.0
DB	0.6	0.3	0.3	0.1	0.0	0.0	0.0	0.0	0.0	0.0	0.2	1.5	37.5
PB	1.0	0.2	1.5	0.3	0.1	-0.0	0.0	0.0	0.0	0.0	0.3	3.5	38.0
ROW	-0.1	-0.0	0.1	0.1	0.0	0.0	0.0	0.0	0.0	0.0	0.0	0.2	10.6
Multi	0.2	0.2	0.2	0.2	0.0	0.0	0.0	0.0	0.0	0.0	0.0	0.8	0.8
Total paym'ts	13.4	2.7	26.5	3.1	-0.0	0.2	0.1	-0.1	0.3	0.9	0.8	47.8	612.1
Reserves	-4.2	1.0	2.4	1.5	0.0	0.6	0.2	0.4	0.9	-2.8	0.0	0.0	
I+F	130.5	80.3	184.5	54.7	50.8	5.3	19.0	37.5	38.0	10.6	0.8	612.1	

Table A5.6 A reconciled WAM for 1975 (in US$ billions)

bloc CT : Current Account Transactions

	US	Japan	EU	OO-ECD	CMEA	MOE	OB	DB	PB	ROW	Multi	Total receipts
US	0.0	15.1	42.0	37.1	3.9	10.2	9.7	7.0	22.9	9.4	0.2	157.5
Japan	17.1	0.0	8.5	6.5	2.9	5.2	7.5	7.2	10.6	5.2	0.1	70.8
EU	32.8	4.7	237.5	56.0	16.5	21.2	17.8	11.5	29.0	13.3	0.4	440.9
OOECD	33.1	9.7	46.2	18.2	6.8	2.6	4.4	3.0	5.8	3.1	0.1	133.1
CMEA	1.2	2.1	21.5	7.1	61.1	1.1	5.6	2.1	1.1	2.6	0.0	105.6
MOE	6.9	19.3	42.7	7.4	2.9	2.5	7.0	1.7	7.9	1.2	0.0	99.3
OB	14.5	3.7	16.1	2.6	6.0	7.1	4.2	1.4	1.6	1.2	0.7	58.9
DB	5.1	7.4	6.7	1.3	1.5	0.6	2.0	0.6	3.9	2.2	0.6	31.7
PB	20.5	7.0	26.5	7.2	2.5	1.2	5.9	2.5	6.7	2.3	0.2	82.6
ROW	11.6	3.2	12.4	3.7	3.2	0.8	1.8	0.9	1.7	1.1	0.0	40.5
Multi	0.4	0.2	0.6	0.4	0.0	0.0	0.2	0.2	0.4	0.0	0.0	2.4
Total payments	143.1	72.4	460.8	147.4	107.4	52.4	66.1	38.1	91.6	41.6	2.4	1223.2

bloc S : Gross National Savings

	US	Japan	EU	OO-ECD	CMEA	MOE	OB	DB	PB	ROW	Multi	Total S
US	226.6											226.6
Japan		165.1										165.1
EU			307.1									307.1
OOECD				111.5								111.5
CMEA					95.2							95.2
MOE						83.4						83.4
OB							29.8					29.8
DB								75.7				75.7
PB									99.6			99.6
ROW										28.4		28.4
Multi											0.0	0.0
Total S	226.6	165.1	307.1	111.5	95.2	83.4	29.8	75.7	99.6	28.4	0.0	1222.3

CT+S	369.8	237.5	767.9	258.8	202.6	135.8	95.9	113.7	191.1	70.0	2.4	2445.6

Note: Figures may not tally due to rounding.

Table A5.6 (Continued)

bloc I : Gross Domestic Investment

	US	Japan	EU	OO-ECD	CMEA	MOE	OB	DB	PB	ROW	Multi	Total I	CT+I
US	212.3											212.3	369.8
Japan		166.7										166.7	237.5
EU			327.0									327.0	767.9
OOECD				125.8								125.8	258.8
CMEA					97.0							97.0	202.6
MOE						36.5						36.5	135.8
OB							36.9					36.9	95.9
DB								82.0				82.0	113.7
PB									108.6			108.6	191.1
ROW										29.5		29.5	70.0
Multi											0.0	0.0	2.4
Total I	212.3	166.7	327.0	125.8	97.0	36.5	36.9	82.0	108.6	29.5	0.0	1222.3	2445.6

bloc F : Capital Account Transactions

	US	Japan	EU	OO-ECD	CMEA	MOE	OB	DB	PB	ROW	Multi	Total inflows	S+F
US	0.0	-0.2	16.3	2.0	0.0	2.1	-0.2	0.8	0.5	1.4	0.0	22.7	249.3
Japan	0.0	0.0	8.2	-4.3	0.0	0.0	0.0	0.0	0.0	0.0	0.0	3.9	169.0
EU	14.7	0.2	4.7	13.1	0.0	28.4	0.0	0.0	0.0	0.1	0.0	61.2	368.3
OOECD	9.1	0.1	8.9	-4.6	0.0	10.9	0.0	0.0	0.1	0.0	0.0	24.6	136.1
CMEA	1.8	0.0	0.0	0.0	0.0	0.0	0.0	0.0	0.0	0.0	0.0	1.8	97.0
MOE	0.7	0.3	0.0	0.0	0.0	-0.9	0.0	0.0	0.0	0.0	0.0	0.2	83.6
OB	0.9	0.2	1.2	0.2	0.1	3.1	0.0	0.0	0.0	0.0	1.5	7.3	37.1
DB	1.9	1.1	0.6	0.2	0.2	0.1	0.0	0.0	0.0	0.0	0.8	4.9	80.5
PB	5.8	0.7	2.6	0.6	0.0	0.1	0.0	0.0	0.0	0.0	1.3	11.0	110.6
ROW	0.4	0.0	-0.1	0.1	0.0	0.0	0.0	0.0	0.0	0.0	0.0	0.5	28.9
Multi	0.9	0.6	1.5	0.6	0.0	0.0	0.0	0.0	0.0	0.0	0.0	3.6	3.6
Total	36.2	3.0	44.0	7.9	0.2	43.9	-0.2	0.9	0.7	1.5	3.6	141.7	1364.0
Reserves	0.8	-0.7	-2.8	2.4	-0.1	3.3	0.3	-2.4	1.3	-2.1	0.0	0.0	
I+F	249.3	169.0	368.3	136.1	97.0	83.6	37.1	80.5	110.6	28.9	3.6	1364.0	

Table A5.7 A reconciled WAM for 1980 (in US$ billions)

bloc CT : Current Account Transactions

	US	Japan	EU	OO-ECD	CMEA	MOE	OB	DB	PB	ROW	Multi	Total receipts
US	0.0	32.5	98.1	64.6	8.9	20.1	16.1	18.6	64.7	23.4	0.5	347.6
Japan	42.5	0.0	21.7	12.7	4.9	15.0	10.1	15.1	26.6	15.5	0.3	164.5
EU	61.1	12.1	613.3	113.7	33.9	62.6	41.0	20.7	70.9	29.8	1.0	1059.9
OOECD	61.2	17.7	95.5	41.1	15.6	8.2	8.8	6.9	16.1	7.7	0.5	279.3
CMEA	1.9	3.2	42.2	14.5	112.2	3.2	10.5	4.2	1.8	6.2	0.0	200.1
MOE	36.5	51.2	90.6	16.2	5.4	8.4	14.2	7.0	25.0	6.1	0.0	260.7
OB	22.1	9.6	40.7	5.9	10.0	9.4	9.2	2.4	4.5	5.6	1.8	121.1
DB	12.1	22.3	14.7	3.3	4.0	5.4	3.5	1.5	8.7	5.9	0.4	81.8
PB	76.9	22.4	60.2	14.8	7.1	7.0	15.6	7.5	22.3	6.0	0.2	240.3
ROW	32.3	8.7	28.9	11.5	5.4	2.8	3.8	2.4	5.6	4.2	0.3	106.1
Multi	0.5	0.4	1.0	0.8	0.0	0.0	0.5	0.7	1.1	0.0	0.0	5.0
Total payments	347.2	180.2	1106.9	299.2	207.4	142.3	133.3	87.0	247.4	110.5	5.0	2866.3

bloc S : Gross National Savings

	US	Japan	EU	OO-ECD	CMEA	MOE	OB	DB	PB	ROW	Multi	Total S
US	435.7											435.7
Japan		327.8										327.8
EU			668.4									668.4
OOECD				197.5								197.5
CMEA					177.3							177.3
MOE						213.7						213.7
OB							60.0					60.0
DB								158.4				158.4
PB									242.6			242.6
ROW										70.8		70.8
Multi											0.0	0.0
Total S	435.7	327.8	668.4	197.5	177.3	213.7	60.0	158.4	242.6	70.8	0.0	2552.3

CT+S	782.9	508.0	1775.3	496.8	384.7	355.9	193.3	245.5	490.0	181.3	5.0	5418.6

Note: Figures may not tally due to rounding.

Table A5.7 (Continued)

bloc I : Gross Domestic Investment

	US	Japan	EU	OO-ECD	CMEA	MOE	OB	DB	PB	ROW	Multi	Total I	CT+I
US	435.4											435.4	782.9
Japan		343.5										343.5	508.0
EU			715.4									715.4	1775.3
OOECD				217.5								217.5	496.8
CMEA					184.6							184.6	384.7
MOE						95.3						95.3	355.9
OB							72.1					72.1	193.3
DB								163.7				163.7	245.5
PB									249.6			249.6	490.0
ROW										75.2		75.2	181.3
Multi											0.0	0.0	5.0
Total I	435.4	343.5	715.4	217.5	184.6	95.3	72.1	163.7	249.6	75.2	0.0	2552.3	5418.6

bloc F : Capital Account Transactions

	US	Japan	EU	OO-ECD	CMEA	MOE	OB	DB	PB	ROW	Multi	Total inflows	S+F
US	0.0	9.0	27.9	16.3	0.0	12.5	0.6	0.3	2.3	10.6	0.0	79.4	515.1
Japan	17.3	0.0	-0.7	-6.2	0.0	32.1	0.5	0.1	2.1	0.0	0.0	45.1	372.9
EU	36.9	2.6	178.5	26.9	0.0	32.8	0.5	0.1	2.2	0.4	0.0	280.9	949.4
OOECD	12.7	2.8	14.4	-6.9	0.0	32.4	0.5	0.2	2.1	0.0	0.0	58.1	255.7
CMEA	1.2	6.3	0.0	0.0	0.0	0.0	0.0	0.0	0.0	0.0	0.0	7.5	184.8
MOE	-3.5	-0.7	-0.5	0.0	0.0	-4.7	0.0	0.0	0.0	0.0	0.0	-9.4	204.3
OB	2.7	0.9	2.0	0.3	0.4	1.0	0.0	0.0	0.0	0.0	4.3	11.6	71.6
DB	1.0	1.3	2.2	0.7	0.2	0.9	0.0	0.0	0.0	0.0	2.4	8.7	167.2
PB	4.1	3.0	7.3	2.6	0.0	0.0	0.0	0.0	0.1	0.0	2.0	19.2	261.8
ROW	1.7	-0.1	0.1	0.2	0.0	0.0	0.0	0.0	0.0	0.0	0.0	1.9	72.6
Multi	2.1	1.1	3.9	1.6	0.0	0.0	0.0	0.0	0.0	0.0	0.0	8.7	8.7
Total payments	76.2	26.2	235.0	35.5	0.6	106.9	2.0	0.8	8.8	11.1	8.7	511.8	3064.1
Reserves	3.6	3.3	-1.0	2.7	-0.4	2.0	-2.5	2.7	3.4	-13.7	0.0	0.0	
I+F	515.1	372.9	949.3	255.7	184.8	204.3	71.6	167.2	261.8	72.6	8.7	3064.1	

Table A5.8 A reconciled WAM for 1985 (in US$ billions)

bloc CT : Current Account Transactions

	US	Japan	EU	OO-ECD	CMEA	MOE	OB	DB	PB	ROW	Multi	Total receipts
US	0.0	43.0	90.2	93.3	4.3	11.4	16.9	19.0	61.7	24.1	1.0	364.9
Japan	84.0	0.0	30.4	17.3	4.0	13.0	13.0	25.5	24.5	14.4	0.6	226.9
EU	102.6	16.7	555.3	129.4	31.0	51.9	33.0	26.8	54.8	19.6	2.3	1023.6
OOECD	118.3	18.7	87.1	25.9	11.3	6.6	9.2	7.5	13.7	6.3	1.0	305.6
CMEA	2.4	2.0	35.7	12.9	119.1	3.4	14.5	5.5	3.2	2.2	0.1	201.1
MOE	7.4	26.6	43.2	3.0	2.1	6.4	13.1	7.5	20.1	5.1	0.0	134.5
OB	21.9	7.4	31.8	6.0	13.0	13.1	8.1	2.3	6.0	2.5	6.1	118.2
DB	13.5	23.3	15.5	3.8	4.1	7.1	6.5	2.2	9.8	9.8	2.0	97.5
PB	77.9	21.1	53.1	10.6	4.6	7.6	16.5	9.7	26.3	7.6	1.3	236.2
ROW	35.0	8.0	17.4	6.2	6.5	2.4	3.8	7.0	4.6	4.1	3.4	98.5
Multi	2.9	1.0	6.0	3.0	0.0	0.0	1.0	1.6	2.2	0.0	0.0	17.7
Total payments	466.0	167.9	965.7	311.5	200.1	123.0	135.6	114.8	226.8	95.8	17.7	2824.8

bloc S : Gross National Savings

	US	Japan	EU	OO-ECD	CMEA	MOE	OB	DB	PB	ROW	Multi	Total S
US	551.3											551.3
Japan		435.1										435.1
EU			537.5									537.5
OOECD				201.7								201.7
CMEA					196.6							196.6
MOE						113.9						113.9
OB							72.0					72.0
DB								160.4				160.4
PB									179.8			179.8
ROW										53.6		53.6
Multi											0.0	0.0
Total S	551.3	435.1	537.5	201.7	196.6	113.9	72.0	160.4	179.8	53.6	0.0	2502.0
CT+S	017.3	603.0	1503.2	513.2	396.7	236.9	207.5	275.2	406.7	149.4	17.7	5326.8

Note: Figures may not tally due to rounding.

Table A5.8 (Continued)

bloc I : Gross Domestic Investment

	US	Japan	EU	OO-ECD	CMEA	MOE	OB	DB	PB	ROW	Multi	Total I	CT+I
US	652.4											652.4	1017.3
Japan		376.1										376.1	603.0
EU			479.6									479.6	1503.2
OOECD				207.5								207.5	513.2
CMEA					195.6							195.6	396.7
MOE						102.4						102.4	236.9
OB							89.3					89.3	207.5
DB								177.7				177.7	275.2
PB									170.4			170.4	406.7
ROW										50.9		50.9	149.4
Multi											0.0	0.0	17.7
Total	652.4	376.1	479.6	207.5	195.6	102.4	89.3	177.7	170.4	50.9	0.0	2502.0	5326.8

bloc F : Capital Account Transactions

	US	Japan	EU	OO-ECD	CMEA	MOE	OB	DB	PB	ROW	Multi	Total inflows	S+F
US	0.0	40.7	55.1	12.3	0.0	9.5	-2.2	2.1	12.2	0.0	-0.0	129.7	681.0
Japan	2.1	0.0	50.2	1.4	0.0	0.0	0.0	0.0	0.1	0.4	0.0	54.3	489.4
EU	7.9	41.8	96.9	27.8	1.3	-0.4	0.0	0.0	0.2	0.5	-0.0	176.0	713.5
OOECD	3.7	18.0	23.5	1.5	-0.0	2.4	0.0	0.6	0.1	0.4	-0.0	50.2	251.9
CMEA	-1.4	0.6	1.9	0.4	0.0	0.0	0.0	0.0	0.0	0.0	0.0	1.5	198.1
MOE	-0.3	2.2	-0.0	0.0	0.0	0.0	0.0	0.0	0.0	0.0	0.0	2.0	115.9
OB	1.9	2.6	4.6	0.2	0.6	0.5	0.0	0.0	0.0	0.0	4.5	15.0	87.0
DB	2.3	5.7	2.4	-0.9	-0.0	0.3	0.0	0.1	0.0	0.0	4.1	14.0	174.4
PB	7.9	-0.1	-2.9	-2.4	-0.2	-0.5	0.0	0.0	0.0	0.0	2.9	4.8	184.7
ROW	0.2	0.1	-1.4	-0.2	-0.2	0.0	0.0	0.0	0.0	0.0	0.0	-1.6	52.0
Multi	2.5	1.5	5.0	2.5	0.0	0.0	0.0	0.0	0.0	0.0	0.0	11.5	11.5
Total outflows	26.8	113.1	235.4	42.6	1.4	11.9	-2.2	2.8	12.6	1.3	11.5	457.3	2959.4
Reserves	1.8	0.2	-1.4	1.7	1.1	1.6	-0.2	-6.1	1.6	-0.3	0.0	0.0	
I+F	681.0	489.4	713.5	251.9	115.9	87.0	174.4	184.7	1.6	52.0	11.5	2959.4	

A7 Appendix to Chapter 7

Table A7.1 The geographical distribution of the market effect (in US$ billions)

	US	Japan	EU	OOECD	CMEA	MOE	OB	DB	PB	ROW	Total
(A) Merchandise trade											
1970-75											
OB											
SITC 0-1	0.3	-0.3	-0.8	-0.2	0.7	0.4	0.1	-0.2	-0.4	-0.1	-0.4
SITC 2+4	0.0	-0.0	-0.1	-0.1	0.1	-0.0	0.2	0.2	-0.2	0.1	0.1
SITC 3	4.8	-1.0	-2.0	-0.1	-0.2	0.0	0.4	-0.0	0.5	-0.1	2.3
SITC 5-9	-0.1	0.3	0.1	-0.8	-0.3	0.4	1.0	-0.0	-0.4	-0.1	0.2
Total	5.0	-1.0	-2.8	-1.2	0.3	0.8	1.7	-0.1	-0.4	-0.1	2.2
DB											
SITC 0-1	0.1	0.1	-0.3	-0.1	-0.1	0.0	-0.1	-0.0	0.2	0.4	0.1
SITC 2+4	-0.0	0.2	-0.1	-0.1	-0.1	-0.0	-0.0	-0.0	0.2	-0.0	0.0
SITC 3	0.2	1.0	-0.8	-0.0	-0.1	-0.0	-0.0	0.1	0.2	-0.0	0.6
SITC 5-9	0.1	0.1	-0.4	-0.3	-0.0	0.2	0.1	-0.1	0.3	0.1	0.1
Total	0.3	1.5	-1.5	-0.5	-0.3	0.2	-0.0	-0.1	0.9	0.5	0.9
PB											
SITC 0-1	0.6	-0.0	-0.3	-0.2	-0.4	-0.3	-0.5	-0.1	0.4	-0.1	-0.8
SITC 2+4	0.2	0.3	-0.4	-0.2	-0.1	0.0	-0.1	0.1	0.3	0.0	0.1
SITC 3	4.5	-2.7	-2.4	0.1	-1.0	-0.1	3.3	0.2	0.4	-0.2	2.2
SITC 5-9	0.8	0.2	-0.5	-0.6	-0.8	-0.3	-0.2	0.1	1.1	-0.1	-0.4
Total	6.0	-2.2	-3.5	-0.8	-2.4	-0.7	2.6	0.3	2.3	-0.4	1.1

(Continued)

Table A7.1 (Continued)

	US	Japan	EU	OOECD	CMEA	MOE	OB	DB	PB	ROW	Total
1975-80											
OB											
SITC 0-1	1.0	-0.3	-1.2	-0.2	1.6	0.7	-0.0	-0.0	-0.8	-0.2	0.5
SITC 2+4	-0.1	-0.1	0.1	-0.3	0.1	0.0	0.1	0.3	-0.3	0.0	-0.1
SITC 3	9.0	-1.0	-4.0	-1.1	-0.4	-0.1	-0.2	-0.2	-0.6	-0.1	1.1
SITC 5-9	0.3	0.4	-0.4	-0.9	-0.1	0.9	0.7	-0.1	-0.3	-0.2	0.2
Total	10.1	-1.0	-5.5	-2.5	1.2	1.4	0.6	-0.0	-2.1	-0.4	1.7
DB											
SITC 0-1	0.3	0.2	-0.8	-0.1	-0.4	-0.1	-0.0	0.1	0.4	0.6	0.1
SITC 2+4	-0.0	0.4	-0.3	-0.1	-0.1	-0.0	-0.0	-0.1	0.5	0.1	0.3
SITC 3	1.9	4.4	-4.3	-0.8	-0.3	-0.1	-0.1	-0.3	0.3	-0.1	0.7
SITC 5-9	-0.1	0.9	-1.0	-0.5	-0.1	0.1	0.2	-0.1	0.4	0.7	0.5
Total	2.1	5.9	-6.4	-1.6	-0.9	-0.1	0.1	-0.3	1.6	1.3	1.6
PB											
SITC 0-1	1.0	0.3	-1.1	-0.2	-0.0	0.2	-0.1	0.0	0.5	-0.0	0.6
SITC 2+4	0.5	0.2	-0.8	-0.2	-0.2	0.1	-0.1	0.2	0.6	-0.1	0.4
SITC 3	8.3	-4.8	-4.4	-0.0	-1.2	-0.3	2.8	0.6	-1.0	2.0	1.8
SITC 5-9	4.2	1.9	-2.5	-1.3	-1.2	-0.5	0.0	0.2	1.4	-0.4	1.8
Total	14.1	-2.4	-8.7	-1.8	-2.6	-0.7	2.7	1.1	1.5	1.5	4.7
1980-85											
OB											
SITC 0-1	0.2	-0.0	0.1	-0.0	0.2	-0.0	0.1	0.1	0.2	0.0	0.9
SITC 2+4	0.0	0.0	-0.1	0.1	0.0	0.0	0.0	0.0	0.0	0.0	0.1
SITC 3	-1.7	0.2	1.0	0.6	-0.5	0.0	-0.2	-0.0	-0.0	-0.2	-0.8
SITC 5-9	-0.4	0.1	0.2	-0.1	-0.4	-0.0	0.2	-0.1	0.2	-0.0	-0.4
Total	-1.9	0.2	1.2	0.5	-0.8	-0.0	0.1	0.0	0.5	-0.2	-0.3
DB											
SITC 0-1	0.0	0.0	0.2	0.0	0.1	0.0	-0.0	0.0	-0.1	-0.1	0.2
SITC 2+4	0.0	-0.3	0.3	0.1	0.0	0.0	-0.1	-0.0	-0.0	0.0	-0.0
SITC 3	-0.2	-2.4	2.1	0.5	-0.5	0.0	0.1	-0.0	0.0	0.0	-0.4
SITC 5-9	-0.0	0.1	0.3	-0.1	0.0	-0.0	0.1	-0.1	-0.2	-0.3	-0.2
Total	-0.2	-2.6	2.9	0.5	-0.3	0.0	0.0	-0.1	-0.3	-0.3	-0.4
PB											
SITC 0-1	0.2	0.0	0.4	0.1	-0.2	0.0	-0.1	-0.0	-0.1	0.0	0.3
SITC 2+4	0.0	-0.3	0.6	0.1	0.0	-0.1	0.1	0.0	-0.1	-0.0	0.4
SITC 3	-6.6	2.0	1.9	0.4	-1.6	0.1	-0.4	-0.0	-0.0	0.1	-4.0
SITC 5-9	6.5	0.2	1.2	-0.3	0.6	0.1	0.1	0.5	-0.8	-0.0	8.2
Total	0.1	2.0	4.0	0.4	-1.1	0.1	-0.3	0.5	-1.0	0.1	4.8

(Continued)

Table A7.1 (Continued)

	US	Japan	EU	OOECD	CMEA	MOE	OB	DB	PB	ROW	Multi	Total
(B) Capital inflows												
1970-75												
OB	0.5	0.0	-0.4	0.1	0.0	-1.8	0.0	0.0	0.0	0.0	0.8	-0.9
DB	0.3	0.0	-0.4	0.0	0.0	0.3	0.0	0.0	0.0	0.0	0.6	0.8
PB	0.1	0.0	-0.3	0.2	0.0	-4.6	0.0	-0.1	-0.0	-0.0	1.0	-3.8
1975-80												
OB	-1.0	0.6	-4.5	-0.6	0.2	1.3	-0.1	0.0	-0.4	-0.5	1.8	-3.4
DB	0.7	7.3	-3.8	-0.4	0.4	-2.0	-0.1	0.0	0.0	-0.3	1.0	2.8
PB	3.3	3.2	-3.7	0.1	-0.1	-4.8	-0.2	0.0	-0.2	-0.7	1.5	-1.6
1980-85												
OB	-0.6	1.2	0.0	-0.1	0.6	1.3	0.1	0.1	-0.1	0.2	1.3	3.8
DB	0.2	2.9	0.0	0.0	0.3	0.8	0.1	0.0	-0.1	0.2	0.7	5.1
PB	-0.8	6.6	0.0	0.3	0.0	3.6	0.2	0.0	-0.1	0.4	0.5	10.6
(C) Foreign debt												
1975-80												
OB												
FDI	0.4	0.0	1.7	0.6	0.0	-0.2	0.2	-0.0	-0.1	-0.6	0.0	2.1
Official	-0.3	-2.1	-1.0	-1.4	0.5	4.7	0.0	0.0	0.0	0.0	-1.0	-0.8
Private	-1.8	-0.2	1.8	-0.1	4.9	0.1	-0.1	-0.3	-2.6	-0.9	0.0	0.7
Total	-1.7	-2.3	2.4	-0.9	5.3	4.5	0.1	-0.3	-2.7	-1.4	-1.0	2.0
DB												
FDI	1.1	0.7	-2.4	0.6	0.0	-0.2	0.3	0.1	0.1	0.1	0.0	0.4
Official	0.4	1.1	-0.4	-1.0	0.6	-1.2	0.0	0.0	0.0	0.0	0.0	-0.5
Private	4.9	5.0	-7.1	-0.7	3.8	-1.1	-0.3	-0.6	-5.9	-2.0	0.0	-4.0
Total	6.4	6.7	-10.0	-1.1	4.4	-2.4	0.0	-0.5	-5.8	-1.9	0.0	-4.1
PB												
FDI	0.5	0.0	-4.4	-1.5	0.0	-0.7	0.2	0.4	0.1	-1.8	0.0	-7.1
Official	0.6	-0.4	-3.2	-1.3	-0.4	-1.7	0.0	0.0	0.0	0.0	6.7	0.3
Private	12.7	1.9	5.6	-1.0	-0.6	-3.3	-0.6	-1.0	-10.6	-3.5	0.0	-0.5
Total	13.9	1.4	-2.0	-3.9	-1.0	-5.7	-0.4	-0.6	-10.5	-5.3	6.7	-7.4
1980-85												
OB												
FDI	0.0	0.6	0.3	-0.3	0.0	-0.0	0.0	-0.0	-0.0	-0.1	0.0	0.6
Official	-0.2	-2.5	-3.4	-3.7	0.3	2.6	0.0	0.0	0.0	0.0	5.6	-1.3
Private	-0.7	0.9	0.8	1.5	0.1	-0.1	-0.4	-0.6	-3.9	-1.9	0.0	-4.4
Total	-0.9	-0.9	-2.3	-2.5	0.4	2.4	-0.4	-0.6	-3.9	-2.0	5.6	-5.0
DB												
FDI	-0.1	2.3	-1.4	-0.7	0.0	-0.0	-0.0	-0.0	0.2	0.0	0.0	0.3
Official	-1.0	0.8	-0.8	-1.5	0.3	-0.1	0.0	0.0	0.0	0.0	3.0	0.6
Private	0.3	16.0	-0.2	2.5	-0.0	-0.4	-0.7	-1.0	-6.8	-3.4	0.0	6.3
Total	-0.9	19.0	-2.3	0.4	0.2	-0.6	-0.7	-1.0	-6.6	-3.3	3.0	7.2
PB												
FDI	0.1	0.5	-0.4	3.6	0.0	-0.2	-0.0	0.0	0.0	-0.4	0.0	3.2
Official	1.3	0.6	-2.8	-0.9	-0.1	-0.9	0.0	0.0	0.0	0.0	6.3	3.5
Private	7.0	50.1	1.3	4.8	-0.7	-2.0	-3.5	-4.6	-32.7	-16.2	0.0	3.8
Total	8.4	51.2	-1.9	7.5	-0.7	-3.0	-3.5	-4.6	-32.6	-16.6	6.3	10.5

Note: Due to rounding columns may not tally.

Notes

Chapter 1

1. As will be explained in Chapter 2, the matrices are linked through the global accounting identity. To satisfy the accounting constraints, the WAM includes a matrix for gross domestic investment and gross national (instead of domestic) saving.
2. See Machlup (1983) for a clear exposition of balance of payments accounting.
3. The term billion signifies 1,000 million.
4. The WAMs for 1970, 1975, 1980 and 1985 are the WAMs described in this study. A series of WAMs for 1985–90, constructed following the same methodology but for different country groups, is described in de Jong, Vos et al. (1993a & b).
5. The title of the half-yearly BIS/OECD publication is: *Statistics on External Indebtedness: Bank and Trade-Related Non-Bank External Claims on Individual Borrowing Countries and Territories.*
6. These and other country groups are defined in Chapter 2, and presented in Table A2.1.

Chapter 2

1. In national accounting, government spending and government savings are usually included separately from similar categories of the private sector. Here, transactions of the government sector are included in total investment, consumption and savings.
2. See Dornbusch (1980) for an exposition of the national income identity of an open economy.
3. The net capital outflow is equal to net changes in the stock of foreign assets adjusted for valuation changes.

4. See for example, the World Bank, *World Debt Tables* (various issues) for data on official and private lending to LDCs.
5. Long-term external debt is defined by the World Bank as debt that has an original or an extended maturity of over one year and short-term debt is debt that has an original maturity of one year or less (World Bank, *World Debt Tables*, various issues). Chapter 4 discusses the debt definitions of the World Bank, among others, in fuller detail.
6. These are the major categories in the balance of payments statistics of the IMF.
7. Capital flight from LDCs is considered as 'asset accumulation of the private sector in LDCs' and will not be treated differently from asset accumulation by other transactors.

Chapter 3

1. The UNTMS is compiled by the United Nations Department of International Economic & Social Affairs (UNDIESA), from the UN Commodity Trade Statistics.
2. For example, the IMF *Balance of Payments Statistics*: includes only three CMEA countries: Hungary, Poland and Rumania; from the MOEs, Brunei, Qatar and the United Arab Emirates are not included; LDCs are included with the exception of Cape Verde, Djibouti, Guinea and Lebanon. In many instances observations are missing for particular years or variables. However, the difference in country coverage is not the only explanatory factor, since there are also – unexplained – differences between the estimates for individual countries.
3. The surplus on the balance for merchandise trade in the period 1973-81 has been analysed by the IMF (1983). The study suggests that the surplus may partly be explained by (1) the use of unduly large adjustment factors to convert import data on a c.i.f. basis to an f.o.b. basis; (2) the timing asymmetry due to world trade in transit, i.e. already recorded by one country as an export, but not yet recorded by another as an import.
4. See IMF (1977) for an extensive list of this type of transaction.
5. The tables are available for US, Japan, EU (except Greece and Portugal), OOECD (except Australia, Iceland and New Zealand), OB (Mauritius, Swaziland, Togo, Zambia), DB (Paraguay, Peru, Thailand, Turkey), PB (Chile, Korea, Malaysia, Panama, Singapore, Uruguay, Venezuela) and ROW (South Africa, Israel).

6. See the country notes in the (BOP) Balance of Payments Statistics (yearbooks).
7. Calculations from the stock tables in Dunning and Cantwell (1987) show that their average share in world assets has been circa 80 per cent; their average share in world liabilities has been circa 50 per cent.
8. The adjustment in the report for credits not matched by debits for 1983 amounted to US$ 12.8 billions.
9. There are some systematic tendencies in reporting of direct investment that lead to an excess of assets and related income over liabilities and related payments. However, a large share of the global discrepancies results from differences in recording practices between individual countries, including the major creditor countries. For example, the US balance of payments statistics included exchange rate-related capital gains/losses on direct investment up to 1990. As no other country followed the US practice, a discrepancy was inevitable (IMF 1987). Another example: a loan for a Dutch subsidiary of a UK parent is recorded as an outward disinvestment by the UK in the UK statistics, but is recorded as outward investment by the Netherlands in the Dutch statistics (Turner 1991: 110).
10. See Dunning and Cantwell (1987), Kragenau (1976, 1987). The UNCTC is currently continuing the Dunning and Cantwell project, but has published results only for Asia and the Pacific (UNCTC 1992).
11. The main reason why the World Bank DRS has been used instead of the OECD Creditor Reporting System, is that the OECD does not provide any detail on the geographical distribution by origin and destination of LDC debt. The DRS is generally seen as the most complete and reliable source for external long-term debt of LDCs (cf. Tims & Waelbroeck 1982, Dooley 1988).
12. Published in the *Maturity Distribution of International Bank Lending* (BIS, various issues).
13. A debt-for-equity swap will reduce total external debt according to the core definition, but will not alter total external debt in the BOP.
14. See, for example, Tims and Waelbroeck (1982). This link is also suggested by the World Bank itself (World Debt Tables, 1988/89).
15. Although Dooley studied capital flight from Argentina, Brazil, Chile, Mexico, Peru, the Philippines and Venezuela, the argument may, to some extent apply to other countries as well. See for example Naylor (1987) for an analysis of 'hot money'.
16. See de Jong et al. (1993a & b).
17. See IMF (1977) *Balance of Payments Manual.*

18. See OECD (various issues) *Geographical Distribution of Financial Flows to Developing Countries.*
19. See, for example, World Bank, *World Debt Tables* (1985), Cuddington (1986), Lessard and Williamson (1987b).
20. See the introduction to the 1988–89 edition of the *World Tables.*
21. Most definitions in the *World Tables* series on the Origin and Use of Resources are from the United Nations (1968), *A System of National Accounts*, series F, No. 2, revision 3.
22. The definitions for domestic transactions in this section are the definitions given in the 1988–89 edition of the World Tables (pp. 7–8). In some instances, the definitions are derived from the WT and presented in an abbreviated form.
23. The missing countries are: Burma, Djibouti, Equatorial Guinea and São Tomé and Principe.

Chapter 4

1. As described in Stone (1977) and Byron (1978).
2. To analyse the world current account discrepancy, the IMF working party used questionnaires designed to expose gaps or inconsistencies in reporting by national compilers. The questionnaires were sent to countries whose transactions seemed likely to have a significant effect on the global discrepancy (IMF 1987: 33).
3. The geographical distribution is as follows: CMEA (17 per cent), MOE (7 per cent), OB (17 per cent), DB (11 per cent), PB (11 per cent) and ROW (27 per cent).
4. This may well be an overstatement of CMEA nonfactor services; especially for travel, CMEA debits are probably very low. The only estimates given in the BOP for CMEA countries are for Hungary and Poland, for 1980 and 1985. The ratio of nonfactor services to merchandise trade for Poland and Hungary in 1985 was 19 per cent and 14 per cent respectively, and for 1980 it was 14 per cent and 9 per cent respectively, while world ratios ranged from 20 to 25 per cent.
5. Similarly, in a world model designed by Cline (1989) nonfactor services are set proportional to merchandise trade.
6. An 'educated guess' in McMillan (1987) places the stock of foreign direct investment of CMEA countries in the range of US$ 4–6 billion.
7. The data in Dunning and Cantwell (1987) cover a limited number of years. For many of countries, data for 1982 and 1975 have been estimated from data for adjoining years.

8. For 1970 and 1975 the stock matrix for 1975 has been used and for 1980 and 1985 the stock matrix for 1982 has been used.
9. According to the definition by the OECD, as used for example in the 1990 edition of *Financing and External Debt of Developing Countries*.
10. As an indicator for the differences in real interest rates in the G-7 countries, the ratio between Central Bank discount rates and the Consumer Price Index (from the IMF, *International Financial Statistics*) for the years 1975, 1980 and 1985 has been calculated. The differences were on average smaller than 0.5 per cent with little variation.
11. US dollar-denominated new international borrowing in OCA was 64.3 per cent in 1985 and 80.4 per cent in 1980, and higher in the 1970s (OECD, *Financial Market Trends*, various issues).
12. This assumption is necessitated by the lack of data. The IMF (1987), using the outcomes of a special questionnaire, estimates the rate of return on equities at 50 per cent of the rate of return on bonds for 1983; the rate of return refers only to the income actually paid or received, and not to revaluations.
13. Weights depend on the rate of growth (g) and the maturity of the loans (n) and the growth rate (g). Changes in g have a marginal effect on the weights:

g	t–7	t–6	t–5	t–4	t–3	t–2	t–1	t
0%	2	5	9	12	16	20	23	12
10%	1	4	7	11	15	20	26	16
20%	1	3	5	9	14	20	29	19

14. OECD, *Financial Market Trends*, various issues.
15. Following the suggestions in the IMF report (IMF 1987), and assuming that debits are reported correctly, only credits have been adjusted. However, to assess the credibility of the exercise a similar check has been carried out with liabilities, using two classes of average spreads, one for OECD countries and one for other countries (from the OECD publication *Financial Market Trends*, various issues). Replacing BOP investment income payments with these calculations would increase the discrepancy on the world account for investment income dramatically. This (1) implies that the generated income in Table 4.4 should be interpreted very cautiously, (2) reduces the credibility of the claim in the IMF report that the world current account discrepancy can be reduced to a negligible amount by increasing investment income credits on the basis of an 'asset-income' check, and (3) indicates that there

is a 'consistent' bias in reporting that leads to under-reporting in investment income, capital outflows and stocks of foreign assets.

16. If more than one estimate was available for the same cell then the more reliable estimate is presented here.
17. As suggested in Tims and Waelbroeck (1982).

Chapter 5

1. Similarly, Cline (1989: 347) observes that adding other countries (including Eastern Europe) provides little explanation for the world current account discrepancy.

Chapter 6

1. See Chapter 2 for a clarification of the country classification, and Table A2.1 for the result.
2. Shifts in the tables are partly affected by shifts in the US dollar. For example, the strong dollar appreciation between 1980–85 explains (part of) the recovery of the US position against Japan.
3. In Chapter 7, the shares S_{ij} and S_i are connected in the market effect in Constant Market Shares analysis.
4. Note that the 'norm' $\beta = 1$ is the norm in a chi-square distribution that is used to test if observed frequencies differ from the (calculated) expected frequencies. In an expected frequency table $\beta = 1$ for each cell.
5. Note that this table is based on current account positions according to balance of payments definition, while in Table 6.5 transfers are transferred to the capital account.

Chapter 7

1. See, for example, Leamer and Stern (1970) for a more detailed exposition.
2. The presentation in this section follows the disaggregation of the four effects in Gerards and Jager (1980).
3. A CMS identity with disaggregation for either products or markets has been called a 'two-level' analysis (Leamer & Stern 1970: 173), as opposed to 'one-level' analysis that only takes shifts and shares in the total trade of a country into account, and the 'three-level' analysis that is presented in identity (7.3). Identity (7.3) without disaggregation by category, i.e. a 'two-level' analysis, becomes:

$$M \cdot \Delta A + \sum_j (A_j - A) \cdot \Delta M_j + \sum_j (M_j + \Delta M_j) \cdot \Delta A_j$$

4. Market shares are subject to many other influences such as (1) differential rates of quality improvement and the development of new exports, (2) differential rates of improvement in the efficiency of marketing or in the terms of export finance, (3) differential changes in the ability for quick fulfillment of export orders, and (4) export policies of own government or the government of trading partners.

References

Allen, C. & D. Vines (1992) 'Some key global adjustment scenarios and their effects on major developing countries, A report to the United Nations', London, Oxford: London Business School and Balliol College.

Armington, P.S. (1969), 'A Theory of Demand for Products Distinguished by Place of Production', International Monetary Fund *Staff Papers*, 16: 159–76, (March).

Bach, C.L. (1983) 'US international transactions, fourth quarter and year 1982', *US Survey of Current Business*, 63(3): 42–68.

Behrman, J.N. (1989) 'Restructuring and reordering the world economy', in K. Fatemi (ed.) *International Trade: Existing Problems and Prospective Solutions*. New York: Taylor and Francis, pp. 11–23.

Bergsten, C.F. (1988) *America in the World Economy: A Strategy for the 1990s*. Washington, DC: Institute for International Economics.

BIS (various issues) *Maturity Distribution of International Bank Lending*, Basle: Bank for International Settlements.

BIS and OECD (various issues) *Statistics on External Indebtedness: Bank and Trade-Related Non-Bank External Claims on Individual Borrowing Countries and Territories*, Basle: Bank for International Settlements.

Brown, R.P.C. (1992) *Public Debt and Private Wealth: Debt, Capital Flight and the IMF in Sudan*, Basingstoke: Macmillan.

Byron, R. (1978) 'The estimation of large social accounting matrices', *Journal of the Royal Statistical Society*, Series A, 141: 359–67.

Chenery, H.B. & A.M. Strout (1966) 'Foreign assistance and economic development', *American Economic Review*, 56(4): 670–733.

Cline, W.R. (1983) *International Debt and the Stability of the World Economy*, Washington DC: Institute of International Economics.

Cline, W.R. (1989) *United States, External Adjustment and the World Economy*, Washington DC: Institute for International Economics.

Cuddington, J.T. (1986) *Capital Flight: Estimates, Issues, and Explanations*. Princeton Studies in International Finance, No. 58, Princeton NJ: Princeton University Press.

Das, D.K. (1986) *Migration of Financial Resources to Developing Countries*, Basingstoke and London: Macmillan.

Dooley, M.P. (1988) 'Capital Flight: A Response to Differences in Financial Risks', *IMF Staff Papers*, 35(3): 422-36. Washington DC.

Dornbusch, R. (1980) *Open Economy Macro-economics*. New York: Basic Books.

Drucker, P.F. (1986) 'The changed world economy', *Foreign Affairs*, 64 (4): 768–91.

Dunning, J. & J. Cantwell (1987) *Directory of Statistics of International Investment and Production*, Basingstoke and London: Macmillan.

FitzGerald, E.V.K & R. Vos (1989) *Financing Economic Development: A Structural Approach to Monetary Policy*. Aldershot: Gower.

Galbis, V. (ed.) (1991) *The IMF's Statistical Systems*. Washington DC: International Monetary Fund.

Gerards, J. & H. Jager (1980) 'De structurele ontwikkeling van de Nederlandse uitvoer: een toepassing van CMS-analyse', *Economische Statistische Berichten*, 16(1): 64–9.

Goldstein, M. (1994) 'Improving economic policy coordination: evaluating some new and some not so new proposals', pp. 298–325 in P.B. Kenen, *The International Monetary System*. Cambridge UK: Cambridge University Press.

IMF (1977) *Balance of Payments Manual*. (Fourth Edn), Washington DC: International Monetary Fund.

IMF (1983) *World Economic Outlook*. Washington DC: International Monetary Fund.

IMF (1987) *Report on the World Current Account Discrepancy*. Washington DC: International Monetary Fund.

IMF (1990) 'Industrial Country Current Account Deficit Widens' in *IMF Survey*, 1: 9–12 (8 January).

IMF (1992) *Final Report of the Working Party on the Measurement of International Capital Flows*. Washington DC: International Monetary Fund.

IMF (various years) *Balance of Payments Statistics*. Washington DC: International Monetary Fund.

IMF (various years) *International Financial Statistics*. Washington DC: International Monetary Fund.

Jellema, T. (1992) 'Methods for automatic reconciliation of accounting frameworks', paper for staff seminar at Growth Dynamics University Institute, Rotterdam: Erasmus University.

de Jong, N., R. Vos, T. Jellema & H. Zebregs (1993a) 'Trade and financial flows in a world accounting framework, balanced WAMs for 1985–88' paper prepared for UN-DIESA and Project LINK, Institute of Social Studies, The Hague and Growth Dynamics University Institute, Rotterdam (mimeo).

de Jong, N., R. Vos, T. Jellema & H. Zebregs (1993b) 'Trade and financial flows in a world accounting framework, balanced WAMs for 1989–90' ISS Working Paper on Money, Finance and Development No. 50, The Hague: Institute of Social Studies.

de Jong, N. & R. Vos (1994a) 'Regional blocs or global markets; a WAM approach to analyzing trade and financial linkages', The Hague: ISS (mimeo).

de Jong, N. & R. Vos (1994b) 'Patterns of international finance between major trading and investing patterns: a world accounting approach', The Hague: ISS (mimeo).

Kaya, Y., A. Onishi & Y. Suzuki (1983), 'Project FUGI and the future of ESCAP developing countries' pp. 237–59 in B.G. Hickman (ed.) *Global International Economic Models*. New York: Elseviers.

Kenen, P.B., F. Papadia & F. Saccomania (1994) *The International Monetary System*. Cambridge UK: Cambridge University Press.

Kindleberger, C.P. (1969) *American Business Abroad: Six Lectures on Direct Investment*. New Haven CT and London: Yale University Press.

Klein, L.R. (1984) 'New developments in project LINK', *American Economic Review*, 75(2): 223–7.

Kragenau, H. (1976 & 1987) *Internationale Direktinvestitionen*, Hamburg: Verlag Weltarchiv GmbH.

Kravis, I.B., A. Heston & R. Summers (1981) 'New insights into the structure of the world economy', *Review of Income and Wealth*, 28(4): 339–55.

Leamer E.L. & R.M. Stern (1970) *Quantitative International Economics*. Chicago: Aldine Publishing Company.

Leontief, W. (1974) 'The structure of the world economy', *American Economic Review*, 64(6): 823-34.

Lessard, D.R. & J. Williamson (1987a) *Capital Flight and Third World Debt*. Washington DC: Institute for International Economics.

Lessard, D.R. & J. Williamson (1987b) *Capital Flight: The Problem and Policy Responses*. Washington DC: Institute for International Economics.

Machlup, F. (1983) 'Autonomous and induced items in the Balance of Payments' in F. Machlup, G. Fels & H. Muller-Groeling (eds), *Reflections on a Troubled World Economy*. Basingstoke: Macmillan, pp. 139–70.

Maizels, A. & M.K. Nissanke (1984) 'Motivations for aid to developing Countries', *World Development*, 12(9): 879–900.

Marris, S. (1987) *Deficits and the Dollar: The World Economy at Risk*. Washington DC: Institute for International Economics.

Masson, P.S., S. Symanski & G. Meredith (1988) 'MULTIMOD Mark II: A Revised and Extended Model' IMF Occasional Paper No. 71, Washington DC: International Monetary Fund.

Matsukawa, M. (1987) *The Japanese Trade Surplus and Capital Outflow*. New York: Group of Thirty.

McCarthy, D., B. Laury, E. Riordan & J.P. Zhou (1989) 'Global accounting framework (GAF), the basic system', GAF Working Paper No.2, International Economics Department, Washington DC: The World Bank.

McKibbin, W. & J. Sachs (1991), *Macroeconomic Interdependence and Cooperation in the World Economy*. Washington DC: The Brookings Institution.

McMillan, C.H (1987) *Multinationals from the Second World*. New York: St. Martin's Press.

Meade J.E. & R. Stone (1941) 'The construction of tables of national income, expenditure, savings and investments', *Economic Journal*, 51(3): 216–33 (June–September).

Meade, J.E. (1951) *The Balance of Payments*. London & Oxford: Oxford University Press.

Naylor, R.T (1987) *Hot Money and the Politics of Debt*. New York: Linden Press/Simon & Schuster.

OECD (1987) *Development Co-operation*. 1986 Report, Paris: Organization for Economic Cooperation and Development.

OECD (various years) *Financing and External Debt of Developing Countries*, Paris: Organization for Economic Cooperation and Development.

OECD (various issues) *Financial Market Trends*, Paris: Organization for Economic Cooperation and Development.

OECD (various years) *The Geographical Distribution of Financial Flows to Developing Countries*, Paris: Organization for Economic Cooperation and Development.

Page, S. (1990) *Trade, Finance and Developing Countries*. New York: Harvester Wheatsheaf.

Richardson, J.D. (1971) 'Some sensitivity tests for a "constant-market-shares" analysis of export growth', *The Review of Income and Statistics*, 53: 300–304.

Riordan, E.J. (1991) 'D/C analytical database: report on methods and data sources national income accounts, balance of payments and other variables', (draft), Washington DC: The World Bank International Economics Department/Analysis and Prospects Division.

Root, F.R. (1990) International Trade and Investment. 6th edn, Cincinnati OH: South-Western Publishing.

Russell, S.S. (1986) 'Remittances from international migration: a review in perspective', *World Development*, 14(6): 677–96.

Stiglitz, J. & A. Weiss (1981) 'Credit rationing in markets with imperfect information', *American Economic Review*, 71(2): 393–410.

Stone, J.R.N., D.G. Champernowne & J.E. Meade (1942) 'The precision of national income estimates', *Review of Economic Studies*, 9(2): 111–25.

Stone, J.R.N. (1977) 'Foreword' in G. Pyatt & A. Roe *Social Accounting for Development Planning with Special Reference to Sri Lanka*, Cambridge: Cambridge University Press, pp. xvi–xxxi.

Tims, W. & J. Waelbroeck (1982) 'Global Modelling in the World Bank, 1973–76', World Bank Staff Working Papers, No. 544, Washington DC: World Bank.

Turner, P. (1991), 'Capital flows in the 1980s: a survey of major trends', BIS Economic Papers, No. 30, Basle: Bank for International Settlements.

Tyszinski, H. (1951) 'World trade in manufactured commodities, 1899–1950', *The Manchester School*, 19: 272–304 (September).

Ulan, M. & W.G. Dewald (1989) 'The US net international investment position: misstated and misunderstood' in J.A. Dorn & W.A. Niskanen (eds) *Dollars and Deficits & Trade*, Boston: Kluwer, pp. 363–95.

United Nations (1968) *A System of National Accounts*. Studies in Methods, Series F, No. 2, Rev. 3, New York: United Nations Department of Economic and Social Affairs.

United Nations (1973) *Input-Output Tables and Analysis*, Studies in Methods, Series F, No. 14, Rev. 1, New York: United Nations Department of Economic and Social Affairs.

United Nations Centre on Transnational Corporations (1992) *World Investment Directory 1992, Volume 1, Asia and the Pacific*. New York: United Nations.

United Nations Department for International Economic and Social Affairs. (various years) *United Nations Trade Matrices System*. New York: United Nations.

United Nations (various years) *National Accounts Statistics*, New York: United Nations.

United States (various years) *Federal Reserve Bulletin*, Washington DC: Federal Reserve Board.

Vos, R. (1986) 'World accounts of trade, finance and accumulation', ISS Working Paper on Money, Finance and Development No.16, The Hague: Institute of Social Studies.

Vos, R. (1989) 'Accounting for the world economy', *Review of Income and Wealth*, 35(4): 310–34.

Vos, R. (1991) *The World Economy, Debt and Adjustment: Structural Asymmetries in North-South Interactions*. PhD dissertation, Free University of Amsterdam. The Hague: Institute of Social Studies.

Vos, R. (1992) 'Aid flows, trade and global macroeconomic adjustment', paper at the Annual Conference of the Royal Economic Society, City University, London, 30 March–2 April.

Wallich, H.C. (1984) *International Capital Movements, Debt and Monetary System*. Mainz, Germany: Hase & Koehler.

Walter, A. (1991) *World Power and World Money: The Role of Hegemony and International Monetary Order*. New York: Harvester Wheatsheaf.

Weale, M. (1984) 'Quantity and price effects in an analysis of world trade based on an accounting matrix', *The Review of Income and Wealth*, 30(1): 85–117.

White, H. & J. Luttik (1994) 'The countrywide effects of aid', Policy Research Working Paper 1337, Washington DC: The World Bank.

Williamson, J. & C. Milner (1991) *The World Economy: A Textbook in International Economics*. New York: Harvester Wheatsheaf.

World Bank (various years) *World Bank Debtor Reporting System*. Washington DC: World Bank.

World Bank (1987) *World Development Report 1985*. New York: Oxford University Press.

World Bank (various years) *World Debt Tables*. Washington DC: World Bank.

World Bank (various years) *World Tables*. Washington DC: World Bank.

World Bank, BIS, IMF, OECD (1988) *External Debt: Definition, Coverage and Methodology*. Paris: Organization for Economic Cooperation and Development.

World Bank, BIS, IMF, OECD (1994) *Debt Stocks, Debt Flows: and the Balance of Payments*. Paris: Organization for Economic Cooperation and Development.

Index